AMERICA,
THE
LAST
DOMINO

AMERICA, THE LAST DOMINO

U.S. Foreign Policy in Central America Under Reagan

STAN PERSKY

New Star Books
Vancouver, Canada

Copyright © 1984 by Stan Persky

First printing September 1984
1 2 3 4 5 88 87 86 85 84

Canadian Cataloguing in Publication Data

Persky, Stan, 1941-
America, the last domino

Bibliography: p.
Includes index.
ISBN 0-919573-36-3 (bound). —
ISBN 0-919573-37-1 (pbk.)

1. United States - Foreign relations - Central
America. 2. Central America - Foreign relations -
United States. 3. United States - Foreign
relations - 1977-1981. 4. United States -
Foreign relations - 1981- I. Title.
F1436.8.U6P47 1984   327.730728   C84-091437-7

The publisher is grateful to the Canada Council for assistance
provided through the Writing and Publication Section.

Printed and bound in Canada

New Star Books Ltd.
2504 York Avenue
Vancouver, B.C.
Canada   V6K 1E3

Contents

List of Maps

Preface

She was an unlikely revolutionary.

Leandra Lopez, or Dona Leandra as everyone called her, had just emerged from the doorway of one of a ramshackle cluster of houses on the outskirts of Esteli, a town of 35,000 in northwestern Nicaragua. It was late-December 1979, five months after the Sandinista National Liberation Front had toppled the nearly half-century family dictatorship of Anastasio Somoza.

I was a Canadian journalist and teacher of political science at a community college who had decided that revolutionary Nicaragua was about as good a vantage point as any from which to contemplate the turning of a decade. The 1980s already promised to be a time of the re-establishment of traditional lines of authority, increased military budgets, and the revival of an anti-communist rhetoric that we mistakenly assumed had faded with the passing of the Cold War. For those of us not inclined to share the enthusiasm for these signs of the immediate future in North America, and disposed toward other hopes, Nicaragua, the site of the first hemispheric revolution since that of Cuba in 1959, seemed worthy of attention.

In Managua, the battered capital of this Central American country of three million people, I'd found an old friend, Margaret Randall, who was writing a book about Nicaraguan women. Margaret had been given the use of a Ministry of Culture jeep and a driver, and invited me to accompany her on one of her interview-gathering trips. From the edge of Esteli, the jeep bounced over pebbled back streets, rocky hillocks and cowpaths to bring us to this house of hard-packed dirt floors and walls of crumbling brick, topped by a slanting corrugated tin roof in front of which Dona Leandra stood.

She was a strong, thin woman, sixty-three years old, about five-foot-two. Her tightly drawn back dark hair was silver just above the forehead, and she wore a white cotton apron over the short-sleeved black dress that hasn't gone out of fashion among country women in Latin America and Europe for more than a century. "I dreamt you were coming," she greeted us, sweeping Margaret, whom she already knew, into her embrace.

Inside, the rocking chairs that are a familiar sight in Nicaraguan households were drawn up. Hens scurried in and out of the kitchen. Dona Leandra was already at the stove making lunch. As we ate, we learned something about this woman who, with a journalist's too facile phrase, I was already thinking of as "the Sandinistas' secret weapon."

"I was born a guerrilla," Dona Leandra began. She was just a girl when Augusto Sandino, the national hero who held off the U.S. Marines during a six-year guerrilla war in the 1920s and '30s, was assassinated by the Somoza clan. "One of my first memories is having cried when they killed Sandino."

She'd always lived in the valleys and villages around Esteli. "I was lucky enough to marry a revolutionary and we went to live in a village named Trinidad." That's a few kilometers down the highway lined with blue morning glories which we had traveled that morning. "We raised eight kids there. My husband died after we'd been married for twenty-five years. Now I'm sixty-three."

Her sons' friends from the Sandinista Front came to her house. She fed them as she was feeding us now, a spread of eggs, beans, cheese and cooked bananas. "All of my children were sympathizers of the Front. They were all against Somoza. There was one son who died at the end of the war." Gradually, her home became a "safe house" where Sandinista rebels hid out. Jose Benito Escobar, whose name didn't mean anything to a foreign journalist, but whom every schoolchild in Nicaragua knows about, spent his last night alive at Dona Leandra's. She remembered staying up late, worrying, and watching for his return.

"It was very dangerous then," she explained. "A lot of people thought that Somoza was the only one who could govern Nicaragua. People would say, If Somoza is thrown out, communism will come, and communism is bad." Dona Leandra was distinctly less terrified by the Red menace than the average North American politician. "They'd say, communism-this, communism-that, but I'd always tell them that the thing about communism is that it's bad for the rich, but it's good for the poor. Of course, communism isn't good for millionaires. No change is good for the millionaire, because he's got everything.

"But for us poor people, who sweat day after day, and don't even have enough to eat, if they call what we're doing communism, I'm not going to worry," she said. Who would have guessed, I thought to myself, that one of the dangerous "subversives" I'd been told about as a kid would turn out to be a grandmother feeding me fried bananas?

A month after the death of her son, Dona Leandra was smuggling medical supplies to the Sandinistas. "People said to me, 'What? Are you doing this again? Have you forgotten they've just killed your son?' I didn't even answer. I just picked up the box of medicine and put it on my head. I thought to myself, They've killed my son, they might as well finish me off and everybody else too. When you really get into this kind of struggle, you lose your fear." As I listened to her I had an image of those elderly women in black dresses, all over Nicaragua, whom one passes, perhaps unthinkingly, on the streets of a town like Esteli, maintaining a honeycomb of secure houses, unobtrusively providing the logistical support that makes a revolution possible.

Later, we all piled into the jeep, bumping through a few cow pastures, and across Highway 1, and then down a dirt road. We were going to see where Jose Benito died. Dona Leandra pointed out the new school named after him. We got out and walked over to a small wooden cross by the road. A tiny earth-darkened arroyo spilled into a little stream below. "This is where he rolled down," Dona Leandra said.

A few people from nearby houses stopped by. Everybody obviously considered it the most natural thing in the world that someone had come more than 5,000 kilometers from someplace called Canada to take a snapshot in the December sunshine of the place where Jose Benito Escobar died.

When we returned to Dona Leandra's house, one of her daughters had arrived with her rather enormously plump baby. Margaret asked Dona Leandra what she felt five months ago on July 19, 1979. "What happened on July 19? Oh, the victory!" she chuckled, amused at having forgotten for an instant the moment of liberation. "Well, I was happy of course, but I was also very sad. So many dead. So many sons and daughters dead. It's as if they're all part of the family. Every guerrilla captured was like they captured my own son or daughter."

In the pastures at the edge of Esteli, as we drove away, kids were flying tiny kites, diamond-shaped bits of paper bearing the red-and-black colors of the Sandinistas.

I don't mean to suggest that the interview with Dona Leandra represents the "truth" of the Nicaraguan revolution, although I must confess to a particular weakness for encounters with a society's elders. As a journalist and teacher, I've been moved by such meetings, especially with women, in places as far apart as China and Poland, and as close to home as the Indian reservation at Mt. Currie, British Columbia. Certainly, other Nicaraguans I talked to presented widely differing views on the meaning of, and prospects for, the Nicaraguan revolution, usually reflecting the perspective of their own position in society, and providing enough diversity to counter any disposition toward sentimentality. Nonetheless, the encounter with Dona Leandra, occurring as it did in the hiatus between the American media's fascination with the moment of revolution and the subsequent officially wary view in which most images of Nicaragua have been mystified, remains memorable. Whatever other questions I would come to have about Nicaragua, the "truth" of Dona Leandra was undeniable, and would have to be taken into account. It was also the moment in which this book was conceived.

America, The Last Domino is a more or less chronological narrative account of U.S. foreign policy in Central America from 1980 to 1984, during the administration of Ronald Reagan. Its title image refers to the "domino theory," the idea that the fall of one country to forces unfriendly to U.S. interests will lead to the inevitable collapse of other adjacent countries. First conjured up in the 1950s and used to justify U.S. military intervention in Vietnam in the 1960s and '70s, this specter has been resurrected in the 1980s and applied to Central America as a rationale for increasing American military involvement there.

I'm not so much concerned with the truth of this theory, since it's a well-known fact that indigenous political movements throughout Central America are at various stages of development that could, ultimately, provide a semblance of veracity to this image. Rather I'm more interested in the logic of the vision of falling dominoes, implying as it does that the United States is the last domino, as a partial explanation of the ferocity with which the present American government is determined to resist changes it considers inimical to its interests.

Let me clearly delineate the modesty of my enterprise. First, in order to focus on one particular aspect of U.S. foreign policy, it means that by and large I've been forced to ignore a much larger ensemble of decision making by the Reagan administration. For the most part I've taken little account of how current U.S. Central American policy fits into the larger picture of America's adversarial relationship with the Soviet Union; as well, I've abstracted Central American decisions from the larger set of Latin American policymaking and even from the Caribbean Basin sub-set. Though I've tried to minimize them as much as possible, resultant distortions are inevitable.

Second, this is a book that is more about events in Washington than in Central America. As such, it contains no spectacular revelations, and though it would have been useful, I have not conducted a first-hand study of the Reagan administration nor have I attempted to have any classified documents disgorged from the maw of government via the U.S. Freedom of Information Act. Here, I must plead poverty of circumstances rather than of imagination. Nonetheless, given my perception of the general public understanding of U.S.-Central American relations, I hope that this generally straightforward narrative based on available sources will be of use to the general reader.

Third, this work is obviously a very provisional account of policy. For one thing, much of the policy is covert and simply unknown, despite significant revelations. In fact, the revelation of the process of policymaking is as much a part of the narrative as the account of the effects of particular policy decisions. For another thing, the events discussed are of such recent vintage that I hope my account will be taken as intended—as a first draft contribution to later historical judgments.

Fourth, I've remained relatively neutral in assessing the political intentions of the Soviet Union, one of the more contentious areas of discussion, given the claims made by the Reagan administration. Though I have tried to weigh the evidentiary substance of U.S. charges regarding the Soviet Union and Cuba, I've not presumed to judge the behavior of those countries. In fact, I've been particularly struck by the fact, in the course of writing this work, of how in North America our knowledge of the Soviet Union and Cuba is thoroughly mystified. While I'm generally disposed to be favorable to socialist aspirations, my experiences as a journalist and researcher in Poland during the period of the existence of the Solidarity trade union has served to insulate me from accusations of pro-Soviet bias.

Similarly, although events in Central America are extensively described here, political developments, particularly in Nicaragua, are only briefly touched upon. I continue to be painfully aware of, for example, how little we actually know about the five-year-old Nicaraguan revolution. Although, as I indicate in the bibliography, I've learned from the wisdom of several contemporary works about the subject, in all my reading only Charles Clements' *Witness to War*, about El Salvador, and Margaret Randall's works about Nicaragua in which Nicaraguan voices are directly heard, provide a substantial sense of reality that goes beyond the pseudo-contact of even the best daily journalism. There has not been, to date, a comprehensive fair-minded account of developments in Nicaragua since 1979; much the same can be said about other Central American countries for the present period.

Finally, because much of this narrative is taken up with an effort to make sense of political rhetoric, particularly that of the Reagan administration, I've been at pains to avoid that indulgence in my own writing. I've attempted to exercise great restraint in this account, often treating the claims of the U.S. government with more respect than they perhaps deserve, at other times giving more credence to criticisms of the revolutionary movements in the region than the facts warrant. Those who know the realities I report better than I do will, I hope, grant me forebearance. Ultimately, I believe, the case is sufficiently clear that my personal outrage in the face of the horrors perpetrated in Central America can be dispensed with. At most, I have indulged in a sort of descriptive black humor to portray various policy processes that seemed to demand something more than objective disinterestedness. I've dispensed with footnotes since this is not a scholarly work and since my sources, whether newspaper accounts, government reports, or books are readily locatable in any medium-sized urban library. In particular instances, references are provided within the narrative itself, and a bibliography and index are available at the conclusion of the text. In general, I've tried to interpose as few obstacles as possible between the story and the reader.

Because of the systematic denial by the U.S. government of the authenticity of revolutionary movements in Central America, as well as of the specific histories of those countries, and the substitution of the specter of Soviet communism as an all-purpose explanation, it has been necessary to interleaf the narrative with brief accounts of the political histories of El Salvador, Guatemala and Nicaragua. They are meant to serve as a reminder of reality for those of us at least vaguely familiar with the region, and as information for readers cognizant of the U.S. preoccupation with Central America but confused by the conflicting claims. In all these matters, I accept the author's usual responsibility for errors of fact and interpretation, and welcome criticism from the readers.

I have received considerable help in the course of writing this book and it is a pleasure to honor some of the debts incurred along the way. All students of contemporary Latin American affairs must be grateful to the publications of the North American Congress on Latin America, and especially the work of George Black, Robert Armstrong and Janet Shenk. As well, I have benefited from the writings of authors Cynthia Arnson, Robert Alan White and Charles Clements, and journalists Warren Hoge, Raymond Bonner and Stephen Kinzer of the New York *Times*, Ben Tierney of Southam News, and Oakland Ross of the Toronto *Globe and Mail*. I have, along with many others, been a beneficiary of various Latin American solidarity committees, research centers and church groups in North America, who have patiently insisted that we pay attention to the issues discussed here and do something about them. Locally, Rick Craig in Vancouver provides an emulatory example of their work.

A number of people have directly contributed to my thinking and the production of this book. Marvin DeVos and Richard Nadeau did the indispensible research work, Richard Clements made available to me his enormous compendium of materials on the Reagan administration, and the people at New Star Books were consistently encouraging and efficient, in particular, Lanny Beckman who sympathetically read a considerable part of the manuscript, Janet Cotgrave who edited it, and Tom Hawthorn who typeset it. I also wish to acknowledge the admirable atmosphere of spirited inquiry I found in discussions among my colleagues at Capilano College, especially Paul Mier, Ed Lavalle, Robert Campbell, Matthew Speier and Paul Avery, and among students in comparative government courses I've taught.

My gratitude to my friends Margaret Randall and Tom Sandborn, both of whom live their lives in ways I find particularly inspiring, is immense. Finally, as a long-standing participant in the tradition of writers who, after a day's work, repair to a local bar to ponder their impudence, my thanks to Brinko at Buddy's, whose wit and wisdom often restored my sense of proportion and enhanced my appreciation of the proportions of others.

S.P.

Vancouver, B.C.
August 1984

AMERICA,
THE
LAST
DOMINO

Central America

Mexico

Belize

Guatemala

El Salvador

Honduras

PACIFIC
OCEAN

Nicaragua

Costa Rica

CARIBBEAN
SEA

Panama

N

1 Dictatorships and Double Standards

> *... traditional autocrats tolerate social inequalities, brutality and poverty while revolutionary autocrats create them.*
>
> *Traditional autocrats leave in place existing allocations of wealth, power, status and other resources... But they worship traditional gods and observe traditional taboos. They do not disturb the habitual rhythm of work and leisure... Because the miseries of traditional life are familiar, they are bearable to ordinary people who, growing up in the society, learn to cope, as children born to untouchables in India acquire the skills and attitudes necessary for survival in the miserable roles they are destined to fill. Such societies create no refugees.*
>
> —Jeane Kirkpatrick, November 1979

They were four American churchwomen engaged in humanitarian relief work in the civil war-torn Central American nation of El Salvador.

On the warm, muggy evening of December 2, 1980, Dorothy Kazel, 40, a nun from the Ursuline Order of Cleveland, Ohio, and Jean Donovan, a plump blond 27-year-old accountant and missionary volunteer, also from Cleveland, waited in the marble mausoleum-like terminal building of the San Salvador International Airport for the arrival of the 7 p.m. flight from neighboring Managua, Nicaragua. Sisters Ita Ford, 40, and Maura Clarke, 46, both of New York City, were returning from Nicaragua where they had attended a conference of the Maryknoll Order to which they belonged.

None of the four churchwomen was a stranger to this crowded coffee-producing country the size of Massachusetts. They had lived among its nearly five million mostly peasant inhabitants who had endured a half-century succession of military dictators and oligarchic pseudo-presidents. Kazel and Donovan worked in the port city of La Libertad which lies southwest of the capital, San Salvador. Ford and Clarke distributed food and clothing to mothers and children made homeless by the civil war in the northern province of Chalatenango. Together, they had experienced their share of a horror largely unknown to most Americans, one which in the previous year had seen 10,000 deaths—from mountainous battlefields dominated by the leftist Farabundo Marti National Liberation Front (FMLN) guerrillas to the middle-of-the-night mass murders by moonlighting government forces operating as rightwing "death squads"—all presided over by the latest configuration of a shaky military-civilian junta that had seized power in late-1979 under banners of reform.

They could hardly be unaware of the dangers they faced. "The Peace Corps left today," Jean Donovan had written to a friend not long before, "and my heart sank low. The danger is extreme and they were right to leave... Now I must assess my own position because I am not up for suicide. Several times I have decided to leave." And yet she stayed. "I almost could, except for the children... the poor bruised victims of adult lunacy." She even maintained a sort of gallows humor to relieve the tension. Another nun, Sister Christine Rody, later recalled that "Jean used to joke that blue-eyed blonds were the safest people in Salvador, because they were so American-looking and no one would kill Americans."

American-looking or not, there were grim warnings. Two weeks earlier, a note tacked to the door of the stucco parish house in Chalatenango where Ita Ford and Maura Clarke lived bluntly declared: "In this house are communists. Everyone who enters here will die. Try it and see." Despite that, the two women had continued to deliver food and medical supplies to those in need. Ford, who with her short-cropped hair and turned-up nose presented the very image of a youthful suburban American housewife, had recently told a journalist, "The colonel of the local regiment said to me the other day that the church is indirectly subversive because it is on the side of the weak.''

But the disapproval of the authorities had not caused her to moderate her criticisms of the regime or of her own government's support for the Salvadoran junta. "It's fearful when you think the U.S. is going to train Salvadoran troops," Ford said in an interview a month before. "It's reprehensible...The United States has to realize it does not own Central America. In my opinion, El Salvador is in a state of war, a civil war.''

As if proof were needed, in the previous week the final possibility of a public political process had been reduced to an obscene mockery when some 200 soldiers and police surrounded the Jesuit high school in San Salvador where key leaders of the opposition Democratic Revolutionary Front (FDR) were holding a press conference. An armed twenty-man death squad, dressed in civilian garb, had entered the school auditorium and abducted a score of people. The next day the bodies of a half-dozen prominent representatives of popular organizations were found. Tensions had run particularly high in the wake of the murders as preparations were made for a public funeral, slated for the following day.

Indeed, recent events had, if anything, made the lonely road from the airport to the capital more ominous. As it was, the microbuses that ferried passengers to San Salvador provided a tense and silent ride. Preferably, friends were on hand to meet one at the airport, as Kazel and Donovan were that evening, to share the trip through a series of army checkpoints along the road.

Unbeknownst to these pilgrims in the land named by Spanish conquistadors for The Savior, events hours earlier augered ill for their safety. When Taca Airlines' 4:45 flight from Managua touched down at the isolated Salvadoran landing strip, it was boarded by three soldiers. Another Maryknoll nun, Sister Marie Rieckleman, en route to Miami, was twice questioned through the stewardess about her destination. "Are you sure you're going to Miami?" Rieckleman was asked at the soldiers' behest. A tape of a military transmission made shortly after the arrival of the afternoon flight was later given to U.S. Ambassador to El Salvador Robert White. "No, she didn't arrive on that flight," said a male voice. "We'll have to wait for the next one."

At about the time the 7 p.m. flight bearing Ford and Clarke landed, a chilling incident was taking place in a movie house in Chalatenango. An unknown man approached one of the parish staff, Father Efrain Lopez, who worked with the two women. The man showed Lopez a sheet of paper with names on it. "Here is a list of people we are going to kill—and today, this very night, we will begin." Ford and Clarke were on the list.

At the airport, a group of Canadian religious people were among the first off the plane and they greeted Kazel and Donovan in the terminal building before moving down the road to San Salvador. Shortly afterward, their party was stopped by uniformed security forces and searched at gunpoint. Meanwhile, the two Maryknoll nuns had arrived and, welcomed by their two friends, the four got into the white Toyota van that belonged to Kazel and Donovan. The eerie terminal, plunked down amid pastures and farmland, receded in the night as they headed toward the capital. They never arrived.

The bodies of the four women, the first Americans known to have been killed in the Salvadoran war, were discovered by a milkman early the next morning near the dusty farming town of Santiago Nonualco, about forty kilometers southeast of San Salvador. The van, fire-gutted and with license plates removed, was found later that day along the airport road. At 10 a.m. the local judge in Santiago Nonualco signed an order authorizing a burial but, frightened, he notified no one. A common grave was dug into the side of a cow pasture, just off the edge of a dirt road, by National Guardsmen and local peasants.

The next day, December 4, the Catholic priest from Santiago Nonualco called church authorities in San Salvador to report that several of his parishioners had seen soldiers burying four women who looked like foreigners. Suddenly, there was a flurry of activity. Ambassador White, church workers, and the media rushed to the gravesite to witness the exhumation of the bodies. Peasants told the press that at about 10:30 p.m. on the night of December 2, they had seen the van pass their houses. Then they heard a short burst of machine-gun fire, followed by three or four single shots. The van then returned the way it had come. The frightened *campesinos* shut their doors and waited until morning.

As the bodies were removed from the grave, nuns prayed over the corpses, while an angry U.S. ambassador surveyed the grisly scene. Each of the four women had been shot once in the head. Two had been found with blood-stained underpants around their ankles. "This time they won't get away with it," Ambassador White muttered. Then, as a contingent of National Guardsmen edged toward him and his aide, he asked, "Are they coming to get us?"

The news of the atrocity reached Washington, D.C. that day. The administration of President Jimmy Carter was in its final days after the defeat of the liberal Democrat from Plains, Georgia a month earlier by 69-year-old, conservative Republican Party challenger, Ronald Reagan, a former movie actor and former governor of California. For a year now the Carter regime had been largely immobilized by a political crisis in Iran where fifty-two employees of the American Embassy in Tehran were being held hostage by the theocratic government of the Ayatollah Khomeini. Even as Carter prepared to turn over power to President-elect Reagan, he remained preoccupied with delicate negotiations for the release of the hostages, working long hours in the White House, seemingly a hostage himself.

The Carter presidency had been relatively unbellicose by American standards. It began by speaking of the importance of "human rights" and noting that "we are now free of that inordinate fear of communism which once led us to embrace any dictator who joined us in that fear." It promised a new morality in American political life. Four years later it had ended in electoral disgrace, but with the modest boast that during its term of office not a single American soldier had died in combat—a claim that could not be echoed by any U.S. president in the preceding half century.

Yet it was an administration that had received savage criticism from both left and right for its vacillation, indecision and lack of coherence. In part, Carter's defeat at the polls seemed as much a matter of a failure of virility as anything else; he had been repeatedly unfavorably contrasted to the horseback-riding cowboy image of the aged but vigorous-appearing Reagan. Now, Carter could only hope that history would offer a more compassionate judgement than had the electorate.

The beleagured president had things other than Central America on his mind—in addition to Iran, that day Soviet troops were reported massing on the Polish border in a bid to intimidate the frail Solidarity trade union movement that had blossomed in the autumn as the first independent working class organization in a communist country; domestically, prime interest rates rose to 19 percent, presaging an economic recession. Still, Carter's Latin American policy had been a central tenet of his approach to foreign affairs.

During his presidency, Carter had concluded a Panama Canal treaty that turned over control of the inter-ocean waterway to the country in which it was located. He had withdrawn political support, briefly but at a crucial moment, from Nicaraguan dictator Anastasio Somoza, thus indirectly contributing to the defeat of the lengthy tyranny, and victory of the Sandinista liberation forces in July 1979. He had insistently, though with marked inconsistencies and dubious success, tied foreign aid to the observance of human rights in the cases of a score of repressive Latin American regimes traditionally allied to the United States.

Despite this noticeable break with tradition, Carter's efforts were little appreciated. Those to the left of the American president's liberal centrism minimized his concern with human rights as insufficient in the light of the continuing savage practices of various Latin police states and they scored Carter for his frequent inconsistencies. Rather than his pressure on the Somoza regime, they recalled Carter's eleventh-hour bid to prop up the tottering Nicaraguan dictator. In a sense, leftist criticism was somewhat disingenuous. It was not as if Carter had pretended to be other than an advocate of America's worldly power, an upholder of traditional capitalist values, and a proponent of nuclear energy and the concomitant arms race (despite his having negotiated a strategic arms limitation treaty with the Russians; it was scuttled when Soviet forces invaded Afghanistan in late 1979). Nonetheless, they refused to grant that, within the limits of American liberalism, Carter was different from his predecessors. Insofar as Carter's human rights policy was appreciated at all, one had to turn to Latin America itself to hear faint praise.

The bulk of the American populace remained stubbornly obtuse about the existence of Latin America. Still smarting from a military defeat in Vietnam, most Americans were puzzled, if not embarrassed, by Carter's unheroic emphasis on human rights. However, among resurgent conservative forces in the U.S.—bolstered by "New Right" religious fundamentalism and the appearence of an intellectual tendency dubbed "neo-conservatism"—one heard loud rumblings of indignation about the decline of American power and the timid use of that power by President Carter. It is to these cries of outrage that we will momentarily attend in observing the fashioning of Central American policy by the incoming Reagan administration.

That night, as the war in El Salvador was brought home to Americans in the only way a people encouraged in political solipcism could understand, the Carter administration pondered its response. Although some Salvadoran government officials initially argued that agents provocateurs of the left had committed the crime, while the most prominent member of the junta, Jose Napoleon Duarte, claimed "this was an action by the extreme right," it was soon apparent there was evidence that government security forces were responsible. Even the most casual and unsophisticated viewer of the evening television news had to wonder why the U.S. was supporting a government whose soldiers raped and murdered innocent civilians.

By the next day, December 5, U.S. support for the trigger-happy personnel of the Salvadoran junta had temporarily diminished. The American State Department announced that U.S. aid to El Salvador—some $25 million slated for economic assistance and military sales credits—was suspended "pending clarification of the circumstances" under which the four American churchwomen had died. In addition, the Carter administration was dispatching a fact-finding mission to investigate the killings. It was led by William D. Rogers, who had been under secretary of state during Henry Kissinger's tenure in that department—this move was designed to increase the likelihood that the results would be palatable to the incoming Reagan regime.

Candidate Ronald Reagan had few doubts as to the precarious nature of the world situation and the source from which all unrest emanated. "Let us not delude ourselves," he urged from the campaign podium. "The Soviet Union underlies all the unrest that is going on. If they weren't engaged in this game of dominoes, there wouldn't be any hot spots in the world.'' Armed with these tidily simple theorems, the presidential candidate, as early as March 1980, in an address to the Chicago Council on Foreign Relations, made clear that U.S. policy in Central America would have to change if the spectre of falling dominoes was to be averted.

"Totalitarian Marxists have control of the island of Grenada in the Caribbean, where Cuban advisers are currently training guerrillas for subversive action against other countries like Trinidad and Tobago, its democratic neighbor,'' declared the conservative challenger. "In El Salvador totalitarian Marxist reactionaries supported by Havana and Moscow are preventing the development of democratic government. Should we allow Grenada, Nicaragua and El Salvador to become 'new Cubas,' new staging grounds for Soviet combat brigades?'' Reagan asked. "Shall we wait to allow Moscow and Havana to push on to the north toward Guatemala and from there to Mexico, and southward toward Costa Rica and Panama?''

By early December, the president-elect and a vast personnel-seeking apparatus of transition teams, advisory panels and policy task forces were still scrambling to fill empty cabinet slots. The men running the transition effort were largely the same ones who had helped Reagan win on election day: campaign manager William J. Casey became chairman of the transition executive committee and would soon be tabbed for the powerful post of director of the Central Intelligence Agency (CIA); 49-year-old campaign chief of staff Edwin Meese III, who had once overseen Governor Reagan's administration, reappeared as transition director, as well as being named counselor to the president with cabinet rank, assuring him continuing inner circle status. Joining Meese to form a trio of ranking presidential aides were Michael Deaver, 42, a longtime Reagan intimate and, as White House chief of staff, James Baker, a 50-year-old Houston lawyer selected to symbolize the politically somewhat-more-moderate forces in the Republican Party which were grouped around Vice-President George Bush.

Perhaps as interesting as the good, grey and expected representatives of the upper class, who would soon be introduced on various Washington stages, was the less visible band of "self-made" millionaires who for years had backed the president-elect with financial and philosophical support. The day after the election a twenty-member cabinet-selection advisory committee held the first of a series of meetings in the Los Angeles law offices of Reagan's longtime personal attorney, William French Smith, 63, a transplanted Bostonian who would eventually become attorney general in the Reagan cabinet. In addition to the inner circle of top aides—Meese, Deaver, Baker, Casey, Bush and Nevada Senator Paul Laxalt— the group included Reagan's informal kitchen cabinet, among them: Smith; 75-year-old millionaire auto dealer Holmes Tuttle; the head of the $2.4 billion Dart Industries, Justin Dart, whose wife, actress Jane Bryan, had starred with Reagan in the 1940s film *Brother Rat*; and Colorado brewer Joseph Coors who, when the group was stuck for an interior secretary, quickly suggested the head of the anti-environmentalist Mountain States Legal Foundation, James Watt, for the job.

While the president-elect shuttled between his Pacific Palisades home and his 688-acre Rancho del Cielo in the hills northwest of Santa Barbara, this self-deprecating elite ("All we are is self-made businessmen concerned about the country," said automan Tuttle) sifted through hundreds of names culled by E. Pendleton James, a former Richard Nixon aide whom Meese had hired a year earlier to do the job-filling groundwork if Reagan were elected. By early December, the lists had been whittled down to the few who would shortly occupy the most prominent of cabinet posts. Former Nixon aide and NATO chief Alexander Haig, currently chief operating officer at United Technologies, was most likely for secretary of state now that George Shultz, Nixon's treasury secretary and currently vice-chairman of the giant Bechtel Corporation, had pulled himself out of the running. Sixty-three-year-old Caspar Weinberger, who had served Nixon in Washington and Reagan in Sacramento and was currently, like Shultz, in the employ of Bechtel, was almost certain to get a cabinet post, probably Defense. Thirty-four-year-old Michigan Congressman David Stockman, who was reputed to understand and support the new-fangled "supply-side" conservative economic nostrums, appeared to be headed for the influential Office of Management and Budget (OMB).

The once contentious debate of a decade earlier about

whether or not there was extensive and unhealthy interlocking between government and capitalism in the U.S. had long since faded from academic rostrums. However, a casual glance at the Reagan roster demonstrated the contention to be an evident truism. About the only noteworthy feature of the alleged new wave of conservatism that had carried the former movie actor to power was how much it resembled (and in fact, consisted of) the old wave of conservatism that had sporadically ruled America in the previous two decades.

The personnel effort represented only a small part of the huge transition operation. Another 250 Reagan staffers were wending their way through the federal government, divided into "issues clusters" and transitions teams for cabinet departments and federal agencies. At the same time, upwards of 400 specialists were mulling over policy options on fifty separate policy task forces. For mental brawn, the new administration was heavily recruiting from the suddenly fashionable idea factories of the right.

From Georgetown University's Center for Strategic and International Studies, located a half-dozen blocks from the White House, founder of the center David Abshire was plucked as group director of the national security issues cluster. A bevy of sub-groupings was soon at work producing recommendations in newly acceptable conservative tones. For example, that first week in December, the CIA transition team policy panel, headed by former Navy secretary and current president of Financial General Bankshares, J. William Middendorf II, was proposing to the new president sweeping changes in the operation of the nation's intelligence program, including increased emphasis on covert action abroad.

Similarly, other corporate-funded rightwing think tanks—the Hoover Institution on War, Revolution and Peace at Stanford University in Palo Alto, California; the San Francisco-based Institute for Contemporary Studies (one of whose founders in 1972 was Ed Meese); and in Washington, the Heritage Foundation (heavily financed by Joseph Coors), and the American Enterprise Institute—were providing second and third echelon personnel from their ranks, including those who would formulate the new administration's Central American policy.

Reagan's Latin policy experts had been active for months, fanning out and carrying the candidate's message to capitals around the hemisphere. By fall, one could find Reagan's chief aide on Latin American policy, Roger Fontaine, somewhere between Rio and Santiago, Chile, ostensibly softening the Republican nominee's hawkish image, but in fact broadly hinting at things to come. Others who carried Reagan's themes south of the border included Pedro San Juan, soon to be on the State Department transition team; former ambassador to Nicaragua, James Theberge, another State Department transition team player; retired General Daniel Graham (who stirred up some notice when he suggested in Argentina that Reagan would favor a NATO-like treaty linking militaristic nations of South America with South Africa); and Georgetown University political science professor Jeane Kirkpatrick, who was also connected to the American Enterprise Institute.

Fontaine, 39, the former director of Latin American studies at the Georgetown think tank and a fellow at the American Enterprise Institute, explained to Argentinians, Chileans and Paraguayans in September and October 1980 that Reagan would "work just as vigorously as Carter for [human rights], but he won't push governments back into a corner." It was just the sort of lightly coded message incumbent regimes wanted to hear. "We must maintain our interest in promoting democracy without getting disillusioned because there's a military coup in Honduras and the generals didn't respond the way we wanted," said the understanding Fontaine.

Reagan's victory in early November was received by conservative Central Americans with fireworks in Guatemala and El Salvador. Nor did the president-elect disappoint their expectations at his first news conference in Los Angeles on November 6. While his criticisms of Carter on the human rights question were carefully couched, the clues they offered were nonetheless clear. "I don't think that you can turn away from some country because here and there they do not totally agree with our concept of human rights," said Reagan, "and then at the same time maintain relations with other countries where human rights are virtually nonexistent."

By the end of November, Reagan's Latin American corps was receiving visitors from El Salvador's private sector and assuring them that the new administration would increase military aid, including combat equipment, to security forces fighting leftist guerrillas. Manuel Enrique Hinds, spokesman for El Salvador's private enterprise Productive Alliance, consulted with Fontaine, Kirkpatrick, Theberge and Constantine Menges of the Hudson Institute, and reported, "They were very clear on the need for strengthening the security forces."

The day that the bodies of the four American churchwomen were found in El Salvador the first semi-official but specific directions on Central American policy from the incoming administration were revealed in the media. A report prepared by Reagan's State Department transition team, put together by veteran government official Pedro San Juan and Frank Carbaugh, a legislative aide of Senator Jesse Helms, the ultra-rightwing Republican from North Carolina, called for a reduction in human rights emphasis and the muzzling of "social reformers" in the department.

The report argued that the new administration should take what it termed a more balanced position toward violence in Central America, "making clear that terrorism is as inhumane as repression." Where the Carter administration had suspended military aid on the grounds of human rights violations, the report countered, "Internal policy-making procedures should be structured to insure that the human rights area is not in a position to paralyze or unduly delay decisions on issues where human rights concerns conflict with other vital U.S. interests."

El Salvador Ambassador Robert White came under fire for backing the Salvadoran junta's modest proposals for change. Ambassadors, said the report, "are not supposed to function in the capacity of social reformers and advocates of new theories of social change with latitude to experiment within the country to which they are accredited." If there was any doubt about White's prospects, they were laid to rest by an accompanying transition team paper on ambassadorial assignments which provided a hit list of some sixty diplomats to be dumped. White and the U.S. Ambassador to Nicaragua Lawrence Pezzullo were prominent among the intended victims.

Jeane Kirkpatrick's idea was that the Carter administration employed a double standard in dealing with dictatorships, tolerating those on the left while being volubly critical of those on the right. In case after case, the United States under Carter had "collaborated in the replacement of moderate autocrats friendly to the U.S. with less friendly autocrats of extremist persuasion." The puzzling irony of this double standard was that in favoring "totalitarianism" over "authoritarianism" (as these two forms of dictatorship came to be dubbed in the debate that followed), such a policy not only didn't serve, but actually undermined, U.S. interests. What America needed, argued Kirkpatrick, was "a morally and strategically acceptable, and politically realistic, program for dealing with non-democratic governments threatened by Soviet-sponsored subversion."

When the 54-year-old professor of political science at Georgetown University was designated U.S. Ambassador to the United Nations on December 22, her views, heretofore confined to the relative obscurity of conservative journals and occasional presentations at the American Enterprise Institute (where Kirkpatrick was a resident scholar), immediately acquired new dimensions, since they bid fair to provide the intellectual foundations of the new U.S. Central American policy.

At first glance, Kirkpatrick, a lifelong Democrat, seemed a slightly surprising choice for the U.N. post. Born in 1926 in Duncan, Oklahoma, she was the daughter of an oil wildcatter who moved his family to a succession of small towns in Oklahoma and Illinois. Kirkpatrick graduated from Barnard College in 1948 and received her master's degree from Columbia University in 1950. Five years later she married Evron Kirkpatrick, a fellow political scientist and Democrat who had once managed a Hubert Humphrey political campaign. After marriage, she took time off to raise three sons, returning to Columbia to earn her doctorate—on the Peronist movement in Argentina—in 1968. For the past dozen years she had taught at Georgetown, achieving tenure and the rank of full professor.

Prominent in the Democratic party, she had become disillusioned in 1972 when what she called the "antiwar, antigrowth, antibusiness, antilabor activists" gained control, securing the party's nomination for Senator George McGovern. Along with other conservative Democrats (among them, Senators Henry Jackson of Washington and New York's Daniel Moynihan), she was a charter member of the Coalition for a Democratic Majority, formed in 1972 to wrest power from the party's liberal wing. In 1976 she supported Jackson for the Democratic nomination, then shifted to Carter. Increasingly unhappy with Carter foreign policy, she published "Dictatorships and Double Standards" in the November 1979 issue of *Commentary*, a neo-conservative magazine edited by Norman Podhoretz.

It was this article that brought her to the attention of the Reagan campaign, through Latin policy advisor and fellow American Enterprise Institute associate Fontaine. Reagan wrote Kirkpatrick a long letter praising the piece and suggested that they meet. "We hit it off very well," she later said, recalling her first meeting with Reagan in spring 1980. The Republican aspirant seemed to be "a nice man" who was "not a rightwing ideologue." The rather patrician Kirkpatrick soon signed on to campaign for the former movie actor.

The week of the churchwomen's murder, Kirkpatrick was at the American Enterprise Institute delivering a paper, a follow-up to her now-celebrated article, entitled "The Hobbes Problem: Order, Authority and Legitimacy in Central America." While the course of foreign policy might be charted by the visceral impulses of longstanding anti-communists, it nonetheless required some semblance of intellectual justification, hence the pivotal role of Kirkpatrick in the thinking of the new administration. And although much of what would transpire in the next four years provides a test of Kirkpatrick's ideas, it's appropriate at this point that they receive some further explication as Central American policy was taking shape in the first months of Reagan's reign.

"Dictatorships and Double Standards" began with a sweeping condemnation of the "failure" of Carter foreign policy ("now clear to everyone except its architects") as evidenced by the giveaway of the Panama Canal, an unanswered buildup of Soviet military might, the related "dramatic extension" of Soviet influence on various African and Caribbean fronts and, as if that were not bad enough, the recent loss of Iran and Nicaragua from the American sphere of domination. In both of the latter cases, Carter "not only failed to prevent the undesired outcome," but worse, had "actively collaborated in the replacement of moderate autocrats friendly to American interests with less friendly autocrats of extremist persuasion."

Of course, despite Kirkpatrick's efforts, from her opening words, to establish a knowing tone that brooked no rebuttal, it was hardly "clear to everyone" that Carter's foreign policy was an unmitigated "failure." One could point to the soon-to-be-outgoing president's successful negotiation of the Egyptian-Israeli peace treaty, his relatively civil relations with China and the USSR (prior to the latter's invasion of Afghanistan), and his temperate, patient response to the Iranian regime throughout the lengthy hostage crisis.

Though Kirkpatrick was irked that the Panama Canal had been turned over "to a swaggering Latin dictator of Castroite bent"—a reference to Panamanian leader Omar Torrijos—it was not entirely clear how the swaggering, imperialistic slogans of Reagan ("We built it, we paid for it, it's ours") constituted a stronger claim to ownership than Panamanian sovereignty. As for the charge of Soviet military superiority, which would soon form the basis for the Reagan administration's advocacy of the most extensive armaments spending program in the country's history, scores of knowledgeable munitions experts would eventually come forth to assert that, at worst, the U.S. enjoyed a rough parity with the Soviets and, by almost all accounts, significant nuclear weapons superiority. Finally, leaving aside the charge that Carter's withdrawal of support for various dictators constituted "active collaboration" in their overthrow (the phrase had a faintly treasonous nuance), it was equally unclear that the characterization of the Somoza dictatorship (which had extended through three generations and forty-five years) as "moderate" autocracy, or the depiction of the Sandinista revolution as autocratic, much less as of "extremist persuasion," was at all accurate. While understandably at odds with liberalism, Kirkpatrick's charges would have to be sustained by something more than polemical assertions.

In calling for a politically "realistic" program to deal with "non-democratic governments threatened by Soviet-sponsored subversion," Kirkpatrick seemed willing to face up to the unpleasantness of "friendly" dictators. But even here, various hidden assumptions were slipped into the argument. The very nomenclature was loaded: friendly dictators were merely "non-democratic"; unfriendly governments were "totalitarian." Nonetheless, in referring to the Somozas of the world, Kirkpatrick conceded that such men "had not been selected by free elections'' and "recognized no duty to submit themselves to searching tests of popular acceptability." Given that they were "confronted by radical, violent opponents bent on social and political revolution," it was admittedly the case that such rulers "sometimes invoked martial law to arrest, imprison, exile, and occasionally, it was alleged, torture their opponents." The implication was that while such acts were not justifiable, they were understandable, even deserving of a sympathetic viewing. Such figures, after all, "were not only anti-Communist, they were positively friendly to the U.S., sending their sons and others to be educated in our universities, voting with us in the United Nations, and regularly supporting American interests and positions even when these entailed personal and political cost." Their Washington embassies, Kirkpatrick noted, even threw good cocktail parties.

While it was true that "traditional autocrats tolerate social inequalities, brutality, and poverty," one had to recognize, in the spirit of realism, that "revolutionary autocracies created them." In an imperfect world, it was necessary to view misery with balanced coolness. "Traditional autocrats leave in place existing allocations of wealth, power, status and other resources which in most traditional societies favor an affluent few and maintain masses in poverty. But they worship traditional gods and observe traditional taboos. They do not disturb the habitual rhythms of work and leisure, habitual places of residence, habitual patterns of family and personal relations. Because the miseries of traditional life are familiar, they are bearable to ordinary people who, growing up in the society, learn to cope, as children born to untouchables in India acquire the skills and attitudes necessary for survival in the miserable roles they are destined to fill. Such societies create no refugees."

The tired, but resignedly "realistic" voice of this passage—speaking in tones inherited from the colonial administrator's complaints about "the white man's burden"—was so smooth as to cause some readers to nod in the face of contrary facts. Other critics, however, such as Tom Farer, president of the Inter-American Commission on Human Rights of the Organization of American States, writing in the liberal *New York Review of Books* a few months after Kirkpatrick's appointment to the U.N., noted that this bucolic account of the preservation of "existing allocations of wealth, power and status" was "a deceptive summary of the goals of Kirkpatrick's 'traditional autocrats'." Such a placid portrait, argued Farer, "misses the dynamic of contemporary Latin American societies." The suggestion that traditional autocrats passively "tolerated" inequalities and "left in place" existing allocations ruled out a model in which the conditions of misery must be actively reproduced on a daily basis, usually through violent coercion, since "ordinary people," despite their love of "habitual rhythms," displayed a disconcerting tendency to dispense with their dictators at the earliest opportunity.

Kirkpatrick's account, replied Farer, "obscures the realities of life under authoritarian governments—not only the torture and murder of political dissidents but also the more subtle yet often more comprehensively destructive acts carried out through the operation and manipulation of economic forces in societies with vast gaps between the power and education and wealth of relatively few people and the rest of the population." Since, in Kirkpatrick's vision, the masses of people were incapable of being actors in history (busy as they were "acquiring the skills and attitudes necessary for survival" in misery), it necessarily followed that occasions of restiveness must be foreign-inspired, and presumably Soviet-sponsored. But apart from this "almost demented parody of Latin American political realities," what in fact happened in the dynamic of authoritarianism was that "universities are purged, political parties dissolved, unions reorganized, dissidents murdered, the Church harassed, all as part of a huge effort first to demobilize the popular classes, and then to direct and strain their demands through new, purified institutions subject to manipulation by the state." Our examination of El Salvador should, in due course, provide an empirical measure as to which of these two accounts is closer to the truth.

Naturally, Kirkpatrick was in favor of the democratization of "non-democratic" governments. But one had to understand that "in the relatively few places where they exist, democratic governments have come into being slowly, after extended prior experience with more limited forms of participation during which leaders have reluctantly grown accustomed to tolerating dissent and opposition, opponents have accepted the notion that they may defeat but not destroy incumbents," etc. To the age-old question of the oppressed, "How long, O Lord?", Kirkpatrick replied, "Decades, if not centuries, are normally required for people to acquire the necessary disciplines and habits."

That was the sober lesson liberals were incapable of grasping. Instead, they succumbed to the utopian beliefs that at the moment of crisis in the reign of a rightwing dictatorship there existed a democratic alternative; second, that continuation of the status quo was impossible; and finally, that any change was preferable to the present conditions. "Each of these beliefs is widely shared in the liberal community," noted Kirkpatrick. "Not one of them can withstand close scrutiny." Worse, such illusions were abetted by the "liberal press" and "left-leaning clerics," who "interpret insurgency as evidence of widespread popular discontent and a will to democracy," oblivious of the dark hand of totalitarianism pulling the strings. In consequence, the strength of sought-for "moderates" in opposition movements against the dictator was overestimated, and the "intransigence of radicals" in such movements grossly underestimated, resulting in the "coming to power of new regimes in which ordinary people enjoy fewer freedoms and less personal security than under the previous autocracy—regimes, moreover, hostile to American interests and policies."

Insofar as the debate in which Kirkpatrick was engaged was confined to the liberal/conservative spectrum of American politics, her argument wasn't altogether implausible. Indeed, it was often the case that it would be impossible to locate pro-American "moderates" to replace the "traditional autocrat," and instead, revolutionary forces would come to office who didn't view American domination benignly. And certainly, the preservation of the status quo might be possible, given sufficient military aid and advice. Finally, if the desirability of change was to be measured solely by U.S. interests rather than the interests of the populations seeking change, one could see how certain changes would be deemed unwelcome. Once outside this narrow spectrum of American interests, however, such concerns considerably diminish in importance, or can be seen at least as the naked interests of empire. As for the theoretical claim that anti-Americanism spelled totalitarianism, or its practical application, in Nicaragua, it was hard to see how Kirkpatrick, writing less than six months after the Nicaraguan revolution, could already discern that "ordinary people enjoyed fewer freedoms and less personal security" than under Somoza.

However, Kirkpatrick's was not a crude appeal to simply ensure the maintenance in power of America's thuggish friends. On the contrary, it was possible that U.S. policy "could effectively encourage the process of democratization, provided that the effort is not made at a time when the incumbent government is fighting for its life against violent adversaries, and that proposed reforms are aimed at producing gradual change rather than perfect democracy overnight." Since El Salvador, Guatemala, Honduras and the late, lamented Nicaragua might all be characterized as having dictators fighting for their lives against armed adversaries, that formula seemed to rule out the advocacy of democratization in Central America at present.

Instead, policymakers had to more "adequately appreciate the government's problem in maintaining order in a society confronted with an ideologically extreme opposition." Taking up the issue once again in December 1980, Kirkpatrick invoked the spirit of Thomas Hobbes, the seventeenth-century political philosopher of order, urging contemporaries to learn his fundamental doctrine—that "the central problem of any society is to establish order and authority." But order was hard to come by in the inherently unstable societies of Central America, and worse, into these systems enter guerrilla violence and groups trained and supported by Cuba and linked to the grand schemes of the Soviet Union.

In Chilean scholar Luis Maira's critical summary of the Georgetown professor's analysis, the guerrilla "forces use terrorism to destroy order, break down the economy and daily life, demoralize the police, and mortally wound governments by proving their inability to protect personal safety and maintain public authority." In Kirkpatrick's words, this terrorism constituted "a form of revolution that replaces mass support with the employment of revolutionary military groups."

The crucial shift in perspective advocated by Kirkpatrick was to see that Central America was an internationalized area where other powers were acting in opposition to the U.S. national interest. In order to develop that "realistic" policy she had called for, it was necessary to learn the neo-Hobbesian lesson that in a case of externally supported terrorism, "the status of a government depends more than usual on its ability to govern, to assure obedience, to punish those who disobey, in sum to maintain order." The policy that flowed from this analysis, observed critic Maira, was one "that stresses the reconstruction of order, even if this takes force and rebuilds authoritarianism as well. After all, these conservative reflections tell us, political democracy is not a suitable model for all countries, especially not for those whose entropic tendencies are accelerated by the seige of international communism. To impede, by whatever means, the rise to power of a coalition opposed to the region remaining in loyal alliance with the U.S. is to serve the U.S. national interest."

Such as they were, these were the seminal ideas offered to, and embraced by, the incoming Reagan administration. All that was required was someone to put them into operation. Al Haig would soon make his appearance.

In Chalatenango, El Salvador, on Saturday, December 6, little girls played with dolls on the steps of the altar as fourteen white-robed priests, led by Acting Archbishop Arturo Rivera Damas, celebrated the funeral mass for Sisters Ita Ford and Maura Clarke who would be buried in this rural peasant village where they had worked. The next day in Cleveland, Ohio, a memorial service was held for slain Ursuline nun Dorothy Kazel. Jean Donovan's body was returned for burial to Sarasota, Florida, where her parents lived.

Outside the Chalatenango church, dark green military vehicles were parked. A few soldiers armed with automatic rifles patrolled the plaza. Inside, Rivera Damas told the mourners, "The government says it is not persecuting the church, but there are certain facts which cannot be explained." The persistence of these elusive explanations would, in the coming months, haunt the policies devised by Jeane Kirkpatrick and others.

2   A Textbook Case

> ...*the insurgency in El Salvador has been progressively transformed into a textbook case of indirect armed aggression by Communist power through Cuba.*
>
> —U.S. State Department,
> Feb. 19, 1981

He proclaimed himself the "vicar" of American foreign policy.

At 56, Alexander M. Haig, Jr., the man President Reagan had chosen to be his secretary of state, was considered to be a master of the power game by virtue of a remarkable career. It included a distinguished series of battlefield tours; service in the Department of Defense during the Lyndon Johnson administration; an apprenticeship under Henry Kissinger, Richard Nixon's national security adviser and later secretary of state; promotion to four-star general; the post of White House chief of staff during Nixon's final days; commander of NATO; and most recently, president of the United Technologies Corporation.

This lantern-jawed workaholic was a man whose world view could be summed up by *Time* magazine "in a phrase: the Russians are coming." He had the reputation of being a tough-minded leader whom conservatives expected could end what another publication called "the post-Vietnam vacillation that has plagued foreign policy during the Carter administration."

The road from four-year-old who took a bugle to bed with him to four-star general began in Bala-Cynwyd, a middle class

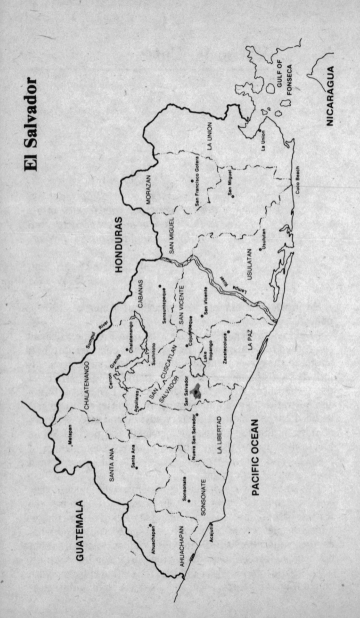

El Salvador

Catholic suburb of Philadelphia, Pennsylvania, where Haig grew up the middle of three children of a lawyer. His younger brother Frank, a Jesuit priest who chaired the physics and computer science department at Loyola College in Baltimore, Maryland, recalled that as a boy Al was the leader of a gang called the Musketeers and in charge of negotiating agreements over neighborhood turf with rival groups.

Haig's father died of cancer when the boy was ten, and a wealthy uncle, John Neeson, stepped in to support the family financially and help Al realize his boyhood ambition to become an army officer. Neeson first got Haig into Notre Dame University and then used his congressional contacts to wangle the youth an appointment to West Point in 1944. Haig was a dutiful but hardly brilliant student who graduated a poor 214th in the 310-member class of 1947. At the military academy, Haig failed to make the varsity football team, but quarterbacked in intramural ball. He continued playing as a young infantry officer serving postwar occupation duty in Japan. Patricia Fox, the daughter of a general who was a senior aide to commanding General Douglas MacArthur, saw Haig on the gridiron and remarked to a friend that he was "like a Greek god." They met and married, and soon after, Haig was posted to MacArthur's staff.

From there he went to Korea, where he saw action in several campaigns and took part in the famed Inchon landings. Later, he did a European tour and picked up a master's degree in international relations at Georgetown University. By the early 1960s he was assigned to the Pentagon, where his work brought him to the attention of Army Secretary Cyrus Vance. When Vance was promoted to deputy defense secretary in 1964, Haig went along, eventually becoming an assistant to Secretary of Defense Robert McNamara. Believing he needed more combat experience if he was ever to make general, Haig went to Vietnam in 1966 as a field commander.

When Henry Kissinger was assembling a national security staff for President-elect Nixon in 1968, Haig had just the background needed to become National Security Council military adviser. He was the White House's eyes and ears in Vietnam, making sixteen fact-finding trips to the war zone for the president and Kissinger. Haig was also one of the important behind-the-scenes players in the inner Nixon circle. As Seymour Hersh reported in *The Price of Power*, his study of Kissinger's White House years, it was Haig who pushed for what eventually became the president's program of secret bombings of Cambodia. When Nixon and Kissinger decided to tap the telephones of journalists and government officials in a bid to stop leaks about the administration's war plans, it was Haig who personally requested the Federal Bureau of Investigation to install the taps.

By 1972, Haig had been promoted to the rank of major general and was one of Nixon's most influential advisers, setting up the president's first trip to China and sitting in on peace talks with the North Vietnamese in Paris. Throughout, Haig was a hardliner, pressing Nixon to bomb Hanoi and mine Haiphong harbor. His White House career was capped in September 1972 when Nixon leapfrogged him from two-star to four-star full general over 240 more senior officers.

But by May 1973, as the Watergate scandal was decimating the ranks of Nixon's White House aides, Haig was asked to return as chief of staff. In the next eighteen months, Haig's relationship with Kissinger, now secretary of state, was transformed from protege to rival. "There were incredible fights between Henry and Al over who would get the bedroom next to Nixon on foreign trips," recalled one insider.

Even as Haig prepared for his Senate confirmation hearings in December 1980, there was still controversy over his role during Nixon's last days, especially on the issue of whether he had participated in what was legally an obstruction of justice. The line between loyalty and illegality was thin. On one of the notorious White House tapes, which congressional investigators were scouring to locate a "smoking pistol" statement that would seal Nixon's fate, Haig could be heard urging the president to sidestep damaging allegations by telling accusers "you just can't remember." After Nixon's resignation, his chief aide was urged to stay on by interregnum president Gerald Ford, but the Watergate affair made it politically difficult. Though Ford wanted to reward the general with the post of Army chief of staff, the position required Senate confirmation, a process that could be embarrassing to both men. Instead, Haig was shipped to Brussels as commander of NATO.

When he resigned in mid-1979, openly critical of Carter's foreign policy, Haig undertook a nationwide speaking tour that he hoped might eventually propel him to the Republican nomination for president. When it became obvious that his White House ambitions were premature, he accepted the top executive post at United Technologies, where he remained until Reagan phoned him with a job offer. At the State Department, Haig would have the opportunity to put into practice his position that the U.S. "cannot recoil from challenging Soviet interventionism wherever it occurs," particularly in Central America.

Meanwhile, as the general about to turn statesmen readied himself to seek Senate approval, Jimmy Carter's representatives in El Salvador were apparently doing more than merely determining whether Salvadoran security forces had murdered the U.S. churchwomen. Fact-finder William Rogers had hinted as much when he said upon departing Washington that his mission would attempt to discover "what kind of government can exercise power effectively in El Salvador's conditions."

Within days of the U.S. mission's departure the Salvadoran government was given a facelifting reshuffle. On the surface, it looked like one of those careful steps toward democratization recommended by Jeane Kirkpatrick, while at the same time satisfying U.S. critics of military rule. Jose Napoleon Duarte, a 55-year-old Christian Democratic member of the current junta, after week-long intense negotiations with the military, was named on December 13 the first civilian president of El Salvador in a half century.

Appearances were deceiving. In exchange for the presidency, the armed forces in fact consolidated their grip on power. First, Colonel Adolfo Majano, the leader of a group of younger officers who had deposed dictator General Carlos Humberto Romero in October 1979, was now himself ousted from the ruling junta. For months, Majano, considered the most liberal member of the junta, had been steadily losing influence to conservative Defense Minister Colonel Jose Garcia and to Colonel Jaime Gutierrez, the most rightwing member of the junta, who had recently replaced Majano as commander of the army. As one foreign diplomat described the situation, it was a quiet coup "being played out over an extended period."

Duarte, who had won the 1972 presidential election but had been thwarted by electoral fraud and then driven into exile, claimed that the shuffle was "an important historic step; the government has been given to the civilians." Knowledgeable diplomats thought otherwise. Gutierrez had been named vice-president and retained his command of the army; Garcia remained as minister of defense. Given that, "Mr. Duarte is an adornment," said one foreign embassy official. Or, as another diplomat put it, "Nothing has changed. Mr. Duarte has made an expensive compromise to realize his dream of becoming president. If the president is not commander in chief, then he is not in command."

For the moment, however, this satisfaction of appearances was enough to permit the U.S. State Department to speedily resume economic aid to the junta. Four days after the shuffle, which the U.S. acknowledged as a "positive development," the $20 million in suspended economic assistance was restored; as well, the U.S. voted at the Inter-American Development Bank for a loan of some $40 million for farm machinery and fertilizer destined for peasant cooperatives under El Salvador's land reform program. Investigator Rogers' report to the president dutifully concluded that the Salvadoran high command was not involved in the missionaries' murders, but that lower-level members of the security force might have been.

Reports and reshufflings aside, the killings continued. In addition to the daily political murders of Salvadoran civilians, two weeks later, on January 3, 1981, the violence again struck close to home. Two Americans working in El Salvador's land redistribution program were sitting with the head of the country's agrarian reform agency in the coffee shop of the Sheraton Hotel, a popular gathering place for the wealthy located on the slopes of one of the volcanoes surrounding San Salvador. The three men—Jose Viera, 43, president of the Institute for Agrarian Transformation; Michael Hammer, 42, of Potomac, Maryland, and Mark Pearlman, 36, of Seattle, Washington, both of whom had been sent by the U.S. labor movement's American Institute for Free Labor Development as land reform consultants—had finished a late meal and were drinking coffee.

At 11:30 p.m., three assassins entered the nearly deserted restaurant. While one guarded the door, the other two walked over to the table, pulled out .9-millimeter and .45-caliber automatic pistols and slew Viera, Hammer and Pearlman. The killers, according to an eyewitness waitress, "calmly tucked their pistols into the waists of their trousers and very calmly left," undetected by the hotel's sizeable security force. Once again, there was the pro forma charge—this time made by junta member Jose Morales Ehrlich, a Christian Democratic party leader—blaming the left for the murders, but as one observer pointed out, "The Sheraton is a fortress; it had to be an inside job." Recently named president Duarte quickly conceded "it was almost certainly an action of the extreme right," whose detestation of the land redistribution scheme was well known. Given that the land program was one of the pillars of reform, by which the effectiveness of the search for a political center in El Salvador would be measured, the killing of its top officials had to be a cause for alarm among the forces represented by Duarte.

As damaging as the junta's inability to control its thugs was to the credibility of the Salvadoran government, it faced a far more serious danger on the battlefield. Ten days before Ronald Reagan's inauguration, on January 10, the Farabundo Marti National Liberation Front (FMLN), the federation of five guerrilla groups fighting to overthrow the junta, launched what it called a "final offensive." As sporadic fighting broke out in various regions of the country, including the capital, Duarte immediately declared martial law and imposed a nationwide dusk-to-dawn curfew.

The emergency, though it would be short-lived, provided the impetus for a further resumption of U.S. aid. Citing what they claimed to be an increased flow of arms to the guerrillas from Nicaragua, a charge given credibility by Ambassador White in San Salvador, the State Department on January 14 announced the resumption of $5 million worth of "non-lethal" military aid to El Salvador. The decision, said department officials who were concerned about maintaining a semblance of consistency, was also based on progress made in the investigation of the killings of the American churchwomen. Three days later, in a less publicized but more important move, the outgoing Carter administration authorized an additional $5 million worth of M-16 rifles, ammunition, grenade launchers, and four Huey helicopters for El Salvador's armed forces, the first time since 1977 that direct U.S. military assistance was being provided. Ironically, on the eve of his departure, Carter was restoring the very policy he had found so objectionable upon taking office.

The rapid provision of this arsenal appeared to be unnecessary. Two weeks after its launching, the guerrilla offensive had stalled. In a statement signed by FMLN commanders, who had overestimated their prospects, the guerrilla leaders conceded that the military actions had failed to spark a nationwide insurrection, as they had hoped. Ambassador White, who had supported the resumption of military aid, and even lent plausibility to a Salvadoran government story that a group of FMLN guerrillas had arrived from Nicaragua via boat, now caustically observed about the offensive, "They gave a war and nobody came." The prematurity of White's battlefield assessment would become apparent within months.

The Nicaraguan government vigorously denied any involvement in a seaborne invasion from its territory. There was also a disclaimer of outside aid by the opposition Democratic Revolutionary Front's recently formed political and diplomatic commission in Mexico City. Nonetheless, the accusations provided a pretext for the suspension of the remaining payments of a $75 million economic aid package to Nicaragua in one of the first moves by the U.S. State Department after Ronald Reagan's January 20 inauguration. This was soon followed by a decision to delay a $9 million wheat sale to the Nicaraguans.

While these were but hints of things to come, the new president was busy sending signals of his administration's interest in making Latin American affairs a high priority item. Two weeks before his inauguration, Reagan, in a "gesture of goodwill" as it was billed, met with Mexico's President Jose Lopez Portillo in Ciudad Juarez, a Mexican border city across the Rio Grande from El Paso. A week after his installation, the first foreign visitor Reagan received at the White House was Jamaican Prime Minister Edward Seaga, a conservative who had defeated the socialist government of Michael Manley at the polls the previous October. Reagan used the occasion to voice his concern about hemispheric security problems. "We are unrelaxed about the status of events in the Caribbean and the instability being inflicted on some countries in Central America and in other places in the hemisphere from the outside," Reagan said.

Alexander Haig's commanding start at the State Department began on Inauguration Day when he handed presidential counselor Edwin Meese a detailed proposal designed to consolidate foreign policy decision making within his bailiwick. The scheme was too ambitious for the president's men and Meese set to work on an amended version intended to protect other government agencies from Haig's designs.

The general moved quickly to outflank Richard Allen, another Nixon era conservative whom Reagan had chosen as his national security adviser. Haig was determined not to see a repeat of the process he had witnessed firsthand as Henry Kissinger's No. 2 man a decade earlier when State Department power was shifted to the White House. Within forty-eight hours of the formal transfer of power, Haig swept grandly into the department, arriving with a half-dozen or so trusted associates whom he called "my nominees," despite reminders from White House aides that they were really presidential appointees. Haig's men were described as "moderate conservatives" with lengthy operating experience; among them: Walter Stoessel, a senior foreign service ambassador as under secretary for political affairs; the staunchly conservative former Senator James Buckley as under secretary for security assistance; and former Haig colleague from Nixon days, Lawrence Eagleburger, named one of the key assistant secretaries. The one exception to this pattern of control was William Clark, a former California judge appointed by Reagan, and now chosen as deputy secretary of state. Clark showed an abysmal ignorance of foreign affairs at his confirmation hearings (asked to name the prime minister of Zimbabwe, he replied, "It would be a guess"), but he had been chosen by Reagan's Californians on the White House staff to keep an eye on Haig.

The new secretary of state also came on strong at the podium. At his first official press conference, he shocked several foreign policy experts by bluntly charging the Soviet Union with "training, funding and equipping" international terrorists. The following day, department spokesman William Dyess was sent in with the water bucket to cool things off. Haig was actually using the word "terrorism" rather loosely, said Dyess, to include Soviet support of national liberation movements and propaganda advocating "armed struggle," as in El Salvador. All of this can be broadly defined as terrorism, claimed Haig's underling, because it "creates a climate in which terrorism flourishes." Despite the effort at moderation, experts on terrorism such as Georgetown University's Professor Walter Laqueur remained puzzled. "I sympathize with Haig's sentiments," said the professor, "but I regret the lack of precision in his words. It is very difficult to know what he means."

Laqueur wasn't the only one having trouble understanding "Haig-speak." The secretary, garbed in rather garish broad-pinstriped suits and employing a disconcerting speaking style in which a quavering whisper was used to underline the dangers posed by America's enemies, appeared to be carrying out search-and-destroy missions against the English language. Amused members of the press soon issued lexicons of "Haigledygook," including such items as "caveat," a key word in the general's verbification program, as in: "I'll have to caveat my response, Senator." There was a string of involuted phrases like "careful caution" and "exacerbating restraint" (as in expressing the hope that the Soviets would do nothing "to exacerbate the kind of mutual restraint that both sides should pursue"). At times, Haig himself seemed to be in on the joke. Asked to clarify a statement at a press conference: "That was consciously ambiguous in the sense that any terrorist government or terrorist movement that is contemplating such actions I think knows clearly what we are speaking of." But the former general didn't look like he was joking.

There was no misunderstanding Haig's message when, less than ten days after taking office and in his first public move, he fired U.S. Ambassador to El Salvador Robert White on February 1, 1981. Although it was standard practice after a change of administration to remove ambassadorial political appointees, the norm for career ambassadors, such as White who had been a Foreign Service officer for twenty-five years, was to keep them at their posts or to offer new assignments. Pointedly, there was no new assignment offer made to White.

When White's name appeared atop the Reagan transition team's hit list of ambassadors slated for removal, the 55-year-old diplomat was engulfed not only in the investigation of the murder of the American churchwomen, but the shakeup of the Salvadoran regime that immediately followed it. It wasn't until a week later that White replied publicly to the criticisms. He charged that the transition team report was undercutting him, making it difficult to influence moderates, and encouraging far rightwing elements in the country, who he said were organizing a coup. "The danger is very real," he said. "There is a lot of pressure being placed on military officers to move this government to the right." During the same interview, White revealed that retired Major Roberto D'Aubuisson, a 37-year-old former Salvadoran Army intelligence officer linked to previous coup attempts as well as to the notorious death squads, was once again in the country. A rightwing coup, White claimed, would plunge El Salvador into an even more fratricidal civil war than already existed. "When civil war breaks out in this country, I hope they get their chance to serve," said the bitter ambassador, referring to Reagan's aides.

Although White had been rumored to be previously opposed to U.S. military aid to Salvadoran forces, when the State Department made the decision to resume military aid on January 14, 1981, in the face of the FMLN offensive, the ambassador was on-side. At a news conference in San Salvador the next day, White testified that "it is my personal conclusion that there has been a change in the amount and sophistication of weapons coming to the guerrillas, and I think they are coming from Nicaragua." The U.S., he added, was "under an obligation. . .to try to help El Salvador interdict the supply of military equipment coming in from the outside." In the internecine departmental rivalries in Washington, the resumption of military aid was seen not so much as a State Department decision but as a policy victory for the Pentagon and the Defense Department, which had been urging such a move for months while the Carter administration continued to seek a political center in El Salvador.

What irked White about the arms resumption decision was that it had been linked to the claim that the Salvadoran government had taken "positive steps" in the investigation of the killing of the churchwomen. Again, White spoke out. "As far as I am concerned, there is no reason to believe that the government of El Salvador is conducting a serious investigation," he said, disputing the official line. "I am not going to be involved in a cover-up. . .There were good reasons for giving the military assistance at this time, but there was no need to misrepresent the situation on the investigation."

Such unusual frankness was of a piece with the line White had taken since being moved into El Salvador by President Carter the previous March. In accordance with Carter policy, White had diligently searched for what he called "a non-Marxist, pro-democratic model of profound change," attempting to hold the right at bay by not arming them to the teeth, and insisting that the self-proclaimed reformers on the junta live up to human rights commitments in return for aid.

It was not White's bluntness that aroused the wrath of the new Reagan administration and its foreign policy "vicar" Al Haig, but their perception of the ambassador as soft on the arms question. As Jeane Kirkpatrick put it in a debate with White on El Salvador three weeks after his firing, "It is widely said by some people who were involved that one of the reasons that no requests for military equipment came forward during Ambassador White's tenure was that he declined to forward them." Although White exploded at Kirkpatrick's catty version of Washington gossip, calling her claim "a total falsehood," when he testified before a sub-committee the following month, he agreed that Haig had dismissed him because he opposed growing U.S. military aid. He was, however, unrepentent. "Last week, this administration informed me that I must leave the Foreign Service," he told congressmen. "I regard it as an honor to join a small group of officers who have gone out of the service because they refused to betray their principles." The group was small indeed. In the State Department's announcement that White would be removed under a provision that a career officer who is not reassigned shall be retired, he became only the tenth ambassador to be separated from the Foreign Service by this procedure since 1947.

Twenty-four hours after dumping White, Haig's department announced that Frederic Chapin, another career diplomat, would be sent to temporarily fill in. White's firing was a good example of the political limitations imposed on the possibilities of American foreign policy. At worst, White's sin was simply to have upheld the liberal position of the Carter White House against more hardline views espoused by the U.S. military-defense establishment. Seen from outside, White's policy didn't appear strikingly different from that of the new regime in Washington. But for Haig, the nuances of difference were enough. The even narrower range than before of what constituted acceptable views was the unmistakeable message of Haig's signals.

Within a week, the word was out that President Reagan, at the urging of his secretary of state, had decided to make El Salvador the subject of his new administration's first major foreign policy initiative. As early as February 6, rumors were afloat that secret documents captured from Salvadoran insurgents provided incontrovertible proof that the Soviet Union, Vietnam, and Cuba, among others, using Nicaragua as a transit point, had agreed to supply hundreds of tons of weapons to the guerrillas. It was not until the following week that it became apparent that Haig's team was about to launch a full-court press on the issue. Not only would the Salvadoran revelations provide a justification for Reagan's course of action there, their disclosure would also offer a paradigm of the conservative regime's hardline on foreign policy. Haig was planning to pull out all the stops: highlevel diplomatic missions to Europe and Latin America, private congressional briefings to garner legislative support for new actions, and a public "white paper" to expose Soviet perfidy. The focus on El Salvador would not only test Soviet resolve; attitudes expressed toward the guerrilla war by European allies, many of whom had previously shown some sympathy toward the leftist opposition, would become an early barometer of their relations with the U.S.

On Monday morning, February 16, Assistant Secretary of State for European Affairs Lawrence Eagleburger was in Bonn, West Germany to present eighteen pounds of intelligence documentation showing Soviet involvement in Central America. It was the first stop of a whirlwind tour that would touch down in Paris, Brussels, the Hague and London. Meanwhile, retired Lieutenant General Vernon Walters, who had been deputy director of the CIA during the Nixon administration, was tramping through Latin America on a similar mission. In Bonn, where the government had suspended development aid to El Salvador because of human rights abuses and a government spokesman had recently said there were "respectable democratic forces" on both sides of the conflict, Eagleburger met with foreign ministry and chancellory officials before hopping the night flight to Brussels where he had hoped to do some arm twisting of

NATO foreign ministers.

While America's "truth squads," as Haig called his messengers, were touring the globe, the secretary of state was busy on the homefront briefing key congressional leaders in a closed-door session. Illinois Republican Senator Charles Percy, chairman of the Foreign Relations Committee, was suitably impressed by Haig's sound-and-slide show. "I think those outside forces should be on notice that this nation will do whatever is necessary to prevent a communist takeover in El Salvador," Percy said after the briefing. Texas Democrat Jim Wright, the House majority leader, added a bipartisan note, declaring that "Central America is probably more vitally important to us than any other part of the world." The secretary had gotten what he wanted: pledges of support for whatever measures of increased "aid" the administration proposed.

The same day Haig also delivered his message to representatives of NATO, as well as of Australia, New Zealand and Japan, in similarly dramatic terms. "A well-orchestrated international Communist campaign designed to transform the Salvadoran crisis from the internal conflict to an increasingly internationalized confrontation is under way," said Haig. Everyone was involved: the Soviet bloc countries, Vietnam, Ethiopia, "radical Arabs," and of course, Cuba and Nicaragua which, given their political orientation, were almost to be regarded as non-hemispheric foreign powers.

By week's end, front-page headlines across the U.S. had picked up the catchphrase "a textbook case" from the State Department memorandum that had been submitted to friendly embassies. In addition to asserting that "the insurgency in El Salvador has been progressively transformed into a textbook case of indirect armed aggression by Communist powers," the document provided a detailed chronology of an arms shopping trip undertaken by Salvadoran Communist Party leader Shafik Handal, and a summary of documentary evidence that Nicaragua's Sandinista leaders cooperated with Cuba in shipping tons of arms to the guerrillas.

The State Department's White Paper, "Communist Interference in El Salvador," was released February 23, 1981, accompanied by a separate volume of nineteen documents to support charges that Cuba, the Soviet Union and other communist countries had organized a "well-coordinated, covert effort'' to bring down El Salvador's government. The report said nearly 200 tons of arms had been smuggled to El Salvador through a pipeline extending from Vietnam, Ethiopia and points east to Cuba and Nicaragua. From there, a sea, air and land courier service had put the guns in the guerrillas' hands. Although the White Paper focussed on evidentiary material—especially the travels of Salvadoran Communist leader Handal—perhaps just as importantly, it offered a political interpretation.

At the heart of this interpretation was the worldwide communist plot to ''overthrow El Salvador's established government'' and ''to impose in its place a Communist regime with no popular support.'' To the latter end, the guerrillas were portrayed by the White Paper as small, squabbling groups of the ''extreme left,'' fragmented until they were welded together, given political direction, and armed by Cuban leader Fidel Castro. Naturally, this naked aggression had to be masked, hence the creation of the Revolutionary Democratic Front (FDR) as ''a front organization to disseminate propaganda abroad. For appearances' sake, three small non-Marxist-Leninist political parties were brought into the front.''

On the other side, according to the State Department version, was the Duarte government, engaged in a ''search for order and democracy.'' Beset by ''the terrorism practiced by extremists of both left and right'' and by a long history in which ''the legitimate grievances of the poor and landless and the growing aspirations of the expanding middle classes met increasingly with repression,'' the Duarte government was ''working hard and with some success'' to introduce reforms. Were it not for this indirect communist aggression, the solution in El Salvador would ''be of the Salvadorans' own making and non-violent.''

With the White Paper released, and its evidence largely unquestioned, the administration now pressed forward with threats and concrete proposals. Presidential counselor Ed Meese, interviewed on television, renewed warnings to Cuba that the U.S. did ''not rule out anything'' in its efforts to halt arms deliveries to the guerrillas. Asked if the ''anything'' could include a naval blockade of the island, Meese coyly replied, ''The president has said many times he would like potential or real adversaries to go to bed every night wondering what we will do the next day. I don't think we would rule out anything." On the day of the White Paper's publication, presidential press secretary James Brady said the U.S. was "drawing the line in El Salvador. We have clear evidence of catching the communists' hands in the cookie jar."

The next day, Reagan, at a brief morning news conference, vowed that his government would continue to support the Salvadoran junta against those committed to its "violent overthrow." Repeating his often expressed views on the "linkage" between aspects of a policy, Reagan suggested that Soviet involvement in Central American arms supply had to be "straightened out" if global arms control negotiations were to proceed. Although Reagan assured the media that he had "no intention" of involving the U.S. inextricably, which was one of the main questions asked by reporters, that afternoon the president delivered an emotional address defending past U.S. involvement in Southeast Asia. American troops were withdrawn, he said, "not because they'd been defeated, but because they'd been denied permission to win."

By then, a National Security Council meeting had been slated to make concrete proposals, and the options being considered were floated in the press by government officials. In addition to boosting military aid, and possibly sending reconnaissance patrol boats to control the waters of the Gulf of Fonseca (which separates El Salvador and Nicaragua), the main idea was to send as many as forty military advisers in addition to the nineteen already present (fourteen of whom were helicopter technicians) to help the Salvadoran colonels win the war.

The following day, February 25, Senate majority leader Howard Baker emerged from a discussion with Reagan to say he supported sending as many as 150 U.S. advisers to El Salvador. Of course, these would not be combat advisers, Baker assured the public. "It is entirely appropriate to dispatch non-combat advisers to tell those people how to defend themselves against Cuba," Baker said. House Appropriations Sub-committee chairman Clarence Long, a Maryland Democrat, who was holding hearings on increased military aid that day, wasn't so sure about advisers. He said the move would be seen as "gunboat diplomacy all over again." Nonetheless, his committee listened to John Bushnell, acting assistant secretary of state for inter-American affairs, talk about increasing the level of military aid from the present $10 million to an amount between $25 million and $40 million.

There was also cheering from the sidelines. Nationally syndicated conservative columnist William Safire, a former Nixon speechwriter, offered a refreshingly vulgar blueprint for victory. "First, we must break the Communist winning streak," Safire told his readers. "Second, El Salvador is a place where we can win." What did Safire mean by "winning"? "Is it supporting a military junta that kills the opposition but by its repressive nature produces more opposition that becomes necessary to kill? If need be, yes." Columnist Safire also offered a step-by-step how-to course: "Let it be known that we are determined to see to it that the anti-Communists win." To do that, "give the government the military supplies it needs along with unabashed advisers who can show it how to use them." Furthermore, "make sure the generals know that somebody like Jose Napoleon Duarte" is "their ticket to all those shiny new gunships that can carry the battle to the terrorists." Next, "buy off the peasants and the middle class" by turning the Central American "minicountry into a garden spot for small businessmen and farmers." Finally, "make El Salvador the showplace for the triumph of free enterprise." It was a breathtaking vision of utopia.

The National Security Council decided at its February 27 meeting to more modestly settle for advisers and increased aid. The plan approved by Reagan and his top aides called for an additional thirty advisers and about $25 million in military equipment. Although the proposal for more American advisers hadn't become public until after the propaganda blitz launched by the administratioon, in fact it had been in the works for some time, as former Ambassador White revealed the day before. In refuting Jeane Kirkpatrick's claim that he had squelched military requests, White related a fascinating tale.

"The chief of the [U.S. embassy] military group came to me on the 19th of January with a five or six-page telegram which gave a rationale and a request for putting something like seventy-five military advisers into El Salvador," White recounted. "Thus, one component of the U.S. mission presented the ambassador with a full-blown telegram without any discussion." White was shocked. "I said, 'Colonel, what possessed you to do this?' He said, 'I'm under instructions to do this from the Pentagon and from South-Com [the U.S. joint military command in Panama].'" After thinking it over, White sent a telegram to his superiors describing the "bizarre message" designed to totally recast U.S. policy in El Salvador. As White saw it, "This was a straight power play by the Pentagon, to have on the desk of the new administration a request for so many military advisers, and to bypass the ambassador."

By now, "momentum"—a concept prominent in American football and politics—was with Reagan. As congressional opponents were conceding that they didn't have the votes to stop a policy they disagreed with, the State Department announced on February 28 the departure of a half-dozen Navy technicians to maintain patrol craft in El Salvador. Secretary Haig was meanwhile sabre rattling in the corridors. "Cuban activity has reached a peak that is no longer acceptable in this hemisphere," said the State Department chief. He reiterated a warning that if the "externally managed" arms flow continued, the U.S. would "deal with it at the source."

A week later, on March 2, the State Department announced that military aid to El Salvador would be expanded by $25 million and that some twenty to thirty military advisers would be added to the present Salvadoran contingent (eventually the total number would reach fifty-four). For all practical purposes, that completed the Reagan administration's first El Salvador initiative, apart from the periodic burst of rhetoric from Haig officials in subsequent weeks.

Walter Stoessel, Haig's under secretary for political affairs, told a Senate Foreign Relations Committee hearing in mid-March that the administration had a wide variety of options under consideration for dealing with Cuba, "not excluding or necessarily including military." Stoessel's boss, testifying at the same time before a House committee, said the Soviet Union had a "hit list" for the domination of Central America. Nicaragua's revolution was only phase one. "Next is El Salvador, to be followed by Honduras and Guatemala," said Haig. When asked by a congressman whether this was "a Caribbean domino theory," the master of Haigspeak replied, "I wouldn't call it necessarily a domino theory. I would call it a priority target list—a hit list, if you will."

Even William Clark, Haig's second in command, who was

getting on-the-job training in foreign affairs, got into the act. Seated behind a giant world globe in his seventh-floor State Department office, a few doors down from that of Al Haig, Clark, asked if the Reagan administration feared a "domino effect," replied, "We do." If El Salvador fell, "then Cuba has prevailed and then it is truly a step in their divine path to go on to Honduras, Guatemala, Belize and then, a true threat to Mexico itself." Although he left out Costa Rica and Panama, Haig's deputy was the first Reagan official to indicate knowledge of the seldom mentioned former British colony that was now Belize.

Viewed purely as a political operation, the reinvention of the "Red menace," as social scientist James Petras later called it, had gone off with few hitches. The ideological side of the initiative had received wide publicity in the U.S. As well, the administration had achieved its practical objectives of increasing military aid and advisers to El Salvador. But there was, to use the techno-language of the day, a "downside" to the operation, partly little noticed but much of it distressingly visible, at least to Haig and Reagan.

One of the items receiving scant attention was Salvadoran Communist Shafik Handal's February 9 denial of the authenticity of State Department documents at the center of the White Paper. Although Handal's rejection of the captured documents as "categorically false" was perhaps to be expected, nonetheless he offered a political argument that received little hearing in the U.S. He described the White Paper as "a maneuver to justify the growing supply of U.S. arms and military personnel to the genocidal Christian Democrat-military junta." That is, it was not the Russians who were "internationalizing" the conflict, but the U.S. who sought to do so as a cover for their own determination to suppress a justified revolution. "No one can honestly be surprised that the Salvadoran people has now taken up arms to exercise its right to self-determination," argued Handal. Rather, he asked, "What is the legal and moral authority of the U.S. government to question this right, being, as everyone knows, the largest supplier of arms to the bloody dictatorships of Latin America?"

Although Handal's denial was belatedly printed in the New York *Times*, a statement from the Revolutionary Democratic Front (FDR) that "our arms don't come from the Soviet

Union or Cuba as a rule...We buy them on the dollar black market'' was largely ignored. As the *Columbia Journalism Review* noted in a critique of the obeisant attitudes of the U.S. media on El Salvador coverage, ''By running only Handal's denial and ignoring the broad-based FDR, the *Times* seemed to be accepting the State Department's view of the situation— namely, that the left opposition was synonymous with the Communist party, while the FDR was a small, insignificant group.''

Totally unreported, except for an article in the small socialist magazine *Monthly Review*, and of interest because it offered an overview contrary to that of the State Department, was the Tribunal on El Salvador held in Mexico City, February 9-11, 1981 just as the White Paper campaign was shifting into high gear. A jury of a private Italian-based group, the Permanent Tribunal of the Peoples (successor to the better-known Bertrand Russell Tribunal that existed during the Vietnam War period), brought together such notables as Nobel Prize winner George Wald of Harvard University, theologian Harvey Cox, the Catholic bishop of Cuernavaca, Mexico, a Swiss parliamentarian, and Vincente Navarro, a Johns Hopkins University public health professor, whose account of the case appeared in *Monthly Review*.

The Tribunal's findings were at startling variance with those of the State Department. Unlike the State Department's version of a government searching for order and democracy, the Tribunal found that ''the junta represents the dominant sectors of the oligarchy, the ultra-right, which, in order to retain power, carry out a brutal system of repression against the majority of the population.'' Power in the Salvadoran state ''is centralized in the armed forces and other state organs of repression.'' Although the Christian Democratic party attempted ''to provide the legitimation that the military junta needs,'' in fact, most members of the party and most of the civilian members of the frequently reshuffled junta had joined the FDR. Far from being a mere front organization, the FDR, said the Tribunal, represented broad sectors of Salvadoran society, from social Christians to communists.

According to the Tribunal, the situation in El Salvador, at least during 1980, was characterized by a ''systematic policy of terror'' carried out under the dictatorship of the junta. Basing its report on statistics from offices of the Salvadoran Catholic church and from human rights groups, the Tribunal reported over 8,000 rightwing political assassinations from January 1 to December 15, 1980, excluding military actions and civilian massacres. In addition, there was systematic repression—including torture, bombings, and "disappearances"—against all sorts of groups, such as trade unions, peasant communities, newspapers, educational institutions, churches and even hospitals. The suffocation of possible opposition had produced at least 100,000 refugees, excluding thousands more refugees in camps within the country—notwithstanding Jeane Kirkpatrick's assurance that traditional autocracies don't do such things. The Tribunal's verdict also sought to expose the much-heralded land reform program, condemned U.S. involvement, and justified the right to insurrection. Although one didn't necessarily have to accept the Tribunal's account in its entirety, nonetheless, had it received dissemination comparable to that of the White Paper, it would have provided grounds for pausing before accepting the U.S. position.

Of more practical concern to the Reagan administration was the generally cool response of U.S. allies to its cries of alarm. Typical of the tone encountered was that of one Mexican official who said, "I don't see why it is any more legitimate for the U.S. to arm the junta than for the guerrillas to get weapons from wherever they can. At the moment, the junta has no more legitimacy than the guerrillas. That's why there must be a cease-fire and a genuine referendum." Even Canada, normally the most pliant of U.S. friends, where Reagan made his first foreign trip as president on March 10, was less than enthusiastic. The president was greeted at the parliament buildings in Ottawa not only by Prime Minister Pierre Trudeau, but also by thousands of heckling demonstrators, some opposed to U.S. policies on acid rain, but most protesting intervention in El Salvador. Although the elegant Trudeau attempted to publicly paper-over differences, at subsidiary meetings between Haig and Canadian External Affairs Minister Mark MacGuigan, America's northern neighbor made it clear that it opposed the arms and advisers policy.

Though it was possible to wring mild statements of concern from European allies, for the most part they, like the others, were more inclined toward negotiated solutions, perhaps on the order of that recently arranged by the conservative British government of Margaret Thatcher in Zimbabwe. But that was precisely what the U.S. was resisting. The FDR, led by Guillermo Ungo, a Social Democrat who had once served in one of El Salvador's post-1979 juntas but later quit in protest, had called for talks with the U.S. as early as January, while the FMLN offensive was in progress. The proposal was subsequently repeated, and as often rejected by the Americans. "This is not a matter into which we are injecting ourselves," said State Department spokesman William Dyess on February 26. "If the insurgents want to talk, they should address themselves to the government of El Salvador."

While foreign support for Reagan's El Salvador initiative was lukewarm at best, congressional opposition to it was still sporadic, limited to statements of concern by noted liberals such as Senator Ted Kennedy of Massachusetts or Connecticut Democrat Senator Christopher Dodd, and in the House, Representative Clarence Long. There was nonetheless substantial and diverse intellectual opposition voiced in the American media. Princeton Professor of international affairs Richard Ullman charged that the Reagan administration's "obsessive concern to demonstrate that the U.S. can no longer be pushed around by the Soviet Union has tied our prestige to the survival of a brutal military regime." Mexican novelist Carlos Fuentes, teaching at Dartmouth College in New Hampshire, asked, "Is the Reagan administration out to prove the born-again machismo of the United States? Does the State Department think that any Latin American will swallow the gruyere-like white paper? Does General Haig think we ignore the fact that in civil strife arms are readily available from all quarters? That four-fifths of the arms used by Salvadoran rebels come from democratic, free-enterprise, gun runners in Florida, Texas, and California?"

While President Reagan might be able to remain oblivious to the dripping contempt of his intellectual critics, the more serious ideological problem he faced was to develop support for the El Salvador thrust among the American populace. From the beginning, reporters began asking a ghostly question they believed was on the minds of the U.S. public. Wasn't all this the first step toward "another Vietnam"? "No, I don't think so," Reagan said the day after the White Paper's release. "I know that this is a great concern. I think it's part of the Vietnam syndrome, but we have no intention of that kind of involvement." The issue continued to dog him. Repeatedly in press conferences, as in the one on March 6, reporters asked, "The U.S. role in El Salvador is being compared with its role in Vietnam fifteen to twenty years ago. Do you think that's a valid comparison?" As often as Reagan denied there was any parallel and assured the public that American troops wouldn't be sent to fight, the image returned.

What else would explain the remarkable news conference on March 12 hosted by the State Department which proposed an about-face on El Salvador publicity? Senior department official John Bushnell told reporters they were exaggerating El Salvador coverage. "This story has been running five times as big as it is," said Bushnell, an astonishing claim given the department's all-out efforts to use the media to arouse American public opinion on the issue. Apparently, the attention directed to the "Red menace" was welcome; however, subsequent publicity given to the dispatch of advisers and arms was less gratifying. As another department official privately put it, "The administration wanted to focus attention on certain parts of the problem. But once they did that, they found they couldn't keep it selective." Now, the growing interest in the subject was deflecting attention from the president's domestic economic program, creating the impression that the administration was "obsessed" with Central America to the exclusion of other foreign policy issues, and proving counterproductive in diplomatic relations with allies.

The reason for the attempted reversal became more apparent when congressmen revealed the contents of mail they were receiving from their constituents. Massachusetts Republican Representative Silvio Conte reported that he had received some 600 letters, "and they're running twenty to thirty to one against military aid and advisers for El Salvador." Key Republican Senator Charles Percy, chairman of the Foreign Relations Committee, said he was getting similar ratios of opposition. A White House correspondence count and a March 14 Gallup poll confirmed the trend. Of 7,224 pieces of mail sent to Reagan, 6,939, or about 98 percent, were against American involvement. The Gallup poll reported that about two-thirds of those surveyed who knew something about the situation were fearful that it could develop into "another

Vietnam." Less than half of the "informed" respondents were in favor of any kind of aid to El Salvador, and an overwhelming 98 percent opposed any possible use of U.S. troops in the region.

For the administration, it was the first public opinion backlash against the popular president. Within White House circles, there was a recognition that the administration had overplayed its hand in making El Salvador such a visible symbol of its determination to draw the line against communism. In the anterooms, Reagan's advisers blamed Haig. Even one of the former general's aides admitted Haig "perhaps opened the jar and he didn't, perhaps, realize how many genies were in it."

Beyond the disapproval of the "silent majority," for the first time since the Vietnam War visible public opposition appeared in the streets and on the campuses of the United States. Demonstrations were held in late March at New York's Columbia University, Ohio State, the University of Michigan and a half-dozen other prominent schools. Chapters of the Committees in Solidarity with the People of El Salvador (CISPES) sprang up in various cities, including Boston, where more than 3,000 people marched. In mid-April, thousands of New Yorkers trudged over to the U.N. building, where former Representative Bella Abzug told protesters, "The same bunch of crazies that brought us the war in Vietnam is now trying to get us involved in El Salvador."

Opposition organizing continued even as career Foreign Service officer Deane Hinton was named to take over Robert White's vacated El Salvador post, and a $5 million military aid measure squeaked through the necessary House Appropriations Committee vote ("To fail to support the president will send a wrong signal to Cuba and the Soviet Union," explained Representative Silvio Conte, whose Massachusetts constituents had been sending precisely the opposite signal). On May 3, the first phase of protests reached its high point in Washington, D.C. when between 20,000 and 100,000 people snaked their way from the Lincoln Memorial, across the Memorial Bridge over the Potomac River, to the mall entrance of the Pentagon. It was the largest foreign policy public protest in a decade.

The expose appeared in the unlikeliest of publications: on the front page of the June 8, 1981 issue of the *Wall Street*

Journal; the headline over Jonathan Kwitny's story declared, "Apparent Errors Cloud U.S. White Paper on Reds in El Salvador." Nearly four months after its widespread and unchallenged publication, State Department policy planner Jon Glassman, one of the principal authors of the White Paper, freely acknowledged to reporter Kwitny that it was riddled with "mistakes" and "guessing," and that parts of it were possibly "misleading" and "over-embellished."

In a three-hour interview, Glassman told the tangled tale of the secret documents. The 37-year-old career diplomat, then deputy chief of the political section of the U.S. embassy in Mexico City was called on January 14, four days after the opening of the FMLN offensive, by then Assistant Secretary of State for Latin American Affairs William Bowdler in Washington. Bowdler, who had accompanied William Rodgers to El Salvador a month earlier to reshuffle the junta, ordered Glassman to San Salvador to look for newly captured documents to supplement a cache acquired in November 1980, including the one detailing the arms soliciting trip believed to have been made by Shafik Handal. Glassman reported in to Salvadoran Minister of Defense Colonel Jose Garcia only to be told, in effect, "yes we have no more documents." But the intrepid Glassman pursued his task, eventually stumbling onto a new heap of captured secrets at the offices of the national police. There was a complicated tale involving Venezuelan journalists and hidden walls in a leftist grocery store—it was the stuff of improbable spy stories, but in any case Glassman had found what he wanted in an operation that had been conducted as a complete end-around on Ambassador Robert White, who was kept in the dark.

The question, however, was: What did Glassman have? According to the *Wall Street Journal*, not as much as was claimed in the White Paper. "Several of the most important documents, it's obvious, were attributed to guerrilla leaders who didn't write them," concluded reporter Kwitny. "And it's unknown who did... The month-by-month arms buildup, of almost blitzkreig proportions, described in the White Paper with such emphatic detail and precision, may lose credibility with Glassman's admissions that he doesn't know who wrote some of the allegedly captured documents on which it is based." Certainly, the story of Handal's supposed trip to the Soviet bloc countries, originally attributed to the Salvadoran

Communist leader, was conceded by Glassman to have been authored by somebody else, perhaps a Cuban communist.

"Also in question," reported Kwitny, "is the most widely publicized statistic in the White Paper—the amount of arms that it said was proved to have been delivered to the insurgents." The White Paper confidently described "the covert delivery to El Salvador of nearly 200 tons of arms, mostly through Cuba and Nicaragua." But nowhere in the actual documents, said Kwitny, was there any mention of 200 tons. "That [200 tons] comes from intelligence based on the air traffic, based on the truck traffic. In other words, it doesn't come from the documents," Glassman now explained. In other words, it came from the CIA. Similarly, the other widely quoted figure of 800 tons of arms committed to the insurgents was now also admitted by Glassman to be an "extrapolation." There was considerably more damaging detail—including questions about Fidel Castro's supposed masterminding role in the unification of the guerrillas—but the main thrust of Kwitny's investigation was that the authors of the White Paper "were making a determined effort to create a 'selling' document, no matter how slim the background material." Perhaps, then, it was appropriate that the expose should appear in a newspaper largely devoted to marketing.

The next day, June 9, the prestigious Washington *Post* published the results of its own investigation into the White Paper, largely confirming the Kwitny report. "The *Post*'s inquiry indicates that on several major points, the documents do not support conclusions drawn from them by the administration. On other points, the documents are much more ambiguous than the White Paper suggested," wrote *Post* reporter Robert Kaiser. Far from the State Department picture of an insurgency armed to the teeth by distant communists, according to the *Post*, "these documents portray a guerrilla movement that is chronically short of arms and scrounging for more of them...In document after document there are reports of rebels short of arms, or looking for ways to buy arms, or exhorting comrades to produce home-made arms, or plotting to kidnap wealthy Salvadorans thought to have access to private arsenals."

Although these belated revelations created a stir among journalists, who were now self-critical about their earlier acceptance at face value of White Paper claims and who would subsequently be more quizzical, their publication, coming long after the event and at a time when public attention was diverted to other affairs, had little impact on the American populace. Mass amnesia had already set in, and was not about to be jogged by mere facts. These periodic administration-inspired arousals about the communist danger, followed by exposure of their fabrication, and public forgetting, would prove to be a recurrent phenomenon.

In mid-February 1981, as the White Paper production was unfolding with maximum publicity, *Time* magazine reported that the investigation into the deaths of the American churchwomen had not only bogged down, but was being "stubbornly" suppressed by Salvadoran authorities. Although the State Department had affirmed a month earlier that the investigation was making progress, thus clearing the way for new military aid to El Salvador, *Time* claimed that while an FBI team had indeed turned up damning evidence, Salvadoran officials were ignoring the clues. Among them: sixteen sets of fingerprints lifted from the burned-out van in which the women were riding the night they were killed; a smear of red paint on the van, confirming reports by peasants in the area of having seen the microbus being towed by a red vehicle; ballistics tests on the bullets that had killed the women, revealing that they had been shot with the type of high-powered rifle regularly used by security forces; and a roster of the twenty National Guardsmen and other police on duty at the time with which the fingerprints could be matched. Despite this, the government had so far failed to take any of the next logical steps, and was "refusing to press the inquiry to the point where their own security forces might become implicated." To make things easier, the State Department reiterated its "concern" about the investigation, but "delinked" it from future aid to the Salvadoran regime.

Not until a month later, in mid-March, did junta President Duarte announce that important new evidence had been uncovered in the murders. A month after that, in mid-April, an American network newscast claimed that FBI evidence in the case pointed to six members of the Salvadoran National Guard as the killers. The announcement that the six had been arrested as suspects was made by Defense Minister Garcia on

May 9. However, justice would not be rushed. "They cannot be declared guilty until they are heard and convicted in a trial," Garcia reminded adherants of due process. The progress of the trial would remain a nagging symbolic measure of the state of human rights in El Salvador.

In the midst of the sputtering investigation, Secretary of State Haig offered a revealing gumshoe theory of his own. The remarks came during Haig's congressional testimony on March 18 in which he was denouncing Cuba's Central American "hit list." Speaking about the murder of the four American churchwomen, Haig mused, "I'd like to suggest to you that some of the investigations would lead one to believe that perhaps the vehicle that the nuns were riding in may have tried to run a roadblock, or may accidentally have been perceived to have been doing so, and there'd been an exchange of fire and then perhaps those who inflicted the casualties sought to cover it up. And this could have been at a very low level of both competence and motivation in the context of the issue itself. But the facts on this are not clear enough for anyone to draw a definitive conclusion." Out of that grammatical jungle, newspapers reported the next day Haig suggesting that the women may have tried to run a roadblock and been killed in an exchange of fire with security forces.

Senator Claiborne Pell of Rhode Island, before whom Haig was appearing as a witness at the Senate Foreign Relations Committee, asked whether that was what the secretary had suggested. Detective Haig was glad to clear up the mystery. He had been misreported. He explained that an autopsy on one woman showed the death bullet to have gone through glass first. That meant, he suggested, that one soldier might have fired through a van window, and then others panicked. "I laid that out as one of the prominent theories as to what happened; and I hope that it does not get distorted or perverted emotionally and incorrectly." Perverted emotionally or otherwise, Pell wanted to know if Haig was suggesting that the women had run a roadblock. "You mean that they tried to violate...?" asked Haig with a tone of amazement in his voice. "Not at all. My heavens! The dear nuns who raised me in my parochial schooling would forever isolate me from their affections."

Pell was persistant. What about the phrase "exchange of fire"? "Did you mean the nuns were firing at the people?"

Haig chuckled and, continuing with an air of levity, replied, "I haven't met any pistol-packing nuns in my day, Senator." New York *Times* columnist Anthony Lewis quickly divorced Haig's speculations from the facts. He pointed out that the women had been killed several hours after leaving the airport, all shot in the head at close range. "None of those facts is consistent with a mix-up at a roadblock," noted Lewis. Nor had Haig's "prominent" theory ever been taken seriously by anyone. An early report about glass fragments was later dismissed as erroneous. Although Haig's theorizing didn't say anything about the case, Lewis thought it said a good deal about its author. "An American secretary of state, talking about the vicious killing of four American women, suggested that they were responsible in some measure for their fate. The next day, challenged, he tried to slither away, joking and expressing amazement and blaming the press," wrote Lewis. Echoing an earlier challenger of those who tried to distract attention by slandering the victims, Lewis rhetorically asked, "Have you no sense of decency, sir, at long last? Have you no sense of decency?"

There was one other chilling image of the "vicar" of foreign policy that spring. On March 31, 1981, Americans once again experienced the numbing horror of political violence at the highest level when a would-be assassin wounded President Reagan in Washington. Less than two hours after Reagan was shot, with the president in hospital and Vice-President George Bush flying in from Texas, and with U.S. television providing continuous live coverage of the situation, Alexander Haig appeared in the White House briefing room. The trembling secretary of state grasped the lectern and in a quavering voice declared to the nation: "I am in control here."

Apart from being wrong about the order of presidential succession (third in line is the Speaker of the House, followed by the President Pro Tempore of the Senate), Haig, far from providing the intended soothing reassurance, resembled a glassy-eyed version of the power-hungry paranoid general portrayed in *Dr. Strangelove*-type satires. It was this image of the maker of American foreign policy in Central America and elsewhere that haunted people's memories, like a television picture dissolving with eerie slowness after the set has been turned off.

3   All Over
Except for the Shooting

> *Save the economy, stop the violence,*
> *have the elections and ride into the*
> *sunset.*
> —Ambassador Deane Hinton,
> July 1981

With the familiar blend of casual slickness and the all-knowing eye that unmistakeably marked *Time* magazine's style, correspondent Bernard Diederich, writing from El Salvador, assured American readers in early March 1981: "Most people now seem to feel that the guerrillas will eventually be defeated...Since their 'final offensive' was blunted by the Salvadoran military and by lack of popular support, the guerrillas have made no headway in their struggle to overthrow the civilian-military junta."

It wasn't clear whom veteran reporter Diederich meant by "most people." Perhaps he meant former Ambassador Robert White, who had reduced the "blunted" January offensive by the Farabundo Marti National Liberation Front (FMLN) to the conveniently aphoristic: "They gave a war and nobody came." Or maybe the bloated San Salvador-based press corps which fed off the droppings of diplomatic tables and handouts from Defense Minister Colonel Jose Garcia. In any case, the death notices they cranked out for the FMLN were greatly exaggerated.

As even guerrilla and Democratic Revolutionary Front (FDR) leaders later admitted, the "final offensive" suffered from the illusion of *triunfalismo*—belief in certain victory. Nonetheless, its impact was considerably more extensive than generally acknowledged. Coordinating a nationwide military action for the first time, the five groups that comprised the FMLN appeared not to have exaggerated in the initial heady days of the offensive. The provincial capital San Francisco Gotera in the eastern province of Morazan fell; the garrison in Chalatenango, where Sisters Ford and Clarke had worked, came under massive attack; and in Santa Ana, the country's second largest city, there was a barracks revolt in which the camp commander was executed while officers and soldiers marched over to the rebels' side. Although the attempted general strike in San Salvador, timed to coincide with the offensive, was said to have fizzled—a non-event the Reagan administration eagerly pounced on as proof that the rebels had little popular support—"in point of fact, the strike was successful enough under the circumstances," according to a later assessment in *Maclean's*, the middle-of-the-road Canadian newsweekly. "More than 10 percent of the labor force walked out, despite death threats and the imprisonment of their leaders," reported the magazine's Val Ross.

Certainly, "most people" who expected a guerrilla defeat didn't include the military planners in the Pentagon. In the midst of Secretary Haig's White Paper blitz in February 1981, the U.S. generals issued an assessment of El Salvador's army, asserting it had "no hope" of defeating the FMLN. According to the Pentagon, the Salvadoran army was "not organized to fight a counterinsurgency" battle nor even a conventional war. It was deemed "more like a nineteenth-century constabulary than a twentieth-century army." Nor did the guerrillas concur with gloomy predictions of their demise. The day after the release of the Pentagon study, in a daring interview held in a Roman Catholic institution in San Salvador, a mere two blocks from the home of Defense Minister Garcia, four rebel commanders pledged that the present "tactical retreat" would be followed by a fresh offensive come the rainy season in May. In fact, their only complaint, despite the White Paper's blow-by-blow account of massive arms shipments, was that they were short of weapons. This claim was confirmed by *Le Monde*'s Francis Pisani. In an article published in the French daily in early March, Pisani reported a scarcity of arms, as well as unevenness of quality, with sophisticated weapons appearing alongside antique relics. "Sixty-odd guerrillas fighting at San Lorenzo had between them a single bazooka and an automatic rifle, which had been taken from the Salvadoran army only a few days earlier," Pisani wrote.

For reporters willing to venture into the countryside, the civil war was all over except for the shooting. On the spot observers quickly discovered that the FMLN was on the offensive. A month after the January push, the FMLN had resumed hit-and-run raids, major highway traffic was down by half, and production of coffee, cotton and sugar was significantly reduced. Intrepid members of the fourth estate returned with glimpses of seldom seen Salvadoran *campesinos*. An hour out of San Salvador where "businessmen discussed condominiums and dollars, and then ordered a steak beside the swimming pool," *Harper's* magazine writer T.D. Allman, in perhaps the account most widely read by American intellectuals in spring 1981, found himself in a forest clearing behind rebel lines surrounded by the unnerving innocence and poverty of the peasantry.

"What is this thing you call a 'guerrilla'?" one of the barefooted peasants wanted to know. When Allman explained, the peasant said, "I would like to become a guerrilla, and have boots, and a uniform to wear, and a gun. Then when the soldiers came, I could fire back. I would not have to run and hide in the forest." In contrast to General Haig's pathological vision of Cuban control, the old man in the woods near Aguilares was simply curious. "Can you tell us how we might contact these Cubans, and inform them of our needs, so that they might help us?" he politely inquired.

By May, the guerrillas had targeted the infrastructure. "They are bombing bridges, knocking down power lines, setting factories on fire, everything they can do to strangle the economy," complained Colonel Garcia. Complaints by civilians, however, were usually about Garcia's soldiers. Typical was a former farmer from the northern province of Cabanas who said he had been an army sympathizer until troops came to his town in March, burned a man alive on a pyre of sticks in the main square and killed a pregnant woman with a machete. Such grisly incidents could be multiplied a hundred times over. Although Garcia argued that the army's villainous reputation was due to "Marxist disinformation," the surviving refugees, doctors, priests and relief officials at La Virtud, Honduras hardly seemed to fit the description. Three months after its occurrence, they described the scene of hundreds of refugee Salvadorans crossing the Lempa River on March 17 while soldiers on an overlooking hillside rained the area with rockets, automatic-weapons fire and grenades. At least 200 of the 4,000 fleeing refugees died in the massacre. There would be other such atrocities.

When FMLN guerrillas penetrated to the center of the eastern port city of La Union at the end of June 1981 for three days of the heaviest fighting since the January offensive, it began to dawn on even the drum-beating Secretary Haig that the insurgents had more popular support and military strength than had been publicly admitted. In Morazan, after a highly publicized sweep to "clean up" the area by 3,000 army regulars in August, the FMLN returned to occupy the town of Perquin for nine days. That same month, U.S. Ambassador Deane Hinton admitted that all ten helicopters supplied to the army had been knocked out of commission by guerrilla ground fire. By mid-October, the steel and reinforced-concrete pylons and the asphalt surface, which were the better part of the longest and most important bridge in the country, lay submerged beneath the Lempa River. Celebrating the second anniversary of the fall of the former dictator Romero, the FMLN severed the main route to the eastern third of the country, further demonstrating not only their military prowess but also their ability to secure rural "liberated zones."

Meanwhile, the social reforms which were meant to justify the Reagan administration's massive aid to the regime advanced at a snail's pace. The land reform legislation, which was originally designed as part of U.S. counterinsurgency strategy in Vietnam in the 1960s, had been much publicized and praised ("Land reform takes hold," said a New York Times headline). Haig stepped up military aid in spring 1981. By summer, however, it was clear that the scheme aided fewer peasants than advertised. The three-phase program was in admitted trouble. Under the first phase of the scheme farms larger than 1,235 acres were expropriated with compensation and turned over to peasant cooperatives. But the coops found themselves unable to obtain bank financing or equipment, and most were operating at a deficit, conceded Peter Askin, director of the U.S. Agency for International Development

(AID) in El Salvador. "It has not been a total economic success," understated Askin. Perhaps that wasn't the point though. "But it has been a political success," he added. "I'm firm on that. There does seem to be a direct correlation between the agrarian reforms and the peasants not having become more radicalized." That, apparently, was what the U.S. was getting for the $62 million it had funnelled to the Agrarian Institute, headed by Jose Viera until his murder.

The second phase of the program, which called for a similar conversion of estates larger than 250 acres, was stalled. It was here that the bulk of coffee, cotton and sugar cane was grown. Many of these lands were owned by the same people who lost their larger estates in phase one, and this oligarchy was intent on drawing the line against further reform. The Agrarian Institute was riddled with corruption—director Viera, it was rumored, had been planning to resign in protest—and as many as half of the beneficiaries of the plan were forced to pay protection money to the army; now, a year after the introduction of the reform, less than 15 percent of the country's farmland was in cooperative hands. Some 385,000 people, less than 10 percent of the population, had received the program's dubious benefits.

The fate of Viera's alleged murderers illustrated another aspect of "progress" in El Salvador. In April 1981, at about the same time that five National Guardsmen were arrested for the killing of the American churchwomen, President Duarte announced that two well-known oligarchs had been charged with the Sheraton Hotel murders of Viera and his two American advisers. Ricardo Sol Meza, a member of a wealthy family with business interests in the Sheraton, the national Coca-Cola concession and a bodyguard service for business-men, was arrested in San Salvador. His co-accused, Hans Christ, the manager of a meat-packing conglomerate and son of a German immigrant who had turned up in Central America at the end of World War II, was taken into custody in Miami by FBI agents. The two men were brothers-in-law and, through marriage, related to half the Salvadoran ruling class.

Sol Meza and Christ were in little legal danger. A Salvadoran Supreme Court judge ordered Sol Meza freed in August 1981, and while the decision had to be ratified by the court, there seemed scant likelihood that either would be brought to trial. Though both were known opponents of the agrarian reform plan and admitted being in the Sheraton that night (having drinks with a National Guard intelligence officer), they denied the murder charges and instead claimed a government frame-up. Viera's chief assistant, Leonel Gomez, who subsequently fled the country, also doubted the "killer oligarchs" theory. The arrests had conveniently taken pressure off the army, which had been suspected of supplying weapons to the assassins and, more importantly, deflected attention from Viera's anti-corruption campaign at the Agrarian Institute in which he had blown the whistle on top army officers for stealing $40 million from the program.

Viera's wasn't the only murder to remain a mystery. A United Nations human rights report, issued in November 1981, estimated that 9,250 death-squad murders had occured in El Salvador in the first six months of the year, more than the 8,000 reported for all of 1980. By year's end, the grim tally topped 13,000, notwithstanding the Reagan administration's efforts to conjure up the image of "human rights progress." When American reporters returned from El Playon, and reported on the expanse of jagged lava rock near San Salvador used as a garbage dump-cum-human dumping ground, junta President Duarte said stories about the place had been invented by foreign journalists; Defense Minister Garcia called it press "sensationalism." The correspondents returned in mid-November to make sure they believed their own eyes: vultures were feeding on eight more human victims. Duarte mumbled that the "violations" of human rights were but isolated "abuses of authority."

Congressional disenchantment set in by mid-spring 1981. On April 29, the Democrat-dominated House Foreign Affairs Committee voted twenty-six to seven to impose restrictions on U.S. military aid to El Salvador. The restrictions would require President Reagan to provide assurances that "indiscriminate torture and murder" by the security forces' death squads was being brought under control. The amendment to the foreign assistance bill called for Reagan to submit semiannual reports to the House certifying that the Salvadoran government was not engaged in a consistent pattern of human rights violations and was making progress on economic and political fronts. Two weeks later, in May, over the objections of State Department officials who called it a "wrong signal," the Republican-controlled Senate Foreign Relations Committee passed a similar measure.

Although the Reagan administration resisted the certification requirement throughout the summer and even as the fiscal year deadline (October 1) approached, it was necessary to secure liberal assent to the $114 million El Salvador portion of the $5.8 billion foreign aid package. An administration-backed measure proposed by Senators Jesse Helms and Indiana Republican Richard Luger to lift the certification amendment was defeated fifty-one to forty-seven at the end of September. When foreign aid differences of opinion were thrashed out between the two houses of Congress in a late-night mid-December Senate-House conference, the reporting requirement survived. It became law when Reagan signed the bill later that month. Minimal though the restrictions were, and open to easy evasion by the administration, the measure was nonetheless a sign that the White House initiative had failed to establish its credibility among American liberals.

Congressional opposition to Central American policy wasn't the only annoyance the Reagan government had to put up with, especially in the latter half of 1981. In something of a departure from previous unquestioning acceptance of U.S. hemispheric dominance, Reagan's policies would be challenged by both regional and international opinion. While American legislators were fashioning modest restraints on U.S. intervention in Central America, Venezuelan President Luis Herrera Campins and Mexico's Jose Lopez Portillo issued a communique in early April opposing "internationalization" of the Salvadoran civil war, by direct or indirect intervention, and calling for a political settlement there. In addition, both governments pledged to continue economic aid to Nicaragua following the Reagan administration decision the previous week to cut off help to the Sandinistas. Drawing an analogy between El Salvador and Poland, where tensions between the Communist regime and the fledgling Solidarity trade union had again that spring brought the Eastern European nation to the brink of general strike, Lopez Portillo argued they were both essentially internal conflicts, and that efforts to explain them as the result of outside agitation—the U.S. charge in El Salvador and the Soviet contention in Poland—were "an insult to intelligence." Said Lopez Portillo, "In our continent, social injustice is the true womb of unrest and revolutionary violence. The theory that foreign subversion is the origin of our ills is unacceptable to the democratic nations of the area.''

The idea of a political solution in El Salvador, though far from the thinking of White House and State Department hardliners, was sporadically but persistently raised throughout the year, beginning as early as January when the FDR, in the first days of the FMLN offensive, proposed negotiations. The Salvadoran military was no more amenable to the notion than the Pentagon planners. The most prominent of these initiatives, put forward by the Socialist International (the worldwide organization of social democratic parties) and endorsed by the FDR, was rejected in early May by Salvadoran commander in chief of the armed forces Colonel Jaime Gutierrez, who made it clear that outside mediation was unthinkable.

For the FMLN, the most supportive international diplomatic gesture of the year came at the end of August 1981 as the guerrillas continued to daily demonstrate their potency as a military force. In a joint declaration on August 28, Mexico and France recognized El Salvador's guerrilla-led opposition as a ''representative political force.'' In striking contrast to the Reagan administration dismissal of the FMLN as an insignificant minority of extremists, the Franco-Mexican statement said the guerrillas had a right to take part in negotiations aimed at ending the conflict, and called for a restructuring of El Salvador's armed forces before ''authentically free'' elections could be held there.

The unusual joint declaration provided the FMLN an opportunity to launch a diplomatic drive for additional support in order ''to demonstrate that the Salvadoran conflict is not an East-West issue, despite what Washington claims,'' as an FDR spokesman put it. For Washington, the task was to contain the damage. A few days later, after meetings with Vice-President Bush and Haig, Argentine Foreign Minister Oscar Camilion said that Argentina would join Colombia and Venezuela and perhaps others in issuing a statement supporting the Duarte government and accusing France and Mexico of interfering in El Salvador's internal affairs, a charge the Mexicans dismissed as absurd. Said Mexico's Foreign Minister Jorge Castaneda, ''We didn't create the guerrillas. But they are a reality. They control part of the territory and they have the support of a substantial part of the population.''

France was not the only American ally in Europe to vex the U.S. on the El Salvador issue. When a resolution came to the floor of the United Nations in November 1981 calling on ''the Salvadoran parties involved'' to arrive at a negotiated political solution, its sponsors, in addition to France, were Greece, Denmark, and the Netherlands, all members of the NATO alliance, as well as Ireland, Sweden, Algeria and Yugoslavia. Publicly, U.N. Ambassador Jeane Kirkpatrick minimized the dispute as ''regrettable but not serious''; privately, she worked furiously to tone down and delay the resolution. The measure, calling on the junta to negotiate with the FDR prior to any attempt at elections, and appealing to all countries to get out of El Salvador, passed during the December 16 meeting of the general assembly sixty-eight to twenty-two, with the U.S. voting against.

Whether or not negotiations were genuinely feasible, and irrespective of the limited clout a U.N. resolution carried, it was nonetheless a clear rebuff to the course the Reagan administration had sought to chart from its first days in office.

As the focus of U.S. foreign policy diversified in the latter half of 1981, El Salvador faded from the front pages of American consciousness. The Central American neighbors—particularly Nicaragua, Guatemala, Honduras and Costa Rica—remained largely invisible in the U.S. popular imagination. However, since the policies of the Reagan administration in that part of the hemisphere would increasingly have to be seen as an ensemble of interlinking strategies, a brief survey of contemporary events is in order.

Six months before his murder by government death squad on July 28, 1981, Reverend Stanley Rother, a 46-year-old American Roman Catholic priest in Santiago Atitlan, Guatemala, wrote a letter to a friend in Oklahoma City describing the terrifying abduction of one of his parishioners. Late one Saturday night in January, four kidnappers intercepted a 30-year-old father of two on the steps of the church rectory and were shoving him into a waiting car as Rother arrived on the scene. ''They had broken the bannister where the rectory porch joins the church, and I just stood there wanting to jump down to help, but knowing that I would be killed or taken along also," Rother wrote. "The car sped off with him yelling for help but no one was able to do so. Then I realized that I had just witnessed a kidnapping of someone that we had gotten to know and love and were unable to do anything about it. They had his mouth covered, but I can still hear his muffled screams for help."

That muffled cry went unanswered innumerable times in Guatemala in 1981. The country of 7.2 million people was ruled by General Romeo Lucas Garcia, the latest in a quarter-century line of military dictators that was initiated when a CIA-sponsored coup deposed the freely elected reformist President Jacobo Arbenz in 1954 because the U.S. saw his moderate regime as a communist threat. Notwithstanding Jeane Kirkpatrick's thesis about the gradual democratization of authoritarian regimes, Guatemala had yet to return to democratic rule. Instead, it had been the subject of rigged elections (the next one was slated for spring 1982), military coups, death squads, and as in El Salvador, a civil war that had taken thousands of lives. In tragic Central America, history repeated itself not as farce, as the celebrated aphorism of Karl Marx had it, but as sheer horror.

The only modest interruption of U.S. support for Guatemalan dictatorships had occurred in 1977 when President Carter suspended military assistance on the grounds of continuous human rights violations. Four years later, in April 1981, just as the U.S. Congress was attaching conditions to further Salvadoran military aid, Reagan administration officials were looking for a way to restore relations with the Lucas Garcia regime. The problem was complicated by the fact that in Guatemala, unlike El Salvador, there was no facade of land reform and the like to mask the campaign of increasing repression. The violence had been starkly documented by such organizations as Amnesty International, which counted some 11,000 instances of "extrajudiciary executions" that year, mostly directed against opposition political figures, intellectuals, and the country's native Indians who comprised half of Guatemala's population (a demographic distinction shared by no other Central American nation).

Undeterred by such unpleasantries, Acting Assistant Secretary of State for Inter-American Affairs John Bushnell told U.S. senators in early May that the Reagan administration was disposed to resume military aid to Guatemala to combat a "major insurgency" underway there. Days later, word was out that Secretary Haig's senior adviser, retired general and former CIA deputy director Vernon Walters, would be shipped to Guatemala to discuss conditions for restoring military aid. In Guatemala, Walters did nothing to dispell the impression that little more was involved than the improvement of table manners. The Guatemalan government, declared Walters, deadpan, was defending "peace and liberty" and "constitutional institutions," a remark that raised eyebrows among liberal American editorialists who wondered how such an estimation could be squared with the country's "grim reputation as the hemisphere's worst human rights offender." Despite American pleas that Lucas Garcia temper the brutality, the Guatemalan dictator was unmoved. "We've been told to shove it," said one American official.

By year's end, the Guatemalan army remained locked in combat with the country's four guerrilla organizations, in a war that raged across the western and central highlands, irrespective of the regime's scorched-earth style counter-insurgency campaigns.

The Reagan administration's approach to Central American policy, said Rodrigo Carazo, was wrong in two ways. Carazo was president of Costa Rica, the "Switzerland of Central America," so called for the dismantling of its military apparatus in 1948 and the subsequent decades of pacifism and liberal democracy that made the country unique among its neighbors. "First, the officials in Washington have an almost total ignorance of the realities of our countries," Carazo explained. "And secondly, their policies respond not to the common interest but to 'he exclusive interest of the United States." Considering Costa Rica's pro-Americanism and the fact that it seemed to be an almost perfect model of what the U.S. claimed to be seeking in Central America, Carazo's remarks constituted a particularly damning criticism. Moreover, he added, 90 percent of Central America's problems were economic.

Certainly, that was the case in Costa Rica that year, as economists and headlines proclaimed, "The fiesta is over." After several years of an annual 6 percent growth rate, the Costa Rican economy was suddenly squeezed between high oil prices and low returns on its coffee exports. "In 1970, one bag of coffee bought one hundred barrels of oil," is the way Economic Minister Jose Alfaro graphically put it. "Today, one bag of coffee buys just three barrels of oil." That single illustration explained growing unemployment, out-of-control inflation, a devalued currency, the prospect of a stagnant growth rate, and the reluctance of international bankers to finance an increasing trade deficit.

Although Costa Rica's needs appeared to be clearly economic, Jeane Kirkpatrick, who passed through as part of a six-nation Latin American swing in August 1981, offered the instant analysis that Costa Rican democracy was being undermined by communist subversion. "There is a very great deal of economic disruption in the Costa Rican economy that has been directly linked repeatedly to the Soviet Union," she decided. The American solution? "We can help them with some training for their police."

Replied the editorial in a local newspaper in the capital of San Jose: "We appreciate the generous offer of police training, but a little cold cash to help bail Costa Rica out of its economic crisis would go a lot further toward preserving local stability than would pseudo-military assistance." President Carazo accused Kirkpatrick of "exaggeration and falsehood," and flatly stated, "Costa Rica does not want military aid." Social Democratic politician Luis Alberto Monge, who was heavily favored to win the February 1982 presidential election, concurred. "We can deal with communism without weapons or military training from the U.S.," Monge said. "Costa Rica offers a great opportunity for the U.S. to show that the problems of an economic crisis and underdevelopment can be dealt with democratically. I can't tell people not to take the Marxist-Leninist road if we can't show them an alternative." Sneered another opposition politician more succinctly, "Now that someone has noticed us, we're being given the scratched record of anti-Communism."

Feisty dismissals aside, Kirkpatrick had dropped an ominous hint of things to come.

Honduras, the poorest country in the Americas after Haiti, was, partly as a result of pressure from the former Carter administration, halfway through an electoral process that would restore civilian government. However, the legislative victory in April 1980 by the Liberal party, a right of center formation that was nonetheless to the left of the military-linked Nationalists, had altered conditions little by the time that Reagan took office. The same army general who had ruled prior to the national assembly vote, Policarpo Paz Garcia, was still president; the Honduran economy—weaker than that of Costa Rica—was experiencing the brunt of a recession led by inflated oil prices; and corruption remained rampant (as one foreign aid official put it, ''It doesn't take much to realize that a lieutenant colonel cannot build a $250,000 house and buy a $60,000 Mercedes on a salary of $1,500 a month''). So far, this impoverished land of four million people had escaped political violence due to a combination of circumstances: it had no powerful independent oligarchy since its main export crop, bananas, was in the hands of U.S. companies; further, the successive military governments of the past two decades had not yet felt the need to squash press freedom or repress leftist students.

Nonetheless, while the generals considered whether it was really necessary to go through with the presidential elections slated for the end of 1981, violence was at the Honduran borders. Rather than constituting a threat to the regime in Tegucigalpa, the capital, it promised a lucrative new industry for the country's uniformed rulers. As early as April 1981, the country was hosting on its Nicaraguan border several hundred former National Guardsmen of the late Anastasio Somoza's regime. Clashes between the would-be counter-revolutionaries and the Sandinistas had already required sporadic closings of the frontier and the exchange of angry diplomatic notes. On its Salvadoran border, peasant refugees were spilling across, in flight from the civil war at home. By summer, U.S. ''green berets'' in camouflage jungle gear and toting M-16 automatic rifles were helping the Honduran army to patrol the border. In addition to boosting the local economy through military tourism, the Reagan administration promised to double military aid to $10.7 million in fiscal 1982. The possibility that Honduras' principal economic activity would be its transformation into a gigantic military staging area was not difficult to envisage.

Although General Paz Garcia had last minute misgivings about the November 29 presidential election, the Supreme Council of the Armed Forces decided, the weekend before the vote, to go ahead with democracy. Liberal party candidate Dr. Roberto Suazo Cordova, a 53-year-old family physician from La Paz, handily captured 54 percent of the 1.2 million votes cast. The meaningfulness of this demonstration of the democratic process could be gauged by the fact that most political speculation centered not on the presidency, but on who would be appointed the next head of the armed forces. Police chief Gustavo Alvarez was said to have an inside track. In any case, both the major parties promised during the campaign to leave all national security questions in the hands of the army, granted the armed forces council veto power over cabinet appointments and pledged not to sponsor any investigation into military corruption. Hardly an inspiring program, but one that appeared to guarantee that an immediate military coup would not be required.

Jimmy Carter had "lost" Nicaragua, according to an unforgiving Jeane Kirkpatrick. The Reagan government had not been in office a month before it took up the question of whether that loss was irreversible. Even as Alexander Haig, in February 1981, launched the ideological war against Central America's first leftist revolution, the fledgling Sandinista government was confronting a more immediate war. For more than a year former Somocista National Guardsmen had been conducting raids from across the Honduran border. "Every revolution faces a counter-revolution," militia commander and revolutionary hero Eden Pastora observed the month of Haig's White Paper, explaining why Nicaragua's junta had ordered the creation of a 20,000-person militia. "If there is a real threat, we need a real defense," said Pastora, whose remarks, as we'll eventually see, would come back to haunt him. For the American administration, however, it was simply evidence of the revolution's ambition to "export" itself.

Our concern here is not simply with developments in Nicaragua, but also the image of its revolution as seen through the prism of the American media. The light it shed would condition U.S. popular support for, or opposition to, whatever the Reagan administration had in mind. That image, of course, was heavily colored by the increasingly critical remarks of the U.S. secretary of state—his claims of February that the Sandinistas were a conduit for Soviet-Cuban arms shipments to El Salvador, escalated by November to the

accusation of a Nicaraguan "drift towards totalitarianism."
Nonetheless, the mythological demon of communism that
Secretary Haig sought to locate seemed to evaporate upon
examination.

Accused of human rights violations, the Sandinistas opened
their jails to foreign reporters in March, the month the Reagan
administration cut off economic aid to the country. The New
York *Times'* Alan Riding talked privately to prisoners and
"heard no stories of torture and only occasional complaints
about individual guards." He found "most Nicaraguans
clearly unafraid of the Sandinista authorities." The murderers
and torturers of the previous regime had been jailed, but not
executed. The authority on hand, Interior Minister Tomas
Borge, a founder of the Sandinista Front for National
Liberation (FSLN) and a former victim of the jails he now
oversaw, was self-critical and "shocked by the filthy
conditions" in which the prisoners were living. "Despite our
mistakes, which we admit, we are for human rights," said
Borge.

A similar absence of self-righteousness could be heard in
mid-year when Nicaraguan government officials talked about
their relations with the Miskito and other Indian peoples living
in the northeastern Atlantic Coast portion of the country.
Many of them had fled across the Honduran border, including
the most influential Miskito leader, Steadman Fagoth Muller,
and been subsequently shaped into a counter-revolutionary
force. "It's a terrible mess," conceded Sergio Ramirez, a
member of the three-person "junta of national reconstruction." Atlantic Coast Minister William Ramirez concurred:
"We've allowed small mistakes to turn into a big problem,"
he said of the hasty moves to integrate the heretofore
politically isolated native population into the revolution by
diverse means, including much criticized relocations of Indian
communities.

Indeed, the new regime had practised sporadic censorship of
La Prensa, the chief opposition newspaper; it had also briefly
jailed both prominent businessmen and Communists, and
then backtracked in embarrassment by ordering their early
release. In the face of economic woes that were little different
from those of liberal Costa Rica or authoritarian Honduras,
the Sandinistas proclaimed a state of economic emergency in
fall 1981, bringing with it the inevitable proliferation of

government regulation and the predictable cries of repression. For all that, 60 percent of the economy and 80 percent of production remained in private hands, there was freedom to move in and out of the country, *La Prensa* criticized the government daily, and opposition political parties survived. As Sandinista founder Borge put it, "Nothing will work unless it is economically and politically pluralistic." If this was the voice of totalitarianism, it didn't sound like its preconceived stereotypes.

Justified criticisms might be offered of the Nicaraguan revolution. The problem for much of the American media, however, was an inability to conceive of a political situation that "didn't fit the mold" as New York *Times'* correspondent Warren Hoge put it in an all-too-rare effort at a balanced assessment. Given the peculiar limits of the narrow liberal-conservative range of American political thought, more sophisticated Latin and European perspectives were simply not available to most U.S. analysts. For Americans, revolution was by definition incipient totalitarianism, notwithstanding reporter Hoge's observation that Nicaragua "for better or worse, is being governed for the first time by people who were not installed from the outside." Though he insisted that "the embattled Nicaraguan revolution is a movement far from the political definitions that outsiders are still trying to force upon it," *Time* magazine, in a year-end evaluation that was perhaps more characteristic of the tone of the American media, had no trouble pegging the FSLN regime in neat phrases that lent weight to Al Haig's rumblings about totalitarianism.

The optimism that followed the overthrow of Somoza, according to *Time*, had "all but disappeared"; "a kind of bunker mentality seems to have settled over" the Sandinista leadership; worse, it was "stridently pro-Cuban and pro-Soviet," and its rhetoric had taken on "a decidedly paranoic tinge." With respect to the last, *Time* grudgingly allowed that U.S. naval maneuvers off the Honduran coast in October may have "helped along" the revolutionaries' mental distress. (As we shall soon see, however, the revelation of decisions affecting Nicaragua, which were made by inner councils of the Reagan administration, would render *Time*'s psychiatric diagnoses sheer quackery.) Even "signs of reasonableness" by the Sandinistas were dismissed by *Time* as "no more than a temporary tactical accomodation," although, curiously, the newsweekly didn't have similar misgivings about the occasional moderation of bellicosity by the American government.

Though the Reagan administration's first major foreign policy initiative in El Salvador played to mixed reviews, most of the new regime's first year in office was marked by a series of legislative triumphs, with much of the credit going to Reagan himself, who was quickly dubbed "the great communicator" for his effective speeches and affable persuasiveness. With its main emphasis on U.S. domestic economic measures, the administration basked in success as it maneuvered a package of tax cuts, social service spending reductions and an increased military budget through the Congress.

There were even occasional foreign policy-related coups. During summer naval exercises in the Mediterranean, U.S. jets strayed into a shootout with Libyan aircraft, and downed two of Colonel Muhamar Khadaffi's planes, thereby displaying resurgent America's no-nonsense attitude. Even a minor flap over the failure of White House aides to waken the sleeping president during the conflict seemed but a sign of restored confidence in American abilities. When the administration decided to sell AWACS radar planes to Saudi Arabia in the face of opposition from the Israel lobby in the Senate, the president was portrayed as rolling up his sleeves and pitching into the fray. "There he goes again," cried an admiring press as the Senate acceded to his will and approved the sale in October.

On the perenially troubled international scene the U.S. contented itself with treading water. In autumn 1981, Egyptian President Anwar Sadat was assassinated, presaging new difficulties in the Middle and Near East. Throughout Europe that fall, there were unprecedented and massive demonstrations against nuclear weapons, especially against the Cruise and Pershing missiles about to be deployed on European soil and aimed in the direction of Russia. A nuclear disarmament speech by Reagan in November was designed to furbish his peacemaking image, but had little impact on the stalled arms limitation talks with his Soviet counterparts.

The occasional setbacks experienced by the Reagan team in

its first year were more in the nature of embarrassments than defeats. For example, National Security Adviser Richard Allen was forced to step down at the end of the year when an unreported $1,000 gift from a grateful Japanese magazine was found in his safe. (His replacement was Reagan crony William Clark, who was shifted to the White House from his State Department post.) More serious were the musings aloud by the government's budget director which found their way into William Greider's widely read article in *Atlantic* magazine, "The Education of David Stockman." Reagan's chief numbers-cruncher said, in effect: "We don't know what the numbers mean," a not particularly reassuring assessment from the accountant responsible for the most extreme national economic program in recent years. After what he called "a visit to the woodshed" with Reagan, the chastened and now tight-lipped Stockman was kept on, perhaps, as some said, because he was the only one who even vaguely understood the "voodoo economics" being practiced by the administration. Apart from such minor peccadillos, the president's honeymoon with the public and press lasted well beyond the normal duration, even as the international capitalist recession made its appearance toward the end of the year, marked by declining productivity, impossibly high interest rates, and 8 percent unemployment.

The change of tack in U.S. Salvadoran policy was announced on July 16, 1981 by Assistant Secretary of State for Inter-American Affairs Thomas Enders, the administration's new point man on Latin matters. Speaking before the World Affairs Council in Washington, Enders, in a bid to stem public criticism of the government's warlike noises, committed the Reagan administration to a political rather than a military solution to the conflict in El Salvador, and pledged support for free elections there.

It was an odd voice to hear piping up for peace. The six-foot-eight-inch pinstriped Connecticut Yankee from a wealthy banking family had served as deputy chief of the U.S. mission in Cambodia from 1971 to 1974 where he helped preside over the collapse of the U.S.-supported government in Phnom Penh. It was rumored that Enders had personally transmitted some of the target coordinates in the massive U.S. bombing of civilians in what eventually became Kampuchea—a charge he denied, although he coolly added that noncombatant casualties were always an inevitability. Now, the man admiringly described by *Time* magazine as "aloof, even cold, and almost cynically pragmatic" had snared a prestigious State Department post that required him to sound like a dove.

"Just as the conflict was Salvadoran in its origins, so its ultimate resolution must be Salvadoran," cooed Enders, in a marked departure from Al Haig's heretofore official line about Soviet machinations, international terrorism, and all the rest. State Department officials noted the deviation too, for they went out of their way afterward to insist that Enders' speech represented a "clarification," not a change in U.S. policy. Department spokesmen admitted that Enders' conciliatory oration was aimed primarily at the American people who, they conceded, were turning against the administration actions in the region.

In El Salvador, though the junta had appointed a three-man electoral commission in March to organize Constituent Assembly elections for early 1982, there was considerable skepticism about the efficacy of such a "political solution." At least there was outside the confines of the American embassy where U.S. Ambassador Deane Hinton burbled: "Save the economy, stop the violence, have the elections and ride into the sunset."

For one thing, while the phrase "political solution" meant elections as far as the U.S. and the Duarte regime were concerned, for the FMLN and much of the international community it meant negotiations. Across a spectrum of opinion, there were questions about the feasibility of a narrow electoral strategy. "How can there be elections?" asked one business leader. "What are we going to do? Campaign with loudspeakers mounted on top of our armored cars?" In reference to Enders' invitation to FDR leader Guillermo Ungo to run for office, a church official asked, "If you were Mr. Ungo, would you participate in the elections?" Or as a Swedish Social democratic official summed it up: "Elections with death lists of the opposition—you might as well hold them in the cemeteries."

Misgivings aside, the legislative elections were touted throughout the year. Gradually, radio and television spots were filled with get-out-the-vote commercials, despite the occasional glitch (one public service announcement showed a family grieving over a body covered by a sheet while a narrator urged viewers to vote to end the violence; it was pulled after market research showed Salvadorans were troubled by the negative approach associating elections and democracy with death). Like it or not, the Salvadorans were going to get elections: junta President Duarte plumped for them through the summer; an autumn "political forum" worked out the details; at the Organization of American States meetings in December, Secretary of State Haig finessed a resolution of support for the balloting; by year's end much of the country was plastered with blue-and-white posters declaring, "El Salvador deserves your vote."

Concurrent with the U.S. emphasis on elections was an additional ameliorative gesture—the evolution of an encompassing American aid program that would ultimately be known as the "Caribbean Basin" plan. (This novel geopolitical term used by the Reagan administration designated "the islands of the Caribbean as well as the mainland nations of the circum-Caribbean.") News of the embryonic plan was filtered to the public through the summer; by early June it was reported that President Reagan, at a National Security Council meeting, had approved a plan for increased economic and military aid to the region in order to counter communist gains there. The trial balloons floated for the scheme were met with some misgivings by Latins, who had been entangled by American handouts before. Mexican President Lopez Portillo, who visited Washington in mid-June, insisted that the proposal should not involve military aid and should not exclude any country in the region, a clear reference to the leftist governments of Cuba, Nicaragua and Grenada. But when Thomas Enders presented a preview of the plan in September, it was apparent that "containment of communism" was still one its main features.

Though the focus on political solutions and aid packages seemed to betoken a new moderation in the ranks of Reagan policy makers, there was a less publicized and far more ominous underside to U.S. Central American strategies. Only six weeks after Ronald Reagan was inaugurated, he deposited a document known as a "finding" with the congressional intelligence oversight committees, contending that U.S. national security called for clandestine operations in Central

America. The "Presidential Finding on Central America" of March 9, 1981 said the secret activities would consist mostly of propaganda efforts, improved capabilities to gather intelligence on the shipments of arms to Salvadoran guerrillas, and a paramilitary operation to "interdict" the traffic.

The same month, U.S. reporters stumbled onto former members of the Nicaraguan National Guard training in camps in Florida for counter-revolutionary attacks on the Sandinistas. Although the Nicaraguan government sent a protest note to Secretary of State Haig charging possible violations of the U.S. Federal Neutrality Act (which forbids conspiracies to injure or destroy the property of the government of a nation with which the U.S. is not at war), the objection was brushed aside by department officials who said the training was legal because it was taking place on "private property." "But how would the American government react," asked Sandinista leader Daniel Ortega, "if suddenly in Nicaragua, where there is private property, it should occur to some ranch owner to loan his property to train Puerto Ricans to fight for the independence of their country?"

Less visible to the American public were the recruiting activities of the CIA in Central America. Although knowledge of its covert organizing remained secret for some time, by summer of 1981 the U.S. intelligence agency was busy fashioning the Nicaraguan Democratic Force (FDN) out of various Somocista groups scattered along the Honduran border.

In November 1981 the National Security Council laid out a ten-point covert plan which Reagan approved and signed on December 1, 1981, even as Secretary Haig was busily outlining America's more conciliatory economic aid package to members of the OAS. The secret plan called for initial funding of $19 million to create a modest 500-man force which would conduct paramilitary operations against Nicaragua. CIA director Casey, in presenting the operation to the congressional oversight committees, gave the impression that the operation would be carefully limited in terms of numbers and scope of activities, an issue that would subsequently become contentious.

The initial stage of an undeclared war against Nicaragua wasn't the only aspect of actual American policy during the period. In a significant shift in July, the Reagan administration ordered U.S. delegates to international development banks to support loans to Chile, Argentina, Paraguay and Uruguay, thus reversing Carter's stand of not voting for such loans on human rights grounds. Nor was that the only gesture of renewed friendship with repressive regimes. Jeane Kirkpatrick gave it the personal touch during her summer Latin tour, announcing in Santiago, Chile that the U.S. intended to "normalize completely its relations with Chile in order to work together in a pleasant way." This was indeed pleasant news to Chilean dictator General Augusto Pinochet, who promptly expelled from the country four leaders of the democratic opposition two days after Kirkpatrick's departure.

While Assistant Secretary Enders was preaching peace and prosperity, his chief, Al Haig, was pondering military options. Unfortunately, the most immediate of them seemed to be a tendency to shoot himself in the foot. In early November it was reported that the Reagan administration had reached a consensus that the civil war in El Salvador was stalemated. "Stalemate," said Haig, "could ultimately be fatal." Beyond that, the administration was apparently having difficulty in agreeing on what to do about it.

Haig, according to the ever helpful grapevine, was pressing the Pentagon to examine possible military action in El Salvador, as well as against Cuba and Nicaragua. The "vicar" had stamped "rush" on his requests. But over at the Department of Defense, Secretary Caspar Weinberger and his chief deputy, Frank Carlucci, a former CIA administrator, were playing dove to Haig's hawk. The Joint Chiefs of Staff were especially opposed to the use of American combat forces in Central America, doubting both the feasibility of the options and the likelihood that they could muster any support in the Congress or among the public. Presidential counselor Ed Meese and National Security Adviser Richard Allen were also said to be skeptical of military initiatives.

In short order, the general at State was embroiled on two fronts. Upon learning that Washington columnist Jack Anderson was about to publish a piece suggesting the secretary had "one foot on a banana peel" and was soon to fall, Haig unsheathed his telephone and told the columnist that the rumors were the work of a top White House aide who was waging a "guerrilla campaign" against him that was tantamount to "sabotage of the president." Although the aide wasn't named, Reagan called in Haig and Richard Allen and ordered them to stop sniping at each other, and get back to the guerrillas in El Salvador. As for the identity of the White House guerrilla, Allen said afterwards: "I don't know. My solution is polygraphs at thirty paces."

While he was patching up a truce with Allen, the secretary of state opened a new skirmish with Defense Secretary Weinberger. The day before his Oval Office meeting with Reagan and Allen, Haig, appearing before the Senate's Foreign Relations Committee to explain the administration's $180 billion plan to upgrade the nuclear arsenal, casually remarked that NATO contingency plans included the option "to fire a nuclear weapon for demonstrative purposes" to deter a Soviet thrust into Europe. The next day, Weinberger went before the same committee and directly contradicted Haig's warning-shot-across-the-bow doctrine. "There is nothing in any plan that I know of that contains anything remotely resembling that, nor should it."

A week later, in mid-November, the president was assuring the nation, "We have no plans for putting Americans in combat any place in the world and our goal is peace." Having distanced himself from Haig's contingency plans, Reagan also declared peace between his chief cabinet officers. "We're a happy group," said the president, before heading off to the Oval Office-cum-woodshed to deal with his loose-lipped budget director, David Stockman.

President Reagan's group, assertions aside, didn't appear noticeably happier. However, by year's end, it seemed that Haig had gotten much of what he was seeking. At a series of meetings with Mexico's Lopez Portillo, before the Organization of American States' December gathering on St. Lucia Island, and testifying at various congressional hearings, the secretary of state had continued to issue a stream of harsh warnings about Nicaragua's "drift toward totalitarianism," its potential as a Central American "superpower," and how "the hours are growing short." Though the facade of a more moderate policy had been placed before the American public to staunch domestic criticism, by December the National Security Council had launched a secret war against Nicaragua; the inevitable escalations of military aid to the region's repressive regimes were in the legislative pipeline; and on December 15, Under Secretary of Defense Fred Ikle informed a Senate sub-committee that, Secretary Weinberger's hesitations notwithstanding, the Joint Chiefs of Staff had prepared contingency plans for American military action in Central America. As well, Ikle announced that the U.S. would train some 1,500 Salvadoran soldiers in the U.S., mainly in counter-insurgency techniques, at a cost of $18 million. Though the internecine rivalries within the administration had produced their share of fireworks and buffoonery through the autumn of 1981, it was obvious that such policy differences as there were amounted to no more than a debate over emphasis.

Nearly a year after the murders of the four American churchwomen, the judge in charge of the official Salvadoran government investigation announced that his inquiry was at a "dead end."

As for the families of the dead Catholic missionaries, the year had amounted to a lengthy runaround from the State Department. "I've had a crash course in dealing with the U.S. government," said William Ford, a 45-year-old Wall Street lawyer and brother of murdered nun Ita Ford. "If by radicalization one means that I've come to realize that the U.S. is supporting a government in El Salvador which is no more than a group of gangsters in uniform, then I've been radicalized."

Michael Donovan, brother of the slain lay-missionary Jean Donovan, had hoped family connections would be helpful in getting government action on the case. His father was a former executive of United Technologies, the firm Al Haig headed before taking over as secretary of state. The effort to utilize this business association led nowhere. "It's been very educational," Donovan wryly noted. "I was a Republican. I'm a registered Democrat now." Donovan had been one of the speakers in May at the giant Washington protest demonstration against U.S. support for the Salvadoran junta.

Judge Mario Rivera sat in his rocking chair in a nearly barren office in Zacatecoluca, the city near where the church-women's bodies had been found, and showed reporters what he had after a year of probing. It didn't amount to much. Rivera said the case was technically still open, but "there is nothing more I can do." The half-dozen National Guardsmen who had been arrested in May, and confined to their base since then, would probably be released.

4 Under the Volcano

All of us were born half-dead in 1932.
—Roque Dalton

On the night before the insurrection, January 21, 1932, the volcanoes erupted. The tremors began in neighboring Guatemala. In El Salvador, Izalco volcano, the westernmost of a chain of fiery mountains that runs through the heart of the country, spewed a fine ash. The particles hung in the air at dawn the next day as *campesinos*, armed with no more than machetes and a few rifles, marched across the trembling earth toward Sonsonate, a town of 20,000 and the commercial center of the western coffee-growing region.

It was the first communist-led revolutionary uprising in the western hemisphere. Yet it was far from the later stereotyped images of foreign-inspired Bolshevik conspiracies carried out with calculating precision. Nor did it conform to that other school of mock-history: condescending accounts of slightly comic but violent buffoons who strut across the landscapes of quaint "banana republics." Rather, it was a desperate, ill-timed and doomed gesture.

Its communist leader, Augustin Farabundo Marti, already jailed at the moment of the revolt, was no imported Soviet or Latin agent, but a homegrown leftist labor organizer of the Regional Federation of Salvadoran Workers which, by 1932, had incorporated more than 10 percent of the nation's workforce into its ranks. Marti, the son of a medium-sized farmer from La Libertad province, was attracted to Marxism during his university days. A student activist, he was arrested in 1920 at a protest rally in San Salvador and exiled. Eventually he moved to Guatemala, where with other regional intellectuals he became a founder of the Central American Socialist Party in 1925.

Returning to his homeland later that year, Marti worked as an organizer for the Salvadoran workers' federation until 1928. During that time the federation united various unions, set out a national program of land reform, advocated the eight-hour day, and even ran a People's University, a literacy program for workers and peasants. Its organizers were particularly active in western El Salvador, where the Indian population was embittered over the expropriation of their traditional communal lands by the coffee-growing oligarchy.

One of the contemporary sources of inspiration for men like Marti was the resistance to American domination of the region led by Augusto Cesar Sandino in neighboring Nicaragua. Sandino had refused to submit to the occupation of his country by the U.S. Marines, and in 1927 formed a small band of guerrilla fighters who would hold off the invaders for the next six years. The Salvadoran workers' federation decided to send a contingent to support Sandino's struggle, and Marti found himself in northern Nicaragua, a colonel in the Sandinista army. Contrary to the monolithic image of lock-step agreement among revolutionaries, there were ideological differences between the Marxism of Marti and the narrower anti-imperialist nationalism of Sandino's movement. In 1929 Marti returned home; two years later he was among the small group of intellectuals and workers who gathered on the shores of Lake Ilopango, near San Salvador, to form the Communist Party of El Salvador.

The causes of the 1932 rebellion were no less indigenous than its leadership. With the Great Depression the coffee market, upon which the Salvadoran economy was dependent, collapsed. Whereas a hundred kilograms of coffee brought in $15.75 in 1928, by 1932, the average price of a hundred weight had tumbled to $5.97. With the crash of the market came the crumbling of the oligarchic sector that had controlled the government for the past dozen years. For the presidential election of 1931—perhaps the first and last free election in the country's history—a half-dozen candidates appeared on the scene to fill the power vacuum. Three of them were backed by various factions of the ruling oligarchy; two of them were generals representing a rising social group located in the recently modernized armed forces; and one of them, Alberto Araujo, was a social democrat who spoke of reform and hoped to build a labor party.

An unprecedented popular coalition of workers, peasants, and professionals carried Araujo to power at the polls, where he rolled up over 100,000 votes to 62,000 for his nearest rival. Although there had been talk of a coup, the military remained in its barracks when one of its candidates, General Maximiliano Hernandez Martinez, was named vice-president. The nine-month reign of Araujo was disastrous: it was marked by inefficiency, corruption, and a wave of popular protests, often put down with violence by government troops. When Araujo attempted to crack down on leftist organizations, Farabundo Marti led a protest march on the president's house, for which he was jailed. But after a month-long hunger strike, the government capitulated to popular protests and freed Marti, who emerged as a national hero and a symbol of opposition. Neither the protests nor the falling price of coffee could be halted.

On December 21, 1931, the flawed Araujo experiment was ended by military coup. The new president was General Martinez, the initiator of what would be a half century of military rule in El Salvador. Martinez, a theosophist who dabbled in the occult and often used the presidential palace for seances, decided, despite the coup, to go ahead with the January 1932 municipal elections. Though the fledgling Communists had formed too recently to affect the 1931 presidential balloting, they expected that the subsequent year of discontent would lead to sizeable gains at the municipal level. They were not mistaken. The new ideology which they propagated—communism—proved attractive both to the people in the countryside and to the small but emerging working class in the capital. Its goals seemed familiar to the Indian communities of western El Salvador, who recalled the time within living memory when they shared a communal life. Many thousands inscribed their names on the electoral rolls as supporters of the Communists, and a surprising number of the new party's candidates won at the polls.

The Martinez dictatorship, however, didn't like the results and refused to certify the Communist victories. Caught between the rising expectations of the poor and the power of the dictatorial state, the Communists asked themselves the question faced by all revolutionaries: what is to be done? One segment of the party said that unless it prepared for insurrection, there would be a spontaneous uprising that would be crushed, setting back the popular movement for years. More cautious members replied that the thought of insurrection was premature, that the party was too weak to lead a revolutionary upsurge. In the end, the majority opted for insurrection and a date was chosen. The peasants would march on town halls in their communities; sympathetic officers would lead a garrison revolt; the workers would strike.

Four days before the slated uprising, Marti was arrested. During the next two days, the hoped-for barracks rebellion was aborted. Mass arrests began. A last minute bid to countermand the call to insurrection came too late.

Shortly after dawn on January 22, the ill-prepared rebels were met in Sonsonate's town square by the army. Despite the latter's superior fire power, the soldiers were forced to retreat to the town fort before the machete-wielding peasantry. Repeatedly, the rebels attacked the gates of the fortress only to be driven back by rifle and machine-gun fire. At mid-morning they withdrew, retreating to a nearby town.

Martinez quickly mobilized to crush the revolt, calling out the army and a hastily assembled Civic Guard. The rebels fell back from their encampment near Sonsonate to the village of Izalco at the foot of the volcano. The army closed in. Although scattered fighting continued for several days, the rebellion was finished.

What followed was the horror—the *matanza* or massacre. Terrified by the appearance of the populace on the stage of history for the first time, and by the threat it represented to their domination, the ruling class alliance wanted vengeance. In Izalco, groups of fifty men were tied together by their thumbs and shot down at the wall of the Church of the Assumption. The roads were littered with bodies as the National Guard indiscriminately killed anyone they met. Victims were forced to dig mass graves into which they were machine-gunned. The Communist party was almost wiped out. Using the January electoral rolls, the army systematically eliminated its members and sympathizers. Farabundo Marti died before a firing squad on February 1, 1932. When the *matanza* ended, there were no official death tolls (estimates ranged from 4,000 to 50,000 dead) and the oligarchy had ceded the task of governing El Salvador to the armed forces, beginning with Hernandez Martinez, whose dark era would last a dozen years. As Salvadorans prepared to troop to the polls in 1982, a half century after its traumatic occurrence the *matanza* remained their formative political experience.

Before they cast their ballots, a brief disinterrment of Salvadoran history may be illuminating. In bringing it to light, we unearth what the Reagan administration had to studiously ignore in order to recite its extraordinarily simplified version of Central American events, replete with numerically insignificant extremists, Soviet-and-Cuban conspirators, embattled democrats of the center, and passive peasants seeking peace and a return to the "traditional rhythms of work and leisure" as Jeane Kirkpatrick so quaintly put it. Naturally, such an examination, abbreviated as it must be, runs the risk of leaving us with the complexities of reality rather than the comforting nostrums of anticommunist demonology.

When the sixteenth-century Spanish Conquerors arrived and whimsically bestowed the name of The Savior on this volcanic plot of the Central American isthmus that stretches a mere 400 kilometers from the mountains of Morazan in the east to Lake Guija on the Guatemalan border in the west, they found a corn-growing Mayan people whose fertile ash-enriched soil also produced beans, pumpkins, chilis, cocoa and a cornucopia of other crops.

The Spanish Crown, which reorganized the Mayan economy by force of arms in order to satisfy its need for raw materials, particularly cocoa and balsam, initially sought a self-interested balance of power in its Central American colonies. One measure, which had the effect of somewhat limiting the grasp of its conquistador settlers, was the creation of Crown-protected land on which the indigenous population would continue to collectively grow their food. However, the Crown's continuing European adventures produced a chronic capital crisis. Unable to directly reward its colonial servants, it soon joined forces with them to wrest both labor and land from the Indian communities.

Equally important for its impact on the lives of the inhabitants were two major changes in the mode of agricultural production, both of which consequently altered the relations of production, much to the disadvantage of El Salvador's original population. In the late eighteenth century, the industrial revolution made possible the rise of European textile production, thus creating a demand for dyes which could be met by increased production of Salvadoran indigo. To exploit this export crop more profitably, the settlers sought the acquisition of more land, in the form of large plantations or *haciendas*, the number of which increased steadily through the early nineteenth century. A second and more enduring transformation occurred in mid-century when, for economic reasons, the *hacienda* owners began to shift from indigo to coffee production. Whereas indigo required little tending (and thus non-intensive labor), grew everywhere, and seldom interfered with traditional subsistance farming, coffee-growing produced profound changes in labor and land owning patterns. It required extensive labor and vast armies of workers to harvest. Further, it grew best on the higher slopes of the volcanoes and much of that land, especially in western El Salvador, consisted of the communal and subsistance plots of the peasantry.

Between indigo and coffee, the degenerative weakness of the Spanish Crown resulted in a shift in political power which made it possible for the Central American agricultural oligarchy to wrest independence in 1821. The next two decades were marked by violent struggle between competing segments of the ruling class. The formation of a national government in the 1840s is often seen in idealistic terms as reflecting some level of "political maturity" or "stage of socio-economic development"; however, it is probably more realistic to see the creation of these state entities as structurally securing the gains of that portion of the oligarchy which had proved triumphant in the preceding infra-class struggle. At the same time, the world market upon which El Salvador's economy was dependent shifted from the Spanish motherland to the banking houses of England and France, eventually to be supplanted by those of the United States.

With state power in its hands, and a coffee magnate as president, the oligarchic "Fourteen Families," as they came to be known, moved in the latter part of the nineteenth century to overcome the last obstacles to their dominance. On the grounds that neither the Indian communities nor the municipalities were making efficient use of their common lands, in 1881 the government simply decreed the elimination of all forms of landholding other than capitalist. In addition, draconian labor legislation was enacted to control the dispossessed peasantry and recruit them for work on the coffee *fincas*. Unsurprisingly, so radical and rapid a change in the relations of production was cause for resistance, and indeed there were sporadic peasant revolts to the end of the century.

Again, contrary to the widespread North American notion that state institutions are relatively unconnected to each other or are spontaneous in their origins, it was the "need" of the coffee barons to reproduce their relations of control over the peasantry that led them to urge the buildup of the army in the early twentieth century. Similarly, the creation of a special security force, the National Guard, in 1912 had the specific purpose of maintaining labor order and enforcing the landowners' laws in the rural areas.

As the possibilities for popular organization in the first decades of the twentieth century transformed the peasantry into a self-conscious social force capable of entering into alliance with the nascent urban working class, there was a corresponding emergence of the military as a distinct class entity. Made up of the sons of small farmers, artisans and professionals, its initial role as paid watchdog was gradually enlarged. In the wake of the failed 1932 rebellion it came to encompass the formal control of state power, which could no longer be risked in legitimate elections. The recognition of these historical roots ought to go some way toward dispelling the contemporary image purveyed by the American government of a beleaguered and legitimate Salvadoran state fending off the depredations of external forces.

The succeeding half century of more or less military rule in El Salvador, punctuated by coups, staged successions and rigged elections, saw the country subject to the vicissitudes of a variety of development strategies, carried out under the tutelage of the hemisphere's imperial power. The mystically repressive regime of *El Brujo* or "the wizard," General

Martinez, endured until 1944, increasingly megalomaniacal even as its power eroded. Near the end, when the archbishop of San Salvador asked the general in the name of God to stay the execution of those who had tried to topple him, Martinez replied, "In El Salvador, I am God."

Nonetheless, Martinez had efficiently protected the interests of the coffee growers, discouraged further industrialization, and maintained the order that later analysts such as Jeane Kirkpatrick found so appealing. However, when he sought to alter the constitution to prolong his stay in power, a formidable opposition coalesced—uneasy oligarchs worried about their fiefdoms as World War II came to a conclusion, younger officers seeking outlets for their ambitions, a new generation of professionals inspired by the rhetoric of the Allied war effort, and, as always, the restive population. When a coup attempt ended in bloody retribution, a groundswell of popular indignation against Martinez broke out in the form of a general strike. Among the thousands of strikers who took to the streets was a 25-year-old son of a shoemaker named Salvador Cayetano Carpio, who was making a reputation for himself as an effective organizer of the bakers' union; eventually he would become a leading Communist, and emerge three decades later as one of the leaders of the FMLN. More immediately, three weeks into the paralyzing strike, the "master", as Martinez liked to be called, resigned and fled the country. This bizarre despot, who believed in such doctrines as reincarnation, bought a *hacienda* in Honduras and awaited a political rebirth that never came. In 1966, he was murdered by a ranch hand.

In the ensuing melee for power, the pro-Martinez forces successfully rallied against the would-be reformers. The farcical election that was staged in 1945 brought another general to office who, despite attempts at further general strikes led by Carpio's bakers' union, remained in power until a coup in December 1948. Led by Colonel Oscar Osorio, who represented a new breed of technocratic soldier, the coup marked a breach within the heretofore unified ranks of the oligarchy. On the one side were the entrenched landowning families—the "agro-front" as they were sometimes called—committed to the maintenance of stability against a regional tide of change which, in neighboring Guatemala and Costa Rica, had brought genuine middle-class reformers to power after World War II; on the other side, a group of modernizing oligarchs, intent on diversifying their own wealth as well as the country's economic base. It was the latter who courted a younger segment of the officer caste, a group of professionals and technocrats who saw in the military the possibility for something more than a school for butchery and who shared the modernizers' desire to rescue the country from one-crop dependency.

Under Osorio, whose position was formalized in the presidential spectacle of 1950, the government adopted a strategy that would remain the essential framework of rule in the country until the present. It consisted of developmentalism—the creation of legislative conditions and a physical infrastructure of electrical power and roads to permit the expansion and modernization of the economy—and repression—a ready use of force to violently mark the boundaries of permissible change—leavened with reformism. Thus, the legislation of the 1950s recognized the rights of trade unions and of the new middle classes brought to birth by modernization; in addition, a modicum of political stability was achieved through the regularization of political parties and a one-term presidency. (Incidentally, it was in the year of Osorio's ascension that the son of a Palestinian merchant family, Shafik Handal, joined the Salvadoran Communist Party. The man whose globe-trotting travels would be recounted in such detail in the State Department White Paper of 1981 began his journeys in 1952 when he was first exiled for political activities that excited the regime's repressive rather than reformist impulses.) Osorio's political reforms resulted in a less traumatic succession of power, as exemplified by the easy election of his hand-picked successor, Colonel Jose Lemus, in 1956.

Lemus's term in office, less sophisticated and more corrupt than that of his predecessor, coincided with two crucial external events: the worldwide recession of the late 1950s in which, among other things, coffee prices plunged; and the surprising Cuban Revolution of 1959 led by Fidel Castro. Both developments provoked demands for harsher repression by a nervous oligarchy and more militant forms of resistance from the opposition. Lemus obliged his patrons but, even within the army, the regime's corruption and its jails stuffed with political prisoners appeared excessive. In late October,

1960, junior officers informed the colonel that his services were no longer required.

An all-too-brief interlude of possible reform followed. A new junta combined junior army officers and independent professionals from the university world; it promised free elections and a massive literacy drive. In essence, the new junta represented the political moment in which the emerging middle class found a vehicle of capitalist reform. Some weeks after the election of John F. Kennedy in the U.S., the Christian Democratic party (PDC) of El Salvador was founded by a small group of men. Among them was a civil engineer and contractor, Jose Napoleon Duarte, who happened to be an alumnus of Notre Dame University, the school far less successfully attended by Alexander Haig. The Americans were unimpressed by such developments. As civilian junta member Fabio Castillo later recalled, the U.S. charge d'affaires at a meeting with Castillo and a conservative financier "said that the U.S. embassy did not agree with the holding of free elections and that he supposed that we were not talking seriously."

Three months later, in January 1961, a clique of colonels led by Julio Rivera seized power and established another junta, which was immediately recognized by the recently inaugurated Kennedy. A year later, Rivera was made president. For much of the 1960s, El Salvador was the beneficiary of Kennedy's Alliance for Progress, an economic-military program designed to contain Castroism. On the military side, in addition to providing counterinsurgency training for local security forces, the U.S. pushed for and in 1964 obtained the creation of the Central American Defense Council (CONDECA), designed to assure regional stability by enabling one national army to aid another.

The industrialization policy of the 1950s, import substitution (replacing manufactured imports with domestically produced goods), faced a constant threat of stagnation because the extreme poverty of the peasantry meant that El Salvador's internal market was too small to absorb the increased production. The logical solution would have been to increase consumer purchasing power through a land reform which would create a class of small farmers or cooperative members. But land reform was beyond the political pale; it would violate a tacit agreement between modernizers and the agro-front not to disturb existing ownership patterns.

Instead, two more convenient paths were chosen. The Central American Common Market was founded in 1961 around the ideas of making the region a free trade zone, permitting an unrestricted flow of goods, capital and people among the five republics; and of planned, balanced development, with specific industries assigned to each country. The scheme was particularly appealing to El Salvador and Guatemala, the two relatively most developed economies of the region. In addition, foreign investment was made more attractive at just the time when a U.S.-led capitalist boom was generating corporate investors seeking to increase their holdings. During the 1960s, nearly fifty multinational corporations opened subsidiaries in El Salvador, often as joint ventures with the local oligarchy. U.S. direct investment increased several times over, from about $20 million in 1950 to better than $60 million by 1970—still a relatively modest figure, but nonetheless having considerable impact on the Salvadoran economy.

Notwithstanding the palpable successes of modernization, the underlying economic structure of the country remained vulnerable. For instance, while the country's manufacturing sector grew by an impressive 24 percent in the decade 1961 to 1971, the number of people employed in those factories grew by a meagre 6 percent. Industrialization based on capital-intensive technology forced small artisan producers out of business. At the same time it disappointed the hopes of thousands of peasants who streamed in from the countryside seeking work, resulting in burgeoning slums in the capital. In addition, a birth rate of 3 percent a year and the absence of land reform meant that conditions in the countryside only worsened for the peasantry and the landless laborers.

In these circumstances a variety of social and political forces came to maturation. Although the 1967 presidential election produced a smooth succession in which Colonel Rivera was replaced by another modernizing colonel, who was the candidate of the Rivera-created party of National Conciliation (PCN), the Christian Democrats also became a formidable political entity. Duarte was thrice elected mayor of San Salvador and, by 1968, PDC candidates had scored victories in nearly eighty cities and towns, as well as securing a sizeable number of National Assembly seats. However, the Christian

Democratic party was more complex than the simple drawing of a fish which was the party's quasi-religious symbol. From the beginning, there were two tendencies within the PDC: one, which counted such figures as Ruben Zamora, espoused a serious intellectual examination of the relationship between Christianity and politics—influenced by Marxist scholarship, it moved in the direction of "social Christianity"; the other current was more pragmatic, more oriented toward electoral-machine politics, less ideological, and found its ideal charismatic figure in Jose Napoleon Duarte.

To the left of the Christian Democrats were two smaller parties. The National Revolutionary Movement (MNR), a group based among middle class professionals, favoring social democratic politics, was led by law professor Guillermo Ungo. The party of Renovation (PAR) was headed by the dean of the medical school Fabio Castillo, a former member of the short-lived reform junta of 1960; it espoused a more radical position and employed grassroots tactics, taking its campaign to the countryside. Within a developing ideological ferment, which was international in scope, one found the radical student leaders who, a decade later, would be at the head of the guerrilla forces, among them: Joaquin Villalobos and Eduardo Castaneda (the latter better known by his nom de guerre, Ferman Cienfuegos).

At the same time, two major props of the oligarchic state had substantially shifted position by the end of the 1960s. The Roman Catholic Church, for four centuries a conservative if not reactionary force in Latin America, was experiencing an internal ideological and material crisis of its own. Faced with declining membership and revenues as well as theological dissent that made it increasingly difficult to attract a dynamic priesthood, the church underwent a modernization of its own in the 1960s. It inaugurated liturgical reform and a new political debate on the church's relation to its often impoverished laity. For Latin Americans, one of the highpoints of this development occurred at the 1968 conference of bishops in Medellin, Colombia, where the "theology of liberation" made its appearance, promising a new orientation toward revolutionary Christianity. Already, in the ranks of the priesthood there was an identification with the living conditions of their parishioners. In terms of state structure, the oligarchy was faced with the problem of replacing an institution that had performed an important function of social control and mystification.

Equally important was the changing focus of American attention, which became increasingly preoccupied with the war in Vietnam. The Alliance for Progress program was allowed to lapse in 1971; as well, the economic consequences of American involvement in southeast Asia rippled across the capitalist world, and would shortly be exacerbated by the oil crisis of the early 1970s. In Central America, the common market, which provided unequal benefits to the countries involved, was coming apart at the seams. An expression of the renewed economic crisis could be found in the 1969 "football war" between El Salvador and Honduras. Although ostensibly erupting out of a local soccer rivalry between the two countries, in fact, the clash dramatized the tensions created by a spillover of peasant emigrants from overcrowded El Salvador into the less densely populated Honduras, and also by Honduran dissatisfaction with the workings of the common market. Politically, the brief five-day war, which resulted in 2,000 deaths, boosted the reputation of the Salvadoran military regime as it invoked all the bathetic trappings of national honor and patriotism.

Finally, in surveying the ensemble of maturing forces that set the stage for the revolutionary situation of the late 1970s, an important rightwing development must be taken into account. In the early 1960s, General Jose "Chele" Medrano, head of the National Guard and later one of the heroes of the Football War, founded a rural paramilitary organization whose acronym was ORDEN (the word for "order"). By the end of the decade, the first "disappearences" had occurred. Once more, it is crucial to see that paramilitary formations and subsequently, the death squads, represent not an outburst of zealousness unconnected to the Salvadoran state, but rather a "logical" response by the ruling military-oligarchic structure to a new level of development by the reformist opposition. Far from being an aberration, such forces were instigated, controlled, and staffed by state personnel. While the professed theory of the Salvadoran state in the period 1969-79 revolved around ideas of modernization and reform, in practise it incorporated "terrorism" as a mode of control, and took on features of what political scientists call an "exceptional capitalist state formation" associated with fascism. Without belaboring the point, a failure to see the interconnectedness of these social forces and acceptance instead of the mirage of formal distinctions between institutions, leaves one with a caricature of Salvadoran politics in which left and right "extremists," both independent of the state, are equated as twin evils arrayed against the good, democratic centrists who comprise the Salvadoran government.

El Salvador was ripe for revolution. It only took one more mockery of the possibility of electoral politics to provide the impetus for choosing the revolutionary option. As the presidential election of 1972 approached, many thought it would provide an opening similar to that which had brought Araujo to power in 1931: the economy was weakening, the rigid political framework of the right was showing signs of stress, and a variety of social forces had developed sufficiently to translate the grievances of the peasantry into political power.

The most important development in 1972 was the electoral unity of the left. After years of debate over strategy, the clandestine Communist party had created a legal electoral entity in 1969 called the Nationalist Democratic Union. Seeing the chance for a united opposition, the social democrats, led by Ungo of the MNR, mediated between the communists and the Christian Democrats. In the year of the presidential election, the three parties formed the National Opposition Union (UNO, an acronym meaning "one") as an electoral coalition. Its presidential candidate was the popular Duarte; Guillermo Ungo was named as his running mate.

The right splintered. The PCN candidate was a lackluster career officer, Colonel Arturo Molina. A significant sector of the ultra-conservative agro-front had come to the conclusion that the PCN was becoming dangerously "soft" on subversion and increasingly inclined toward reforms. The agro-front chose ORDEN founder General "Chele" Medrano as its candidate. Even that didn't exhaust the possibilities of the rightist spectrum: the far right, which regarded the PCN as positively socialist, put up a lawyer named Jose Rodriguez Porth as a presidential candidate (a decade later Porth would be the Miami-based backer of Major Roberto D'Aubuisson).

On February 22, 1972, the Central Election Board announced a squeaker win for the PCN's Molina—314,000 votes to UNO's 292,000. That afternoon, however, the San Salvador election board declared that a mistake had been made with respect to returns from the capital. Recalculating the results, a new tally was produced: UNO 321,000; the PCN, 315,000. At that point, the powers-that-had-always-been stepped in and imposed a three-day news blackout. By February 25, the ballot boxes or *tamales*, as they're colloquially known, had been adequately stuffed and a creative recount yielded a Molina victory. A month later, a moderate army colonel made a bid at a coup attempt—and after considerable soul-searching, cheated candidate Duarte threw in his lot with the would-be rebels—but it was quickly and bloodily suppressed, at a cost of over 200 lives. Duarte was briefly imprisoned, tortured, and then exiled to Venezuela.

After the 1972 election, fraud, intimidation and repression as a fact of everyday life became, if anything, even more blatant than before. To cite but one of dozens of possible illustrative examples: two weeks after the inauguration of Molina, the National University was attacked by tanks, planes and artillery. More than 800 people were arrested; among others, the university's president and medical dean Fabio Castillo were flown to forced exile in Nicaragua; for two years the university gates remained locked.

At the same time, in a bid to recapture the momentum of the previous decade's economic boom, Colonel Molina devised a plan for "national transformation" designed to turn El Salvador into "another Taiwan." Again, the infrastructure was modernized at public expense, free trade zones were established to permit foreign companies to operate strike-free and tax-free, and the requisite uninterrupted productivity of labor was guaranteed at gunpoint. Foreign investment, led by American capital, climbed from $66 million to $104 million between 1970 and 1975, with firms from Texas Instruments to Maidenform Brassieres establishing Salvadoran plants. There was even, near the end of Molina's term, the heretical breath of "agrarian transformation" ("We don't use the term agrarian reform," explained the president-colonel, "because that's Marxist terminology"). That was too much for the oligarchy. When the 1977 election rolled around, the agro-front put an end to such dangerous flirtations, selecting Defense Minister and ORDEN director General Carlos

Humberto Romero as the PCN candidate, thus marking a significant shift in the ruling party away from the previous decade-and-a-half of "modernizing."

Within the Communist party, the debate over armed struggle was brought to a head by the party's secretary general Salvador Cayetano Carpio in the late 1960s. In vain, the former bakers' union organizer argued that the solution in El Salvador must be similar to that taking place in Vietnam. Unable to overcome the resistance of party moderates led by Shafik Handal, Carpio, at age fifty, broke with the party in 1970 and formed the first significant guerrilla group, the Popular Liberation Forces (FPL). In short order during the early 1970s, other armed groups emerged.

The most prominent group was the People's Revolutionary Army (ERP). Formed by leftwing Christian Democrats disenchanted with the apparently futile pursuit of electoral victory, and by members of the independent left intelligentsia, the ERP carried out an audacious series of political kidnappings designed both to shatter the image of the oligarchy's impregnability and to raise ransom money for the purchase of weapons. Within this group, during a bitter mid-1970s debate over whether to pursue a strategy of immediate insurrection or to attempt the construction of a broader popular base, violent factional infighting exploded. Among its victims was poet Roque Dalton, murdered at the hands of his comrades. Although years later the ERP would acknowledge that "pragmatism, nearsightedness, the thirst for power, and excessive militarism" had led to "tragic consequences" for the organization, for years the group remained isolated from the rest of the Salvadoran left, and underwent a series of vituperative splits.

The largest of the groups to emerge from this division was the Armed Forces of National Resistance (FARN), led by Ferman Cienfuegos. These three groups (FPL, ERP and FARN) comprised, by the end of the decade, about 80 percent of the estimated 4,000 guerrilla troops. Rounding out the revolutionary forces were two smaller groups: the Central American Workers' Revolutionary Party (PRTC), devoted to the old dream of a unified revolutionary movement in the Central American isthmus; and finally, in early 1979, a Communist party guerrilla organization, the Armed Forces of

Liberation (FAL).

For thousands of Salvadorans, the decade of the 1970s was a prolonged and painful search for an appropriate revolutionary form. The multiplicity of popular organizations and guerrilla forces that this search spawned ought to serve as an indicator of the illusory character of the mystification presented to North Americans in the stereotyped image of "the revolutionary." Were these initially small groups of armed guerrillas no more than isolated expressions of Salvadoran discontent, they would have been quickly consigned to historical obscurity; in fact, they were but spearheads, albeit uncoordinated, of a massive popular mobilization of every sector of Salvadoran society—peasants, teachers, students, trade unionists, slum-dwellers, even the church—notwithstanding the dismissive claims of the U.S. State Department and others about the absence of popular support for the revolutionaries.

Far from the monolithic demon of "the guerrilla," or the corollary reduction of political debate to "doctrinal squabblings" as it is portrayed in the American media, the development of El Salvador's revolutionary forces occurred unevenly over a ten-year period. It was marked by political differences, a panoply of strategies ranging from the ERP's ransom kidnappings to Carpio's "prolonged popular war," and by successive organizational recombinations. It was often punctuated by tragic and violent internal divisions, such as the historically unforgiveable murder of Roque Dalton. But just as the record of their development shows the revolutionaries not to be supra-humans possessed of angelic purity, so also were they not undifferentiated "Marxist-Leninist terrorists" as caricatured in the pat catchphrases of American political rhetoric. Without entering into the specialised discourse of this leftist debate, it will be sufficient to appreciate that the forces which emerged from it are at least as complex and variegated as the divisions among Christian Democrats, the military, the church and the oligarchy.

There were two Romeros in El Salvador. Unrelated by blood or beliefs, recently elected President General Carlos Humberto Romero and newly appointed Archbishop Oscar Arnulfo Romero offered two poles around which much of Salvadoran politics gravitated from 1977 to 1979.

For five consecutive days after the implausible election results—three to one for the PCN—that put Humberto Romero in office, nearly 50,000 people crowded into downtown San Salvador's Plaza Libertad, camping out under the covered arcades and surrounding the statue of the woman representing Liberty at mass rallies denouncing the patently fraudulent outcome. At 1 a.m. on Monday, February 28, 1977, with the crowd reduced to about 4,000, trucks bearing members of the army and the security forces pulled up. The square was sealed off—first there were high-powered hoses to disperse them, then tear gas when many sought shelter in a nearby church, and finally bullets. By 4 a.m., Plaza Libertad had been emptied. A reporter who had only heard the screaming and the shooting, got into the square after it was over "and found it literally covered with blood, although the bodies had been removed. But perhaps the most horrible thing was when I returned again an hour after that to find they had hosed down the plaza and there was a chill as though nothing had happened at all." But not quite nothing.

From these chilling attempts to make terror invisible a new popular form of organization arose. It had happened first two years earlier, in mid-1975, when a student protest march was turned into a massacre in broad daylight on one of the capital's busiest streets. In the aftermath, hundreds of people occupied the Metropolitan Cathedral; there, representatives of diverse groups adopted a new collective identity, the People's Revolutionary Bloc (BPR)—an unprecedented type of mass organization in El Salvador. Similarly, out of the slaughter in Plaza Libertad there came the People's Leagues of February 28 (LP-28), marking a further maturation of the oppositional forces.

Like the Romero chosen for the presidency, Oscar Romero had been selected for the post of archbishop because he was a reliable conservative. As he later confided, he had been named to curb the radical priesthood: "My job was to finish you off." Unlike the other Romero however, the one picked to be the spiritual leader of El Salvador underwent a conversion. The resurgently aggressive ruling bloc had recently launched an attack on the church, adding priests to their list of targets. One of their first victims was Father Rutilio Grande, a legendary and courageous rural pastor, assassinated less than two weeks after the Plaza Libertad massacre.

It was nearly midnight, March 12, when the archbishop found himself in the modest house in Aguilares where the murdered Grande had lived. Grande's death was a moment of personal crisis for the reserved, scholarly Romero. Despite the state of siege still in effect after the election, he called for demonstrations to mourn the slain priest. He sent a letter to lame-duck President Molina demanding an investigation, and announcing his intention to attend no official functions (including Humberto Romero's inauguration) until the murder was solved. He closed all Catholic schools for three days. At the mass which Romero celebrated on the ninth-day remembrance of Grande's death, 100,000 worshippers gathered inside and outside the cathedral. "If I were looking for an adjective to describe this time of change in the archdiocese, I would not hesitate to call it the hour of resurrection," he wrote in his pastoral Easter message.

The archbishop had ceased to be a conservative, and the Salvadoran church was taking up, in the words of the Medellin conference, "the preferential option of the poor." A year later, in November 1978, as he was leaving the funeral of yet another murdered priest, Romero decreed: "When a dictatorship seriously violates human rights and attacks the common good of the nation, when it becomes unbearable... the church speaks of the legitimate right of insurrectional violence."

Civil war, as Salvadoran political history demonstrated, is not a spontaneous familial eruption, but rather the expression of a slow evolution of social forces. The result of thousands of lesser ideological and physical confrontations, it marks an advanced stage in the process of "class struggle," a term whose Marxist connotations make North Americans uneasy. Although it, too, can be reduced to an abstraction by formulaic wear, the concept is perhaps more precise, less loaded, and captures more of the dynamic of the situation than the lexicon in which American political debate is conducted.

In any case, it was soon apparent that the oligarchy's choice of Humberto Romero was an anachronistic blunder. Faced with the failure to stem the growth of the opposition with the blend of economic development and repression known as "modernization," perhaps it was only natural to seek a revivified version of the authoritarian impulse. However, the balance of social relations could no longer support the reimposition of the traditional brutality of rightwing rulers. The Humberto Romero regime lasted a bare eighteen months from the time of the general's election.

Certainly, like other breeds about to become extinct, the regime lashed out in reactionary fury. The toll of civilian deaths, at the hands of ORDEN or the death squads, steadily mounted. The archdiocese of San Salvador, which began a careful count in 1979 under Archbishop Romero's sponsorship, recorded some 600 victims between January and October of that year. No longer, however, could state terror in El Salvador escape international attention. The hitherto obscure Central American dictatorship was now the subject of U.S. congressional examination of its human rights violations, despite Salvadoran government objections to "internal interference." The Carter regime conveyed the new U.S. attitude on human rights by delaying the naming of a new ambassador to the Humberto Romero presidency, instead dispatching State Department human rights officer Patricia Derian to investigate the situation first hand. In July 1977, Washington withheld its approval of a $90 million Inter-American Development Bank loan. To be sure, Carter proceeded with characteristic inconsistency here as elsewhere. When Romero lifted an eight-month state of siege in October 1977, the stalled loan was approved and a new ambassador was appointed. Equally predictably, no sooner had U.S. pressure relaxed, than the PCN-controlled legislative assembly rammed through a *Ley de Orden*, a classic piece of sedition legislation.

But with increasing frequency, El Salvador was a violent image in world news, penetrating even the placid bastion of the American home by way of the six o'clock report. In January 1979, the report of the Human Rights Commission of the Organization of American States condemned El Salvador's human rights record, graphically detailing torture chambers, prisons, and disappearances. A month later, the U.S. State Department's own human rights report ranked El Salvador and Somoza's Nicaragua as "the most serious violators of individual freedoms in Latin America." The one-paragraph column-fillers about murdered priests and kidnapped executives which had been the American media's extent of interest in El Salvador for years, now exploded on U.S. television screens. When in May 1979, 300 protestors of the People's Revolutionary Bloc gathered on the steps of the Metropolitan Cathedral for a peaceful demonstration against the abduction of Bloc leaders, U.S. camera crews were there, recording the arrival of government troops. That night, the lead item on the newscast of Walter Cronkite, the dean of American anchormen, showed troops firing into the crowd, and panicked protestors crawling over dead bodies on the steps of the cathedral. By summer, El Salvador had left the back pages; it was the "next Nicaragua," as commentators compared its situation with that of the collapsing Somoza regime.

Once again, as in 1960, the young colonels stepped into the breach. By late afternoon on October 15, 1979, General Romero and his top aides were packed aboard a plane bound for Guatemala. Militarily, the coup had been effective; politically, the reformist colonels had only the vaguest notion of what should follow. In the hasty negotiations between the officers who had carried out the overthrow and a group of senior, more conservative military officers, whose support would be needed, two slots on the five-member junta were divided between the two factions. Forty-one-year-old Colonel Adolfo Majano represented the reformist group, and Colonel Jaime Gutierrez was named as the compromise candidate of the older colonels in an effort to sidestep such known and unacceptable hardliners as Colonel Garcia and Colonel Vides Casanova.

Three days later, Majano, Gutierrez and the three civilian members of the junta were presented to the public. The three civilians were Roman Mayorga Quiroz, 37, rector of the Jesuit university; social democratic leader Guillermo Ungo; and Mario Andino, 43, manager of the Salvadoran Phelps-Dodge subsidiary, who had been named as a representative of the private sector at the insistence of the U.S. embassy. The impressive cabinet group that had been assembled lived up to one wit's assessment of the change as "the thinking man's coup." Salvador Samayoa, a 29-year-old philosophy professor was to be minister of education; a Christian Democratic economist, Hector Dada, was foreign minister; a millionaire reformist dairy farmer, Enrique Alvarez Cordova received the crucial agricultural post; Ruben Zamora, also a Christian

Democrat, would handle the ministry of the presidency; his brother, Mario, was named attorney general. But as well, the familiar Colonel Jose Garcia appeared among these impeccable democrats as minister of defense; with him came Eugenio Vides Casanova as National Guard commander, and two equally sinister figures to head the National and Treasury Police.

Though the development of Salvadoran political forces, if civil war was to be averted, pointed more than ever in the direction of reform, it hung in the balance whether the still-dominant military would permit that path to be taken. The answer would be provided in short order by members of the junta themselves. Unlike previous gestures at reform, this time the development of mass public organizations (claiming a membership of 100,000 by early 1979) had reached a degree of cohesion sufficient to enable them to render their own judgments on progress.

By December 1979, there were daily demonstrations by the popular organizations; several thousand workers occupied cotton mills and other factories; there were sporadic land takeovers spreading through the countryside. Once more, "extrajudicial executions" became rampant; though ORDEN had been formally dismantled it was promptly reborn under another name. Nearly 300 deaths were recorded in the final month of 1979. Though the junta had seen to the dismissal of about a hundred officers connected with the extreme right and the death squads, gradually most of them were reinstated, excepting only the notorious Major Roberto D'Aubuisson. Increasingly, the power of the hardline colonels eclipsed the presence of the civilians on the junta. Even as the military backed away from the promises of change, Washington resumed military aid and dispatched a training team to teach "riot control" to Salvadoran troops. In mid-December, the army, supported by helicopter fire and armored tanks, "controlled" a strike in which thirty-five workers were slaughtered. The last chance for peaceful reform vanished. The resignations began soon afterward.

Education Minister Salvador Samayoa and Agriculture Minister Enrique Alvarez were the first to go. "We see now that this political project was, from the very beginning, a maneuver against the people," they said in their resignation statement on December 29. "We do not regret having participated in this government...but now that everything is clear, we would regret for the rest of our lives any further collaboration.'' The press conference where Samayoa announced his resignation ended when masked and armed guerrillas entered the room; the former education minister left with them, saying the time for talk had passed. Junta members Ungo and Mayorga followed suit a few days later, on January 3, 1980, along with most of the cabinet, the majority of the sub-cabinet and several Supreme Court judges. Though the pretense of a viable ''center'' in Salvadoran politics would be maintained, particularly by the U.S. whose embassy was already negotiating with the Christian Democrats, the center had in fact collapsed.

A week later, former Foreign Minister Hector Dada, and another prominent Christian Democrat, Jose Morales Ehrlich, who had succeeded Duarte as mayor of San Salvador, along with a nominal independent, took their oaths of office at the Casa Presidencial, joining Majano and Gutierrez in a second revamped junta. More importantly, that same day, also in the capital, another press conference took place. Seated behind a table covered with red and black flags and a small assortment of weapons, sat some of the most wanted people in the country. The leaders of the Popular Liberation Forces (FPL), the Armed Forces of National Resistance (FARN), and the Communist party announced their unification into a coordinated command structure, a moment ending years of factional strife (only the ERP was not present, but negotiations with it were underway). Two days later, in the crowded law school auditorium at the National University, the various popular organizations did likewise. To celebrate the unification of the revolutionary forces, a mass demonstration was called for January 22, the anniversary of the *matanza*. As usual, the thousands of marchers were fired on by the state, irrespective of its current reformist trappings. The Salvadoran Human Rights Commission put the death toll at sixty-seven.

Nor were those the only deaths. Few nights passed in which the death squads did not claim at least five or ten victims. In the first ten weeks of 1980, nearly 700 murders of unarmed civilians were committed. (By year's end the figure would be over 8,000.) The most spectacular individual assassination occurred two days after Roberto D'Aubuisson publicly denounced the Christian Democratic Attorney General Mario

Zamora as a secret communist. Several men pushed their way into the home of the country's chief legal officer and shot him dead. That was enough for junta member Dada. He resigned, as did Zamora's brother, Ruben, a cabinet minister. Ruben then formed the Popular Christian Social Movement, splitting what remained of the Christian Democrats.

Once again, the American embassy, now headed by recent Carter appointee Robert White, met with its Salvadoran clients. The price of continued U.S. aid, Colonel Garcia and other hardliners were told, was the acceptance of Jose Duarte in the junta and a program of modest land reforms, nationalization of the banking system, and state control of coffee exports as proposed by the Christian Democrats. By early March, Duarte was duly installed in the third junta in six months. Whether or not the colonels had been reminded to cease the indiscriminate killings, the implicit warning went unheeded. The murders escalated to about 750 a month. The death squads recognized no sanctuary.

In late March 1980, in his Sunday homily, Archbishop Romero appealed to members of the security forces. "No soldier is obliged to obey an order contrary to the law of God. It is time that you come to your senses and obey your conscience rather than follow out a sinful command." Two days after this near-incitement to mutiny, a man with a rifle appeared in the doorway of the chapel of a hospital for cancer patients where Romero was saying a memorial mass. Raising his arms as he finished the sermon, Romero offered the traditional invocation: "Let us pray." Then he collapsed, as the bullets, muted by a silencer, entered his chest and face. The leader of El Salvador's Roman Catholic Church died instantly.

The formation of the Democratic Revolutionary Front (FDR) in mid-April 1980 was witnessed by more than 5,000 people who jammed the National University auditorium. Though the Carter administration, now thoroughly preoccupied with the Iranian hostage crisis, and later that year the newly elected Reagan regime, would continue to insist on a neat symmetry of right, left, and center, it was hard to see how the FDR could be so conveniently pigeonholed.

Joining the already coordinated mass organizations were the most important democratic forces in the country—

including those Washington had praised as the moderate center as recently as a month before: Guillermo Ungo, Duarte's running mate in 1972 and a member of the first 1979 junta; university rector Roman Mayorga, also a member of the first junta; Ruben Zamora, cabinet minister through two juntas and presently leader of dissident Christian Democrats. Presiding over this broad coalition, which took in 90 percent of the country's organized working class, was Enrique Alvarez Cordova, renegade member of the oligarchic Fourteen Families, and former minister of agriculture.

If the FDR was a repudiation of the credibility Washington sought for the Duarte junta, the next month dashed whatever hopes there were that at least the guerrillas would remain divided. In May, the ERP joined the other armed groups in a formation that by the end of the year would be known as the Farabundo Marti National Liberation Front (FMLN).

There were only one or two more permutations of the opposing forces in El Salvador before they reached their contemporary form. In late November 1980, after a summer of partially successful general strikes, the beginning of international recognition for the Salvadoran left, and the slaughter of over 4,000 people by the death squads, the leadership of the FDR, including Front President Alvarez, while holding a press conference, was abducted and murdered. Henceforth, Ungo and surviving FDR leaders would operate in exile from Mexico City. Correspondingly, there was again a "cabinet crisis"; this time it was resolved, with American advice, by naming Duarte president in early December.

In the brief space between the bid to decimate the FDR and the shuffle which installed Duarte in the Casa Presidencial, the exhumed bodies of four American churchwomen murdered in El Salvador appeared on U.S. television. For a moment, the half-century bloodbath which was Salvadoran history came home to Americans. Just as promptly, the image was exorcised in the alarmist rhetoric of the recently elected Reagan administration.

5 Major Bob

> *For the moment we will have to wear a democrat's skin, like in Little Red Riding Hood.*
> —General "Chele" Medrano,
> November 1981

General Al Haig's second annual pre-spring offensive against Central America began with a search for the "smoking Sandinista." Like the dormant but not extinct Salvadoran volcanoes, the secretary of state opened his campaign with a few warning rumbles.

Appearing before various congressional committees in the first week of February 1982, Haig said that the U.S. would do "whatever is necessary" to prevent the overthrow of the Salvadoran junta, but refused to say whether the administration was contemplating the use of American combat troops. "I am not about to lay out a litany of actions that may or may not take place," huffed the secretary. Days later, just before taking off for Europe to denounce the recent imposition of martial law in Poland, the vicar of American foreign policy shifted into High Haigspeak. "There are no current plans for the use of American forces," he said, but "the sterility of drawing lines around America's potential options constitutes the promulgation of roadways for those who are seeking to move against America's vital interests." While students of syntax were pondering how "the sterility of drawing lines" constituted "the promulgation of roadways," the secretary had moved on to argue that it was wrong to draw parallels between U.S. involvement in Central America and that in Vietnam a decade earlier. "The ambiguities are distinctly different than they were in Vietnam," declared the oracle of Foggy Bottom. Leaving reporters to parse out the ambiguities of his use of the English language, Secretary Haig boarded the flight to Madrid.

Back home in early March 1982, Haig fired the first shots. The U.S., he assured the House Foreign Affairs Committee, had "overwhelming and irrefutable" evidence that the insurgents in El Salvador were controlled from outside the country. However, Haig was not ready to provide details just yet, saying it would jeopardize intelligence sources. The congressmen, who had endured the "incontrovertible" evidence of the State Department White Paper a year before, were not satisfied. Two days later, challenged to prove his contention that shadowy communist foreigners were running the Salvadoran rebellion, Haig leaned into the microphone and in his inimitable quavering whisper casually let slip to Representative Clarence Long, chairman of the House Appropriations Sub-committee, "You might also know, Mr. Chairman, that today for the first time a Nicaraguan military man was captured in Salvador, having been sent down by the FSLN to participate in the direction which is so evident of this guerrilla operation from Nicaragua."

Having reached into his hat and pulled out what the press immediately dubbed the "smoking Sandinista," the far-flung media rushed off to Salvadoran security headquarters for confirmation. (The reference, by the way, was to the decade-old "smoking gun" that investigators searching former President Nixon's Watergate tapes hoped to find to prove the criminal intent of Haig's then-boss.) That evening, CBS Television News had footage of glum Salvadoran Defense Minister Jose Garcia who reported that the captured Nicaraguan had been "snatched" away from Salvadoran officials. Garcia said the Nicaraguan had been captured three or four days ago (rather than that very day, as Haig claimed), and taken to the Mexican embassy in San Salvador to identify a suspected contact. Once there, someone within grabbed the Nicaraguan, pulled him inside, and slammed the door on his captors outside.

The next day, Mexican officials explained that the

"smoking Sandinista," far from being a "military man" or a terrorist subversive, was in fact a 19-year-old Nicaraguan student attending university in Monterrey, Mexico, who, lacking the money to fly to Mexico after a vacation home, had decided to travel overland, passing through El Salvador on his way back to school. Meanwhile, at the State Department that day, where Haig was having a private meeting with Salvadoran Vice-President Jaime Gutierrez, department officials were scrambling to undo the damage. The hoopla over the Nicaraguan student—whose problems seemed more amenable to the ministration of a student loan officer than to an East-West confrontation—might well detract from the "overwhelming, irrefutable" evidence of foreign involvement in El Salvador. Haig's underlings promised to produce a "sanitized" version of the secret information within days.

On March 9, the offensive was officially launched with a slide show for the press. Flanking the screen, and armed with nothing more than school pointers, were John Hughes, deputy director of the Defense Intelligence Agency, and CIA deputy director Admiral Bobby Inman. "Ladies and gentlemen, our purpose this afternoon is to review some of the sensitive intelligence available to us on the continuing Nicaraguan military buildup," Hughes began as the first of thirty-six slides of declassified aerial photographs, taken by SR-71 Blackbird reconnaissance planes flying at 80,000 feet and at speeds of 2,000 mph, flashed onto the screen.

Hughes was an old hand at this sort of thing; twenty years ago he had been the youthful intelligence officer who showed reporters blowup photos of Soviet missile bases on Cuba. As the slides clicked by, Hughes warmed to the task, enthusiastically pointing at "Cuban-style" barracks, "Soviet-style" obstacle courses, "East German-provided" trucks, and reporting that Nicaraguan pilots were learning to fly Soviet MIG-17 aircraft in Bulgaria and Cuba. In case anyone missed it, the communist-influenced architecture and equipment was neatly labelled on the blowups. Although the photographs, shown on American television that night, looked like the ordinary road-and-townsite aerial shots that might be taken of Topeka, Kansas, Hughes' eagle eye was able to pick out the tiniest detail from 80,000 feet up. "There's the Soviet physical training area, situated here, with chin-bars and other types of equipment to exercise the forces," he declared.

It was hard to take this spectacular display of snooping technology altogether seriously. Within days, political cartoonist Garry Trudeau, author of the popular *Doonesbury* strip, was ridiculing the administration's show-and-tell extravaganza. In one panel, while cartoonist Trudeau's prototypical TV viewer was sinking deeper into his easy chair, the administration voice on the tube was saying, "Notice, too, the Soviet-style Cubans wearing Czech-inspired fatigues having lunch with Cuban-trained Nicaraguans in the Bulgarian-built mess tent." "Great photos, General," called out one of the press scrum in the next panel. "What's that they're eating?" Replied the administration voice without missing a beat: "Soviet-style pizza."

What any of this had to do with El Salvador was undetermined. About all that the expensive display of photography proved was that the Nicaraguans were beefing up their defenses. And for good reason, too, it would seem. That same day the Washington *Post* revealed that President Reagan had approved, some three months earlier, a CIA plan to invest $19 million to build a 500-man U.S.-supervised paramilitary force to carry out covert actions against the Sandinista government in Nicaragua. The slide show went up in smoke and the administration stuttered through a series of semi-denials. White House press secretary Larry Speakes, asked whether the U.S. would export terror to Nicaragua, replied, "I don't think so." On second thought, he added, "The answer to that is no. It is not our policy." Latin policy chief Thomas Enders, who was in Santiago shaking hands with Chilean dictator General Augusto Pinochet, pooh-poohed it, "There is always someone saying...someone is in a covert war." However, Republican Barry Goldwater, head of the Senate Intelligence Committee, confirmed that "everything in the *Post* story was true." Said vicar Haig: "It is inappropriate to comment on covert activities...whether or not such exist."

Whether or not such existed, the Nicaraguans were not amused. Sandinista Agriculture Minister Jaime Wheelock, who happened to be in Washington that week, pointed out the overlooked matter of the illegality of spy plane overflights. As for other covert "activities," the Nicaraguans would take their case to the United Nations. "We are accused of converting Nicaragua into another Cuba," said Wheelock, "but what the U.S. really wants is to covert Nicaragua into another Chile.''

The comedy of errors was not over. The State Department approach was to try, try, and try again. It had not been a good week. In addition to everything else, there was a photo of mutilated bodies from the French newspaper *Le Figaro* which Haig cited as proof of Nicaraguan brutality against the Miskito Indian population. *Le Figaro* then issued a retraction, explaining it was an old photo, improperly captioned, of atrocities committed by the ousted Somoza regime. Then there was the rumor of two defectors from the Nicaraguan Air Force who were supposed to tell of their involvement in the Salvadoran insurrection. At the last minute, they failed to show because, as a department official with a slight case of Haigspeak put it, ''The new material is not ready to meet the press.''

But on Friday, March 12, the State Department believed it had finally gotten it right. At a Washington press conference, it produced 19-year-old Orlando Tardencillas, a Nicaraguan captured a year before in El Salvador while fighting with the guerrillas, who would confess that he had been trained in Cuba and Ethiopia and then sent to El Salvador by the Nicaraguan government. However, when presented to the media to confirm Nicaraguan, Cuban and even Ethiopian involvement in El Salvador, Tardencillas coolly announced that he had never been to Cuba or Ethiopia, that though he had indeed fought with the Salvadoran rebels he had not been sent by his government, and that while in El Salvador he had never seen another Nicaraguan or Cuban. Furthermore, all previous statements to his Salvadoran and CIA captors had been made under coercion. ''An official of the U.S. embassy told me that they needed to demonstrate the presence of Cubans in El Salvador,'' said Tardencillas. ''They gave me an option. They said I could come here or face certain death.'' Trying to put a nonchalant face on this latest fiasco, the State Department spokesman shrugged, ''You win some and you lose some.'' Tardencillas was promptly released to the Nicaraguan embassy and flown home that weekend. Perhaps the department officials heaved a sigh of relief that the latest ''smoking Sandinista'' hadn't claimed on national television that he had been personally tortured by Alexander Haig, which is how the satiric *Doonesbury* version had it the following week. Given the surrealism afoot in Washington, satire seemed to have a limited future.

The appearance on March 20 of the State Department's 1982 White Paper, an eleven page missive titled "Cuban and Nicaraguan Support for the Salvadoran Insurgency," was distinctly anticlimactic, and most recipients promptly deposited it in the circular file. By then, the annual pre-spring offensive was in headlong retreat, pelted by international and media criticism, as well as grumbling in the corridors. An unnamed senior White House official complained that Haig's "frothing" over El Salvador had created unnecessary public fears, and sourly recalled that a year ago the secretary had assured President Reagan that the war there could be "won." Said another administration official, "One of the problems we've had is that Al Haig scared everyone." Certainly Congress was becoming scared. Said Massachusetts Senator Paul Tsongas, co-sponsor of a mid-March bill that would make congressional consent a requirement for any military aid or covert action in Central America, "We're on the verge of a kind of 1950s intervention policy. The domino theory does work, but we're going to be the ones to knock down the first domino" by driving countries into the "Cuban embrace."

The administration's overblown talk also aroused international response. In London, Denis Healey, a prominent and pro-American Labor party figure, warned, "There is a growing feeling in Europe that the U.S. is drifting into a very dangerous posture in Central America." French President Francois Mitterand, visiting Reagan in the midst of the "smoking Sandinista" farce, noted, "Our analysis is different from the start. I think these people must come out of the economic misery in which they are held by the oligarchy. This requires comprehension from the West," the French socialist added, as though slightly dubious about the amount of comprehension possible with Reagan's Keystone Cops corps. Typical of foreign press criticism was the editorially conservative Toronto *Globe and Mail*. Said the national newspaper of America's northern neighbor, "Truth is, of course, the first casualty in any war. But in the Reagan administration's propaganda war over El Salvador, the truth refuses to roll over and die: it keeps coming back to haunt U.S. Secretary of State Alexander Haig." After reviewing the series of blunders that even *Time* magazine called a "curious series of public presentations," the *Globe* concluded, "H.L.

Mencken to the contrary, Mr. Haig is going broke underestimating the intelligence of the American people."

The New York *Times*/CBS News poll published March 20 provided a measure of how much Haig had underestimated American public opinion. When asked what Washington should do in El Salvador, 63 percent said, "Stay out." Only 16 percent even approved sending economic and military aid. Some 60 percent of respondents said they were afraid that the U.S. would "get involved in El Salvador the way it did in Vietnam." What support Reagan's policies did have revolved around fear of communism. Despite Haig's inability to prove it, half of those questioned said they believed Soviet or Cuban troops were present in El Salvador. Of those surveyed, 57 percent agreed that El Salvador was important to American interests. On the whole, however, President Reagan wasn't getting top marks for his handling of the situation: 42 percent disapproved, 26 percent approved, and a solid 32 percent of those polled had no opinion. A week later there were protest marches across the country: 50,000 in Washington, 20,000 attending an interfaith worship service in Philadelphia, and thousands more at similar demonstrations in Seattle, Chicago, Dallas, Los Angeles, Denver and San Francisco. A lot of Americans weren't buying the administration's hard-sell on El Salvador.

While Al Haig was gradually working himself into a state of being fit to be tied, President Reagan had been certifying that El Salvador was fit for military aid and electoral democracy. As the January 28, 1982 deadline approached for the first of Reagan's congressionally required semi-annual confirmations of "progress" in El Salvador, the beginnings of the certification ritual took shape. As essayist and novelist Joan Didion, reporting from El Salvador that year, put it, the flurry of reports, speeches and testimonials "seemed almost cyclical, seasonal events keyed to the particular rhythm of the six-month certification process; midway in the certification cycle things appear 'bad,' and are then made, at least rhetorically, to appear 'better,' 'improvement' being the key to certification."

So, for example, on January 21, the year-old investigation of the deaths of the American churchwomen, which two months before was "at a dead end," was now perceived by the

State Department to be "significantly closer to resolution." Similarly, four days later, the State Department announced that the Salvadoran land redistribution program was a "remarkable success," despite "deficiencies" and "implementation problems." The nod to "deficiencies" was a way of discounting a report made the month before by a Salvadoran peasant organization, the Union Comunal Salvadorena, which described the program as being near collapse because of military-backed terror, illegal evictions and bureaucratic roadblocks.

Unfortunately for the Reagan administration's credibility, the day before the president duly certified to Congress that the junta had achieved "substantial control" over its security forces, the New York *Times* published an account from Morazan province detailing a massacre of peasants near the village of Mozote which had been carried out the month before by the government's crack Atlacatl battalion. The villagers had compiled a detailed list of 733 victims who they said were murdered by uniformed soldiers, some swooping in on U.S.-provided helicopters. "The rebels in this zone are not known to wear uniforms or use helicopters," *Times* reporter Raymond Bonner drily noted.

Whether or not the security forces were "under control," as Reagan would claim the next day, the rebels were not. The day the Mozote massacre was revealed, the FMLN launched a devastating attack on El Salvador's biggest air force base, at Ilopango airport near San Salvador. Half the Salvadoran air force, including the Huey helicopters used to slaughter Mozote peasants, were wiped out in the raid. The next day Reagan formally certified to Congress that the junta was making "continuing progress" in carrying out political and economic reforms. The defeat at Ilopango the day before was just one more reason to provide additional aid. "We cannot allow terrorists committed to achieving power through violence to undermine these efforts," said Reagan. It was expected the administration would seek nearly $300 million in military and economic aid for El Salvador for the next fiscal year, as well as an immediate $25 million to replace the lost aircraft.

Not everyone was as sanguine about certification as the president and his underlings, who were dispatched to various congressional committee venues to defend the aid policy. The

American Civil Liberties Union, in an unusual report, declared that "the violations of human rights taking place in El Salvador are not aberrations," but rather "selectively directed" by the junta. A New York *Times* editorial called the certification "cynical humbug." In February, the U.S. Conference of Catholic Bishops reiterated its opposition to more military aid. Said Houston Bishop John McCarthy, "We feel it is our duty to challenge the public policy of the American government which is arming, training and guiding military forces which are obviously repressing its people."

Various congressmen were also uneasy. A three-man delegation visiting El Salvador in mid-February was typical. "A land without justice sums up the El Salvador of today and the last fifty years," said Minnesota Democrat James Oberstar, explaining why the delegation had decided to come out against further military aid. Even U.S. Ambassador Deane Hinton, in a speech to Salvadoran businessmen in late February—his first public statement on human rights since becoming ambassador—appeared to contradict the president's certification claims. The American people understood there would be "some abuses by those engaged in battle," Hinton told the entrepreneurs, but "Salvadoran authorities, and you, the people of El Salvador, have tolerated serious excesses." A Salvadoran human rights worker put it more bluntly: "We invite President Reagan to come down here, to walk the streets of San Salvador at 6 a.m. every day, and see the bodies, then tell us if there is progress in human rights here."

U.N. Ambassador Jeane Kirkpatrick was one U.S. official who remained unperturbed by the certification flap. "We live in an imperfect world," she said at the end of February, putting her world view in a nutshell for an American Legion conference. "Most people are badly governed, and always have been...Therefore, sometimes we are going to have to support and associate with governments who do not meet our standards." That month, President Reagan shipped helicopters and other military equipment worth $55 million into that "imperfect world," using emergency funds that permitted him to bypass the disputatious Congress.

The one bit of genuinely certifiable progress in El Salvador was that of the country's leading military men through the ranks. Notwithstanding the Ilopango disaster, Colonels Garcia, Gutierrez, and Vides Casanova (commander of the

National Guard), promoted themselves to general. Apart from being a morale booster for those involved, the move was generally taken to signal Garcia's pre-eminence in the power structure.

With Central America being battered by the same recession that was taking its toll in the U.S., President Reagan announced his Caribbean Basin aid program on February 24— a $350 million emergency economic assistance package. Despite urgings from Mexico and other Latin nations that he stick to philanthropy, Reagan, as one editorialist put it, "spoiled an otherwise admirable speech" with hardline political rhetoric. "Very simply, guerrillas, armed and supported by and through Cuba, are attempting to impose a Marxist-Leninist dictatorship on the people of El Salvador. If we do not act promptly and decisively in defense of freedom, new Cubas will arise from the ruins of today's conflict," claimed Reagan. "Simple and puerile," responded the New York *Times*. "It is shouting, as if addressing the slow-witted... By debasing debate, the administration impairs support for even modest levels of aid."

In mid-March, the administration sent Congress the Caribbean Basin bill. It looked more like a Salvadoran aid bill. More than a third of the $350 million request—$128 million—was targeted for El Salvador. (Costa Rica, Jamaica, Honduras and the Dominican Republic would receive lesser amounts.) This emergency legislation included no military aid figures; they were still in the works, said spokesman Thomas Enders. Given that the package was but a fraction of the $5 billion which the Latin nations had suggested was required, any notion that the much-heralded plan marked a shift in American policy from its military emphasis was quickly forgotten. In a less noticed move at about the same time, the Reagan administration also submitted a fiscal 1983 military aid request to Congress that included for the first time since 1977 money for Argentina, Chile and Guatemala. In any case, by then the Haig ideological offensive was in full swing, devouring whatever attention Americans were prepared to pay to Central America.

It was going to be a wonderful election. The people would turn out in vast numbers and "repudiate" the guerrillas. The good guys—Napoleon Duarte and the Christian Democrats—

would win handsomely. Ambassador Deane Hinton would beam like the suburbanite host of a pleasurable backyard barbeque. El Salvador at last would be placing one timorous foot before the other on the road to democracy. President Reagan and his policies would receive vindication. Best of all, the whole thing would be beamed live to America via satellite.

It all happened. Everything as expected. Except for one small detail: Major Bob.

Major Roberto D'Aubuisson, a 38-year-old former officer in the G2 intelligence division of the National Guard, had long been regarded by American diplomats as a member of the rightwing lunatic fringe with more than shadowy connections to death-squad terrorism. Five-feet-six-inches tall, muscular, with strikingly handsome Latin features and a tense-jawed macho self-assurance, D'Aubuisson—head of the recently formed National Republican Alliance party (ARENA)—had emerged in the three-month run-up to the March 28, 1982 National Assembly elections as the surprise darling of the Salvadoran electorate.

Born in Santa Tecla, about fifteen minutes from San Salvador, D'Aubuisson's father was a salesman and his mother a civil servant who was now retired on a state pension. He entered military school at age fifteen and, on graduation, was assigned to the National Guard. According to his campaign biography, he took intelligence courses at private police academies in New York and Virginia and studied "communist infiltration" in Taiwan. According to a former Salvadoran officer, within G2 D'Aubuisson became known "for the success of his interrogation techniques." One of his chilling nicknames was Major Blowtorch.

When reformist junior officers toppled the Humberto Romero regime in October 1979, the notorious G2 division was disbanded and Major Bob was one of the hardline officers cashiered from the military. However, another rightwing commander, Colonel Nicolas Carranza, subsequently deputy defense minister to Colonel Garcia, took the former major under his wing and encouraged him to remain active. His activity, it was widely believed, was running the White Warriors—a death squad thought to be responsible for the murders of Attorney General Mario Zamora and Archbishop Romero.

In May 1980, D'Aubuisson was surprised at a farmhouse

meeting and arrested by Salvadoran authorities while in possession of documents described as "deeply incriminating." Former Ambassador Robert White later told Congress that the papers offered "compelling if not 100 percent conclusive evidence" that D'Aubuisson had ordered Archbishop Romero's assassination. He called Major Bob a "pathological killer." After less than a week in jail, however, D'Aubuisson was released, reportedly due to pressure from Colonel Carranza. He went to Guatemala where he had earlier moved his wife and four children. While there he absorbed the lessons of Guatemala's ultra-right National Liberation Movement (MLN), which would provide much of the ideology and structure of ARENA. As President-elect Reagan was about to take office in January 1981, Major Bob returned to his homeland to sound out possibilities for a new coup.

Now, a year later, D'Aubuisson was making an unexpectedly strong showing in the race for sixty National Assembly seats being contested by a half-dozen parties. To identify the differences between them, one had to slice the rightist spectrum very finely. Napoleon Duarte's Christian Democrats (PDC), although described as a center-left vehicle by Salvadoran standards, was the middle-right party. In the orgy of insults that passed for a campaign, the PDC was most often the target of D'Aubuisson's harangues. Holding up a watermelon and recalling that the PDC's party color was green, Major Bob dramatically chopped it in half with a machete, telling the campaign rallies that it reminded him of the Christian Democrats because, like the PDC, it was also red on the inside. Duarte, the PDC's chief stump speaker, although not a candidate himself (he was on the sidelines, expecting to be offered the provisional presidency by a PDC-dominated assembly), replied in kind, letting it be known that he regarded D'Aubuisson as a fascist.

The Salvadoran Popular party (PPS), mainly supported by shopkeepers, and the Democratic Action party (AD), backed by middle class professionals, were both regarded as middle-to-far-right. The National Conciliation party (PCN), the old-line military-backed organization that had ruled the country until the 1979 coup, and the tiny Popular Orientation party, led by ORDEN founder General Medrano ("For the moment we will have to wear a democrat's skin, like in Little Red Riding Hood," he candidly observed) were the far-right parties. Finally, Major Bob's ARENA was the party of the extreme right. Observers could be forgiven for failing on some days to distinguish the nuances between the "middle," "middle-to-far," "far," and "extreme" of the right; in any case, only one side of the story was being told, albeit in numerous versions.

By mid-March, with less than two weeks until the balloting, Deane Hinton began to contemplate the Frankensteinian possibility of a D'Aubuisson triumph. Although he would cooperate with whoever won, Hinton added, "Of course an extreme government, an extremist government from the left or the right, could complicate the problem of public support in the U.S." There were other problems as well. Senator Nancy Kassebaum of Kansas was heading the U.S. team of election observers, but other countries were balking at officially witnessing the spectacle that had become the centerpiece of American policy. Both Mexico and Canada had rejected the invitation to send observers; from Europe, only Britain was coming; principal South American countries such as Brazil and Venezuela had declined; Japan said it would be difficult to participate since most Western nations had said no. Then there were the bodies to be stepped over on the way to the ballot box. During the three-month campaign 1,500 people had been executed. On top of that, there were widespread reports that the FMLN intended to disrupt the elections (although guerrilla threats received considerable attention in the U.S. media, they only came from particular sectors of the rebel forces).

As with justice, the main thing about this demonstration was that it be seen to be done. On Sunday morning, March 28, 1982, with a 700-member international press corps videotaping everything that moved, thousands of Salvadorans jammed polling places across the country; "the dusty roads...were awash with hundreds of people, walking and walking— sometimes for miles—to cast their ballots." Deane Hinton was on American television, live from San Salvador, hailing the turnout and describing the FMLN as "a couple of thousand terrorist thugs." In Washington, the Reagan administration was jubilant. Democracy was working and Duarte's party was the frontrunner in the early returns. Secretary of State Haig, speaking on NBC's "Meet the Press," called it a display of "awesome courage and civic responsibility...a military defeat for the guerrillas quite as much as a political repudiation." CBS anchorman Dan Rather enthused, "It's a triumph." ABC said it was "inspiring"; NBC called it "one of the most remarkable election days anywhere." *Time* summed it up: "Defying widespread predictions of a dismal turnout, at least 80 percent of the electorate—twice the normal figure—took part...more than 1.5 million men and women braved guerrilla threats—and in some cases dodged bullets—to cast their ballots."

The rosy glow of optimism didn't fade until a few days later. By then, the international press corps had packed its bags and cameras and taken off for fresher war fronts that provided more "bang-bang," as it was called in the trade. But at the U.S. embassy where the staff went on twenty-four-hour shift, ashen-faced officials tried to figure out what to do with an election where the PDC won the most votes, but Major Bob won the race. The Christian Democrats had 35.3 percent of the votes cast, and twenty-four of sixty assembly seats. D'Aubuisson's ARENA picked up 25.7 percent of the ballots and nineteen seats. The old-line National Conciliation party was third, with 16.7 percent and fourteen seats. Democratic Action, with 6.6 percent of the vote, picked up two seats; the shopkeeper-supported Popular Salvadoran party gained 2.6 percent and one seat; General Medrano ran dead last with 0.8 percent and no seats. Significant, but seldom noted, were the 11.4 percent of the ballots that were blank or defaced. Before proceeding to the division of the spoils, it might be well to pause briefly for a recount of the alleged 1.5 million ballots cast.

The Jesuit-administered Central American University didn't get around to producing a tally until June 1982, by which point attention to El Salvador had shifted to more pressing problems on the battlefield and in the National Assembly. The university vote study focussed on the time required for a voter to have his indentification card doublechecked, his hand marked with invisible indelible ink to prevent voting twice, to actually vote, then to have his name and ID number hand-recorded in a ledger, and his ID card stamped. Citing the Central Election Council's own estimates, the researchers concluded that it took a minimum of two minutes for a voter to complete the balloting process. Multiplying the number of balloting stations by the hours they were open, and dividing by two minutes, the researchers argued that it was impossible for 1.5 million votes to have been cast. The actual count, suggested the study, was probably between 700,000 and 800,000 votes, a turnout of about 50 percent, and even then, 10 percent of those ballots were blank. What had happened, concluded the editors of the study, was a fraud in which the vote had been massively inflated, perhaps doubled, in order to "prove the fundamental thesis that the Salvadoran people were against the guerrillas." But perhaps even here an American official seeking reasons for certification would discern "progress." Whereas, in traditional Salvadoran electoral fraud, the official party's count was inflated to give it victory, here "there was a pact between the United States, political parties and the army high command to respect the proportionality of the votes." Thus the number of seats each party received remained unchanged. Although a few Salvadoran officials uttered half-hearted denials, the basic findings of the study were never convincingly refuted.

At the U.S. embassy the day after the election, the kitchen staff prepared paella and fruit custard for the candidates and representatives from the six contending parties. Hinton was hosting a luncheon where he hoped to hammer out a deal. But the five furthest right parties, who had been meeting all morning, already had a deal of their own. Though Hinton and Duarte fought a furious rearguard action for the next several days to keep the PDC from being squeezed out, the most Major Bob would concede was that "we will share the destiny of our country with the PDC," meaning that the Christian Democrats would be awarded a few minor cabinet posts as a consolation prize and that Duarte was through as president.

On April 6, the day Ronald Reagan arrived in Jamaica for a working holiday, ARENA and the National Conciliation party (PCN) formalised an agreement to use their thirty-three-seat majority to control the Constituent Assembly. Two weeks later, on April 22, D'Aubuisson was named president of the new legislative body, and the Christian Democrats were locked out of all key assembly posts.

At the U.S. embassy, American diplomats were still furiously engaged in damage control. While the assembly was lost to D'Aubuisson, the provisional presidency and the cabinet were still up for grabs. Hinton called in the reinforcements. The diplomatic offensive reached a crescendo with the arrival of Haig's roving ambassador General Vernon Walters and Senator Jesse Helms' chief aide, who met with the main political parties, bearing with them a blunt letter from the U.S. secretary of state threatening an aid cutoff unless they gave way on the provisional presidency question.

As usual, the army had the final word. Its candidate was its banker, 56-year-old Alvaro Magana. A lawyer with a University of Chicago economics degree, he headed the country's largest mortgage bank, which specialized in providing loans to military men. Major Bob was furious, accusing junta member General Jaime Gutierrez of "imposing" his choice on the assembly. But this time D'Aubuisson didn't have the votes to stop it. The PCN, the old-line party associated with the army, teamed up with the Christian Democrats to elect Magana on April 29. For its part in the deal, the PDC received one of the three vice-presidential posts created to give them a spot in the ruling apparatus.

Chortled Ambassador Hinton, "Democracy is at work. May free men everywhere, as well as the enemies of the democratic process, take due note." Privately, Hinton heaved a sigh of relief. Using one of those football metaphors Americans were so fond of, he said D'Aubuisson had been stopped "on the one-yard line." Magana played his part with studied correctness. He immediately ruled out negotiations with the guerrillas, and by early May installed a three-party cabinet that gave the Christian Democrats minor roles, kept General Garcia in Defense, dropped General Gutierrez entirely—thus confirming what everyone already knew about relative strengths within the military, and handed the land reform program to ARENA via the Agriculture ministry.

Cosmetics aside, El Salvador was back to grim normality: death-squad killings were up; the military was still in control; and the much-touted democratic elections, if not providing for the "legalization of open fascism" as Democratic Revolutionary Front leader Guillermo Ungo put it, had created a legislature dominated by the far right. If there were any doubts about direction, D'Aubuisson's assembly, in its first substantive legislative act on May 19, put them to rest by annulling the government's power to create more peasant cooperatives out of large farms. He followed that up by suspending the so-called land-to-the-tiller program that allowed *campesinos* to buy the small plots they worked as renters and sharecroppers. Though Senate Foreign Relations Committee chairman Charles Percy threatened that "not one cent of funds shall go to the government of El Salvador" if the land redistribution program was suspended, nonetheless by summer some 5,000 peasants had been evicted, and as a bitter Napoleon Duarte said in early June, "In reality, the concept has been stopped, the practice has been stopped, the process has been stopped."

A week after the Salvadoran election, in early April 1982, Argentina, ruled by the military dictatorship of General Leopoldo Galtieri, seized the British-ruled Falkland Islands in the South Atlantic off the Argentine coast. The international press corps promptly decamped El Salvador for stormier seas, leaving the U.S. to sift through the ashes of its pyrrhic electoral victory, and the various shades of the Salvadoran right to settle their internecine power squabbles in relative privacy.

For the next six months, the focus of U.S. foreign policy shifted from Central America to other venues. No sooner was the Falklands dispute resolved in favor of British firepower, than Israel's rightwing Menacham Begin government invaded Lebanon in early June 1982, purportedly in a bid to drive the Palestine Liberation Organization from close proximity. On top of this, the U.S. was involved in a heated dispute with its European allies over their participation in a joint venture with the Soviet Union to build a gas pipeline from Soviet gasfields to the Western European market.

Secretary of State Al Haig played a central role in each of these crises. While President Reagan could be seen lolling in the Caribbean waters off Jamaica as the British armada steamed toward its island colony to repulse the upstart "Argies," Haig was embarked on an arduous shuttle diplomacy mission (36,000 miles of flights between Buenos Aires and London in a matter of days) to avert the confrontation. Later, in his 1984 memoir, *Caveat*, Haig would somewhat grandiosely call the failed mediation effort "my Waterloo."

Whichever way the conflict was resolved, the U.S. stood to be one of the losers. If, after mediation failed, the U.S. took the side of Britain, which is what Haig advocated, America would find itself at odds with almost all of Latin America (on this issue everyone from fascist Chile to communist Cuba was united in supporting Argentina's historical claim to the islands it called the Malvinas). As well, the U.S. would be castigated as a defender of the last vestige of British colonialism in the Western Hemisphere, thus weakening its Central American strategy. If, on the other hand, the U.S. failed to oppose the Argentine adventure, it would alienate itself from the European government with which it had the closest ties.

To make matters worse, the travel-weary secretary of state was faced with a mutiny behind his own lines. Jeane Kirkpatrick, who had written a Ph.D. thesis on Argentine politics, "vehemently opposed" an approach that condemned Argentina and supported Britain. "Our positions were irreconcilable...because each of us believed that the other's position was contrary to the interests of the U.S.," Haig wrote afterward. Furthermore, the stubborn Kirkpatrick "chose to keep on pushing her own view," and insisted on blabbing, "describing the progress and the meaning of the talks, about which she knew little," Haig said testily.

After it was over, Haig discovered that his task had been even more thankless than it seemed. The "leakers" and backbiters were on the loose again, in Haig's view. From the White House he heard reports that his Falklands mission had been undertaken as a means of upstaging Reagan's Caribbean visit. The fruitless mediation was termed "grandstanding." White House aide James Baker had declared, the secretary was told, "Haig is going to go, and go quickly, and we are going to make it happen."

Nor did matters improve during the Lebanon crisis, a foreign policy tangle involving dozens of figures, parties and countries, and far more intricate than the simplified questions—requiring only a denunciation of "Soviet subversion"—that the Reagan administration appeared to prefer. This time, the villains were Vice-President George Bush, head of Reagan's crisis-management team, and Haig's former deputy, National Security Adviser William Clark who, according to the would-be vicar, "seemed to be conducting a second foreign policy...by-passing the State Department altogether." Added Haig, "Such a system was bound to produce confusion, and it soon did." On that point, there was little dispute: as the Israelis made their savage way toward Beirut, Washington was enmeshed in a web of acrimonious exchanges and crossed signals with the Zionists, Saudis, Syrians, various Lebanese factions, and even diverse segments of itself.

By the time Haig was aboard Air Force One with the president, on route to the June 1982 Versailles summit of Western leaders, the secretary was pondering the possibility of resignation. The White House was already way ahead of him. After a final mid-month kafuffle over who commanded the lines of authority to America's mid-East envoy, Haig told Reagan on June 23 that he had prepared a letter of resignation, but hadn't decided whether to submit it. The next day Reagan decided for him.

After a National Security Council lunch during which the White House aides sat, as one of them later said, "knowing what was about to happen, and knowing that Haig didn't know," Reagan summoned Haig into the Oval Office. "On that matter we discussed yesterday, Al," the great communicator said, "I have reached a conclusion." He then handed his former secretary of state an unsealed envelope containing a single typed page that began, "Dear Al, it is with the most profound regret that I accept your letter of resignation." As the slightly stunned Haig wrote in his memoir, "The president was accepting a letter of resignation that I had not submitted." Even in hindsight, Haig didn't seem certain of what had hit him. "To me," he wrote, "the White House was as mysterious as a ghost ship; you heard the creak of the rigging and the groan of the timbers and sometimes even glimpsed the crew on deck. But which of the crew had the helm?"

Hours before Reagan gave Haig the axe, his National Security Adviser, Bill Clark, was on the phone placing calls to the new man at the helm, offering him Haig's job. He was 61-year-old George Shultz, president of one of the world's largest construction and engineering conglomerates, Bechtel Corporation, and former secretary of the treasury in the Nixon administration. When he was sworn in in the White House Rose Garden the following month, Reagan joked, "Today I am reminded of the old saying, 'Let George do it.' And George, I think I'll have a few things for you to do." In fact, George wouldn't do it; instead, as Bill Clark told Al Haig near the end of his tenure, "You'd better understand that from now on, it's going to be the president's foreign policy."

El Salvador's civil war, now well into its second year, continued irrespective of the media's sporadic attention span. In 1981 it had been learned that, despite periodic announcements of their imminent demise (a practise that would continue), the FMLN guerrillas were capable of fighting the war at least to a stalemate. In 1982, the press corps, with their journalistic curiosity piqued by the persistence of the "faceless" revolutionaries, began to produce what in contemporary American sportswriting was known as an "up close and personal" portrait of the opposition.

When New York *Times* reporter Raymond Bonner went "behind the lines" in Morazan province in January 1982, he believed much of what he had heard: that the guerrillas were well armed by the Communist-bloc countries and that there were Cubans and Nicaraguans fighting with the FMLN.*

From conversations with scores of *campesinos*—grizzled old men, pre-adolescent couriers, women, and guerrilla fighters—Bonner pieced together "a rough profile of the peasant revolutionary in Morazan: born and reared in the province and quite likely never traveled beyond it; only two years of formal education; at least one parent, child or sibling murdered by the government soldiers, frequently after having been hacked with a machete; living family members part of the revolution. It is, in short, a homegrown, predominantly peasant revolution."

This matched what Atlanta *Constitution* correspondent Clifford Krauss found in Chalatenango province in early 1982. "I met few people who had not lost at least one relative at the hands of the army, the National Guard or the paramilitary Orden force," Krauss wrote. As did Bonner, Krauss "saw no Cuban or Nicaraguan advisers, no planeloads of guns and ammunition and no abundance of supplies." Notwithstanding the Reagan administration's repeated claims of a constant flow of arms to the guerrillas, "masking tape and string secured the stocks of their Korean War M-1 carbines," wrote Bonner. "A few had more modern German-

---

*Bonner's account, in addition to the dispatches published in the *Times*, is contained in *Weakness and Deceit: U.S. Policy and El Salvador*. The most important eyewitness report to date on the FMLN is Dr. Charles Clements' *Witness to War*, a record of his experiences in the Guazapa region where he practised in 1982-83. See bibliography for details.

made G-3 automatic rifles, the stenciled numbers on the butts indicating that they had once been issued to government soldiers.'' Krauss reported the same thing: ''Hundreds of militia fighters had nothing more than pistols and machetes with which to fight, against an army equipped with U.S.-leased helicopters and artillery.'' The guerrillas, according to Bonner and Dr. Charles Clements, were particularly touchy about insinuations of outside aid. ''It is an insult to say that Cubans and Nicaraguans are helping us,'' one guerrilla fighter told Bonner. ''We are *campesinos*, but we can do it ourselves.''

Wandering in rebel-controlled Guazapa region just north of San Salvador, in spring 1982, among youngsters in rebel schools, fields of cabbage and yucca belonging to neighborhood cooperatives, assemblies of peasants electing local courts, and primitive clinics, the New York *Times*' Warren Hoge thought he discerned the rudimentary lineaments of a new social order. ''The people who are conducting the fight against the government are at the same time busy installing the kind of society you want,'' local FMLN commander Raul Hercules told Hoge and other American reporters.

At times the machetes seemed more than a match for the choppers, as in the spectacular Ilopango airbase raid in January that wiped out half the Salvadoran air force. Other results were more equivocal. After an early February raid on the town of Nueva Trinidad, about fifty kilometers northeast of the capital, the government claimed the guerrillas had massacred 150 civilians. But when reporters arrived on the scene, the death toll was scaled down to approximately fifty, more than half of whom were government soldiers and civilian paramilitaries, although some non-combatants had also been killed. The February fighting was worrisome enough to bring Lieutenant General Wallace Nutting from the U.S.'s SouthCom in Panama to review the troops and to consider the possibility of sending American advisers to accompany Salvadoran soldiers on combat missions. There were also setbacks for the FMLN, as in the March elections when plans to militarily disrupt the balloting fizzled, and produced a temporary retreat to rethink strategy and iron out differences among the guerrilla components.

Overall, however, the guerrilla strategy of sapping the economy appeared to be succeeding. Only the quarter billion

dollars in U.S. aid that year was keeping El Salvador from
going broke, conceded the president of the Central Bank.
Ambassador Hinton estimated the enormous capital flight
from the country at $750 million. Production of cotton, coffee
and sugar was drastically down; as *Time* magazine sourly
noted, "With its economy virtually prostrate, El Salvador's
main export is its people. Officially, some 600,000 have left
for other parts of Central America, Mexico and the U.S."

By mid-June 1982 the FMLN was on the offensive again,
poking holes in the government's "nine-to-five" army, seizing
Perquin in Morazan province, and capturing Deputy Minister
of Defense Colonel Francisco Castillo after shooting down his
helicopter. Leaving behind 200 dead government soldiers, and
carting away a cache of captured weapons, the guerrillas
backed off only under intense bombing raids by the
government's newly acquired A-37B Dragonfly jets. American
officials wondered why the FMLN was stronger now than
when the civil war began despite some $125 million in U.S.
military assistance.

No sooner had the Salvadoran high command, in
September 1982, issued one of its periodic declarations that
the guerrillas' capacity was confined to "occasional spectacular
attacks," than the FMLN appeared in force. General Garcia
had claimed the insurgents were in a "desperate" situation.
Their death rattle, he said, was audible. Within days, the
rebels launched an October offensive whose scale seemed to
surpass all expectations. Though the army was soon rushing
5,000 troops, fighter-bombers and helicopter gunships into
Chalatenango province, for the next six months the FMLN
would hold the initiative and sustain a rhythm of continuous
attacks.

While the D'Aubuisson-dominated Constituent Assembly
squabbled, and the Salvadoran Army remained pinned down
by the FMLN, in Washington the semi-annual flurry of
"progress"-producing gestures was underway in preparation
for the administration's mid-year certification of "tangible
signs of progress" in El Salvador. Early in July, the State
Department said it was putting "plenty of pressure" on
Salvadoran officials for social and economic changes.
Ranking Latin policy official Tom Enders flew into San
Salvador for a first hand look two days before the
certification.

When the presidential report came on July 27, it hardly amounted to a ringing endorsement. Couched in language that seemed little short of apologetic, the report admitted that "the strife continues to produce serious and frequent violations of basic human rights." Although civilian killings were reported to have declined from about 4,000 in the last six months of 1981 to about 2,500 in the first six months of 1982, many congressmen wondered whether the reduction in civilian carnage marked an improvement in respect for human rights. Senator Christopher Dodd called the seal of approval a "sham." "By any analysis, land reform has virtually stopped," he said.

Even President Reagan, at a post-certification news conference, was less than completely upbeat: "I grant you that things—I'm quite sure that there are unfortunate things that are going on and that are happening." Nonetheless, the great communicator claimed to be able to discern a "great turnaround." Within days, the administration team fanned out among congressional committees to seek additional El Salvador aid. The Senate-House conferees finally got around to hammering out approval for a $14 billion supplemental appropriation bill in late August. Although it contained the $350 million requested for Caribbean Basin aid, the amount earmarked for El Salvador was reduced to $75 million from $128 million, and military aid as well as foreign military sales loan guarantees were also slightly slashed.

One route to resolution of the Salvadoran conflict—negotiated settlement—received only sporadic attention throughout the year. In January 1982, the five commanders of El Salvador's guerrilla movement sent an open letter to President Reagan calling for negotiations "without preconditions," meaning prior to ceasefire. The following month, Mexican President Lopez Portillo, speaking in Managua, made a similar appeal, warning his "good friends in the United States" that American intervention in the region would be a "gigantic historical error." FDR leader Guillermo Ungo echoed the Mexican appeal prior to the March 1982 Salvadoran elections.

To all this, the U.S. was distinctly cool, although Secretary Haig took time out from his spring offensive to meet with Mexican Foreign Minister Jorge Casteneda in New York. State Department officials later said privately that the meetings, more symbolic than substantive, were meant to "massage" the Mexican ego. Nonetheless, the Mexicans persisted, suggesting in March that the U.S. pursue a dialogue with Cuba to ease tensions throughout the region. Lopez Portillo insisted that U.S. security interests were not threatened by Nicaragua, El Salvador or even Cuba, challenging a fundamental tenet of American policy. "I would turn it around," he said. "The risk is for Nicaragua, El Salvador and Cuba."

The U.S. interest in talks oscillated. Toward the end of March, the Americans appeared willing to try talking, even going so far as to send the ubiquitous General Walters to a secret meeting in Havana with Cuba's Castro. Soon, however, their interest waned. As one puzzled observer suggested, the U.S. seemed to be engaged in "supply-side" foreign policy— guns, elections, aid programs, talks—trying out everything to see what would stick. Pressed by Thomas Enders for a gesture, Salvadoran provisional President Magana established a "peace commission" in September 1982 to take up the possibility of talks with guerrillas. The prospects were hardly encouraging. When the FMLN again issued a call for negotiations in the midst of its successful October offensive, Constituent Assembly President D'Aubuisson made it clear that the possibility was not only "absurd," but it was an act of "vile traitorship" to even consider it.

Notwithstanding that *Newsweek* magazine's cover story expose of the U.S.-sponsored covert war in Nicaragua ran the week of the mid-term American congressional and gubernatorial elections in early November 1982, Central America was hardly an issue in the campaign. Nor were any other foreign policy questions, although U.S. Marines had landed in Lebanon six weeks before the vote on a peacekeeping mission as the Israeli invasion of that country promised to turn into a quagmire.

In the midst of the continuing recession, the issue was Reagonomics, the president's conservative economic program. Recalling the old show business saw, "But will it play in Peoria?", the president stumped the economically troubled American midwest, including the Illinois town where 16 percent of the population was out of work as a result of layoffs by the Caterpillar tractor company. Echoing

Gloucester in Shakespeare's *King Lear*, who cried, "I am tied to the stake and I must stand the course," Reagan pleaded with voters to "stay the course" and give his policies more time to work.

When the ballots were tallied, although the electorate didn't order Reagan to reverse course, they clearly told him to at least trim the sails. While the Republicans maintained their fifty-four to forty-six majority in the Senate, the Democrats picked up twenty-six seats in the House of Representatives, increasing their majority to 267 to 166, and they gained seven state governorships to give them a thirty-four to sixteen margin in the fifty states. Although the incumbent president denied that voters wanted a mid-course correction, as the vote was analyzed it became clearer that Reagan, for all his amiability and folksiness, was not invulnerable. The Republicans, in fact, had suffered a more serious setback than at first thought.

Not since 1922 had the party in the White House lost as many seats as Reagan in a first mid-term election. Overall, the popular vote for House members was split 57 percent to 40 percent in favor of the Democrats. At the state level, Republicans had been badly routed. Even in the Senate, where the Republicans maintained their hold and thus were able to deny voter rejection, the significance of the count was less in the outcomes than in the margins. The Democrats had come within a whisker of a landslide—a shift of a few thousand votes in a half-dozen states would have deprived Reagan of his Senate majority. White House strategists, however, hoped that economic recovery would swing the pendulum back in the president's direction in time for the 1984 election.

Speculation on changes of course abruptly shifted to the USSR with the death of Soviet leader Leonid Brezhnev in mid-November and his replacement by KGB head Yuri Andropov.

While Salvadoran provisional President Magana continued to make the ritual cosmetic gestures required of him (among them, the creation of "peace" and "human rights" commissions, and the announcement of 1984 presidential elections), the Constituent Assembly remained locked in a stalemate that paralyzed the ability of either D'Aubuisson's far-right or the Christian Democratic-military center-right to carry out its program. Though a so-called Pact of Apaneca in

August 1982 attempted to paper over differences, the ARENA-PDC dispute remained unsettled; if anything, the situation became more rigid the following month when the far right lost control of the assembly because the National Reconciliation party (PCN) was unable to reconcile its own differences. Five members of the old-line party moved toward an informal coalition with the Christian Democrats, while its nine other representatives formed a new grouping allied with ARENA, thus leaving the assembly deadlocked 31 to 29, with the tilt favoring the center-right.

In the face of the FMLN October offensive, and the accompanying proposal for dialogue, all the fierce divisions within the regime resurfaced. The government crisis had its counterpart in the armed forces, with mounting conflict between officers pragmatically supporting the American policy thrust, and traditionalists who opposed it. Upon that division was superimposed a second split between officers willing to accept U.S. military leadership and its modernizing counterinsurgency tactics, and those who insisted on conducting the war themselves. At times, a combination of crosscutting categories led to further confusion, as when officers favored new military techniques but were adamantly opposed to political reforms, or vice-versa.

One such indicator of tension in autumn 1982 was the conflict between D'Aubuisson and Defense Minister Garcia over the latest turn in the case of the American land advisers murdered a year and a half before. In September 1982, Garcia announced that two National Guard officers, Lieutenant Isidro Lopez and Captain Eduardo Avila, had been charged as the men responsible for ordering two corporals to kill the Americans and land reform director Jose Viera.

According to the confessions of the corporals, on the night of the murder Lieutenant Lopez, a former security aide to D'Aubuisson, went with his bodyguard to the home of businessman Hans Christ, one of the two "killer oligarchs" originally charged with the murder. There, they got in touch with Captain Avila. Eventually, the men went to the Sheraton Hotel, where they spotted the Americans and Viera. While there, they met Sheraton part-owner Ricardo Sol Meza and a National Guard major. At 11 o'clock, Lopez, Avila and Christ went into the hotel parking lot where Lopez ordered his bodyguard to assassinate the land reform officials. "You are going to kill them," Lopez told his corporal. When the man responded, "By myself, lieutenant?", Lopez went to a nearby parked Toyota RV and ordered the bodyguard of the major who'd been with Sol Meza to join his own corporal in performing the killing. Businessman Christ then led the corporals into the hotel and pointed out the intended victims.

D'Aubuisson was furious at Garcia for having decided to sacrifice the officers—the first such instance of senior officials being charged—at the behest of American controllers of the aid purse strings. On national television before the Lopez case reached court (Avila had fled to Guatemala), Major Bob testified that the two officers "are my colleagues and my friends, just like all those who through twenty years of military service I knew and lived with." The judge in the case got the message. On October 1 he abruptly decided that there was "insufficient evidence" to hold Lopez. When Garcia tried again, only to have a second judge confirm the release of Lopez, it was the Americans' turn to be outraged. In early November, Ambassador Hinton delivered a blistering speech to Salvadoran businessmen denouncing the rightist "mafia," calling the legal system "rotten," and threatening an aid cutoff.

Major Bob was not the sort to forgive and forget. By early November, Christian Democratic leader Duarte claimed that D'Aubuisson was seeking "a legal coup d'etat." The ARENA leader, claimed Duarte, "sees Garcia as his problem and wants to get rid of him." Asked what D'Aubuisson was doing to unseat the defense minister, one diplomat explained, "Talking to officers." Garcia, for his part, wasn't idle. He responded with a shakeup of top commanders, including D'Aubuisson patron Colonel Nicolas Carranza.

Army infighting broke into the open in January 1983 when Lieutenant Colonel Sigifredo Ochoa, military commander of the northern province of Cabanas, refused an order from Garcia transferring him to the post of military attache in Uruguay and declared himself to be "in rebellion." Describing the defense minister as "a little Hitler," Ochoa demanded Garcia's resignation. "I will not resign," Garcia said on Salvadoran television. "I have the support of the president and the armed forces." But Ochoa, holed up with 2,000 loyal troops in Cabanas, was not isolated either. In the loyalties established by military school graduating classes, the

40-year-old northern warlord could claim the support of D'Aubuisson and the commanders of the air force and the army's First Infantry brigade. Furthermore, Ochoa was a favorite of the American military advisers because of his willingness to employ U.S.-favored tactics as compared to Garcia's reliance on old-fashioned large troop-movement strategies.

The embarrassing row about the government's ability to control its own top officers came less than two weeks before President Reagan was due to certify Salvadoran progress; pressure for a deal was intense. It was quickly made. Ochoa ended the rebellion at the behest of provisional President Magana; his posting to Uruguay would be "rectified" (a cushy job at the Inter-American Defense College in Washington would be found). Garcia remained in office, but with his authority in tatters and with a tacit agreement to wind up his thirty-year military career after the suitable decent interval.

Thomas Enders was once more assigned to carry the waterbucket of certification to various congressional committees. The president's seal of approval, issued on January 21, 1983, was distinctly down in the mouth, conceding, "The situation is not perfect and the progress was not as great as desired. But it is progress nonetheless." While admitting that the release of the Salvadoran officers involved in the land advisers' murders was an example of the "systematic ineffectiveness of El Salvador's criminal justice procedures," Enders claimed that there had been significant progress in efforts to prosecute the accused murderers of the four American churchwomen. However, Ohio Democratic Representative Mary Oakar, acting on behalf of the slain women's families, called the certification an "outrage."

Though the certification report claimed political violence was down, a joint statement by the American Civil Liberties Union and Americas Watch replied, "The number of reported and verified political murders demonstrated that the human rights situation is worse than ever." U.S. doctors and nurses who had returned from a group visit to El Salvador that week added that they had seen "unmistakable physical evidence of torture, starvation and malnutrition." Even the administration's claim that land reform had been "vigorously relaunched," was refuted by government and labor officials in

San Salvador. The land reform institute, confessed President Magana, "is in the hands of people who do not like reforms." Criticisms aside, from the administration's point of view, the important thing was that the certification ritual had been performed.

While human rights progress was debatable, reverses on the battlefield were less open to dispute. Ten days after certification, the FMLN captured Berlin, the second largest town in the eastern cotton-producing province of Usulutan. "The war is not at its most brilliant moment," understated Christian Democratic assembly leader Julio Rey Prendes. In Washington, Assistant Secretary of State Enders conceded, in the wake of the guerrilla seizure of Berlin, that American policy was "confused." Two days later the rebels withdrew, but not before much of the town was leveled by what acting Archbishop Rivera Damas called "indiscriminate bombing" by the Salvadoran air force.

In the wake of the latest military fiasco, American officials stepped up the pressure to ease Defense Minister Garcia out of his post. Despite his value as a supporter of political reform, the laggard performance of the military under his direction outweighed his usefulness. By mid-April air force commander Colonel Juan Bustillo was sounding like a labor leader. "We are not going to have a strike because we are not a union, but we could take a position in which we don't recognize the minister of defense." Forty-eight hours later, Garcia took the heavy-handed hint. "I always thought that one day I would give a press conference in which you would have one question and I one answer," said Garcia, announcing his resignation. "Your question has an answer: yes." National Guard commander General Eugenio Vides Casanova was quickly nominated to fill the vacant position.

With General Haig no longer available to lead the charge, the command of the Reagan administration's third annual spring offensive against Central America fell to National Security Adviser William Clark. Clark, who had displayed such amiable ignorance on becoming Al Haig's second in command two years before, proved to be a rapid learner. Having learned, for one thing, that Central America was a formidable opponent, the White House decided to lob its early spring rhetorical shells in the direction of the State

Department, Congress and American public opinion.

Recognizing his own deficiencies as a conceptual thinker, The Judge, as he was called in memory of his California Supreme Court service, formed an unlikely alliance with the administration's intellectual guru on Latin affairs, U.N. Ambassador Jeane Kirkpatrick. She was dispatched to Central America on a fact-finding tour at the beginning of February 1983. For public consumption, Kirkpatrick announced that the Salvadoran rebels were close to being beaten. "The guerrillas are not winning anything," she said, ignoring for the moment the FMLN's recent seizure of the town of Berlin. Inside the White House, Kirkpatrick told a different story: the military situation was deteriorating, the Salvadorans needed more arms, and leaders throughout Latin America were fearful that a guerrilla takeover in El Salvador would lead to stepped-up insurgent activity across the entire region.

President Reagan was caught by surprise at the depth of Kirkpatrick's gloom. As one administration official later said, "Kirkpatrick came back with a different story than what people had been saying to the president." Stepping to the rostrum at the American Legion's annual conference, shortly after his U.N. ambassador reported in, Reagan warned, "The specter of Marxist-Leninist controlled governments in Central America with ideological and political loyalties to Cuba and the Soviet Union poses a direct challenge to which we must respond." When congressional leaders were shepherded into the White House to hear the inside scoop on Central America, the first official called on by Reagan was Kirkpatrick, a clear indicator that she and Bill Clark were in the process of eclipsing Thomas Enders' and the State Department's pre-eminence in Latin affairs.

Though Secretary of State Shultz would henceforth not be a significant player in Central American decision making, for the purpose of delivering the now annual hint of a "crisis," the White House decided to let George do it. Appearing before a congressional committee in mid-February, less than a week after Kirkpatrick's return, Shultz said that the Salvadoran insurgents were "creating hell" with Soviet-supplied weapons. When congressmen continued to nag him about negotiations, the normally placid Shultz became irritated. The rebels had tried to use force to block the Salvadoran elections last March, he noted. "And to now say, let them shoot their way into that government. No dice!"

A few days later, Defense Secretary Caspar Weinberger mentioned to a congressional committee that more military aid was needed. Though the administration had initially requested $63 million for guns for El Salvador in fiscal 1983, to date Congress had only authorized $26 million under an interim funding measure. "One way or another," said Weinberger, the U.S. was "going to get into El Salvador $60 million, I think, as soon as possible." The problem was how. It turned out there was a squabble between "Cap" Weinberger, representing the Pentagon, and the State Department. The Pentagon wanted an immediate increase in aid, but the State Department believed that bringing the issue up now would be a "tactical blunder" and sought to delay the request until later in the year. Cap decided not to let George do it. Weinberger initially proposed that the additional funds come from a special discretionary fund set up in 1961 for use by the president "to provide emergency military assistance to foreign countries," but it was agreed that bypassing Congress would provoke undue anger on Capitol Hill, where lawmakers remembered that the fund had been extensively used during the Vietnam War. Instead, the next day, a presidential aide said Reagan was considering "reprogramming" some foreign security assistance earmarked for other countries. The move would require scrutiny only by the House and Senate appropriations committees, rather than the full Congress. In addition, there would be consultations with the lawmakers.

On February 28 a bipartisan group of congressmen duly appeared on White House premises. Reagan told them that the survival of the Salvadoran government was at stake. That evening, to underscore the seriousness of the situation, as Air Force One winged the president to the west coast for a speech, one of his aides told reporters that Reagan was weighing the possibility of increasing the number of military advisers in El Salvador.

The next day, it officially became a crisis. "There is a crisis," Deputy Defense Secretary Nestor Sanchez, another rising star in the Bill Clark-dominated group of Latin policy makers, told Congress. However, it wasn't like Vietnam, he assured nervous representatives. "We understand the concern of those who remember the specter of Vietnam that the war in El Salvador is being Americanized," Sanchez said soothingly.

"But Vietnam was 10,000 miles away. El Salvador is a contiguous region right at our door step. San Salvador is closer to Washington D.C. than is San Francisco." Having provided the geography lesson, Sanchez returned to the crisis. "There has been a high level of fighting over the last two or three months. The real crisis is that we have run out of money in order to supply the Salvadoran military. Depending on the amount of ammunition expended, they could be down to less than thirty days."

If Salvadoran soldiers were on the verge of running out of bullets, then there was indeed a crisis. The media rushed off to check. Deputy Defense Minister Colonel Rafael Flores Lima doubted it was a crisis. "I can't say that it is critical in the strict sense of the word. It is difficult, but we are facing that now." But what about running out of ammunition? The colonel laughed. "I couldn't say that at all. We have enough and much more." The press rushed back home. The story changed. A State Department official said the Sanchez prediction was based on a "hypothetical characterization" involving heavier combat than was now underway. The kind of combat he was talking about, the official said, would develop if, for example, "Nicaragua decided to invade El Salvador with a 40,000-man army." Even though there was presumably a considerable difference between fighting a rag-tag guerrilla operation and a 40,000-man invasion, few people blinked at the sleight-of-lip.

President Reagan, who was in California hosting Queen Elizabeth of England, told the Commonwealth Club in San Francisco that the U.S. "may want to go beyond" the present limit of fifty-five military advisers in El Salvador. The president was worried about dominoes. If the leftist guerrillas "get a foothold," said Reagan, "with Nicaragua already there, and El Salvador should fall as a result of this armed violence, I think Costa Rica, Honduras, Panama, all of these would follow."

The media was puzzled. Why a crisis now, it belatedly asked, not being fully attuned to the rhythm of the annual spring offensive. American television news was especially confused by these subtle maneuvers. Since Salvadoran news had been in remission ever since the March 1982 elections, it took them a while to catch up with the crisis. When Secretary of State Shultz announced in mid-February that war was hell

in El Salvador, the former Bechtel executive failed to appear
on the evening news. Two days later, however, ABC showed
some footage of the battle for Suchitoto, fifty kilometers from
San Salvador, full of gunfire and other scenes of "bang-bang"
favored by the visual media. Although ABC declared
Suchitoto "strategically important" and said that the outcome
of the battle was in doubt, it immediately lapsed into amnesia.
Suchitoto was not mentioned on subsequent broadcasts.
Defense Secretary Weinberger's request for $60 million in
Salvadoran pocket money also went unreported until a few
days later when NBC "confirmed" that the president wanted
the aid increase. Not even Nestor Sanchez' use of the word
"crisis" and his dramatic announcement that the Salvadoran
army was down to its last few rounds of ammo made it into
American living rooms. Only when Reagan pressed the alarm
button, suggesting that other Central American countries
would fall if El Salvador went down, did the networks tune in.
That night, the sound of collapsing dominoes was heard
throughout television land. "Is El Salvador turning into
another Vietnam?" asked earnest correspondents. As for the
question of "why a crisis now?", a congressional source had a
simple answer: "A crisis exists because enough people perceive
a crisis exists. It could have been perceived a month ago...it's
just right now, when the administration wants more aid, that
we have this crisis." Like beauty then, crises were apparently
in the eye of the beholder.

Meanwhile, the cowboys at the White House had some
cutting off at the pass to do. The hombre in the white hat and
cassock was globe-trotting Pope John Paul II, who arrived in
Costa Rica at the beginning of March for a week-long Central
American journey to "share the pain" of the region. The
problem for the Reagan administration was how to undercut
the Pope's inevitable calls for reconciliation, which many,
unversed in Biblical interpretation, would hear as a
recommendation for negotiations with the guerrillas. Bill
Clark's braintrust decided on the Central American cure-all:
elections. Recently named special ambassador for "public
diplomacy" in Latin America, Richard Stone, a former
Democratic Senator from Florida, was put aboard a San
Salvador-bound flight and told to get President Magana to
announce, upon the Pope's arrival, that El Salvador's
forthcoming presidential elections were being moved up to

December 1983. The only hitch came on the return flight of
the secret mission when Stone blabbed to the press, which
immediately upset the State Department because the election
announcement would no longer look like it had been Magana's
own idea. Nonetheless, when the Pope touched down at San
Salvador, Magana dutifully made the election announcement;
the Pope made his expected reconciliation plea; and
Ambassador Hinton, momentarily turned ecclesiastical scholar, declared that various groups should not interpret the
Pope's plea as support for their own position. "The Pope did
not say what kind of dialogue he was talking about,"
pontificated the ambassador.

On March 10, addressing the National Association of
Manufacturers, Reagan made another domino speech, and in
passing told Congress how much money he wanted. "If
guerrilla violence succeeds," said the president, "El Salvador
will join Cuba and Nicaragua as a base for spreading fresh
violence to Guatemala, Honduras, even Costa Rica. The
killing will increase and so will the threat to Panama, the canal
and ultimately Mexico." In the president's apocalyptic vision,
the subversives would soon be peering into Texas. Reagan
knew there were doubters: "I know a good many people
wonder why we should care whether communist governments
come into power. One columnist argued last week that we
shouldn't care because their products are not vital to our
economy. That's like the argument of another so-called expert
that we shouldn't worry about Castroite control over the
island of Grenada—their only important product is nutmeg.
People who make these arguments haven't taken a good look
at a map lately," said Reagan. "It is not nutmeg that is at
stake in the Caribbean and Central America. It is U.S.
national security." In the name of national security, Reagan
proposed an emergency $298 million package for the region,
including not $60 million in Salvadoran military aid, as
originally suggested, but $110 million.

For the next month, the administration and Congress
slugged it out over the aid question. From the beginning,
House Speaker Tip O'Neill was skeptical. "There's just a
strong feeling around here that it's another Vietnam
situation." The feeling became stronger when the Salvadorans, prodded by the administration to show they deserved the
money, announced a two-track campaign to defeat the rebels:

in addition to large-scale military sweeps through regions where the FMLN was active, there would also be a program to separate civilians from the guerrillas, similar to the "rural pacification" program used in Vietnam. Congress, however, wasn't buying. When Republican Senators Nancy Kassebaum and Mark Hatfield expressed doubts in mid-March, the White House began to consider scaling back.

For a moment, it looked like the spring offensive would succeed. Near the end of March, the Senate Appropriations Committee agreed to the $60 million "reprogramming" request, requiring only that the administration agree in writing to take several initiatives to strengthen democratic procedures in El Salvador. The next day, however, the Senate Foreign Relations Committee balked; even though it had never previously claimed jurisdiction over reprogramming requests, it suggested that the $60 million be chopped in half.

The real problem came the following month, in mid-April, when the House Foreign Affairs Sub-committee rejected the president's supplemental request for $50 million in Salvadoran military aid. The committee also hacked at money for the covert war in Nicaragua and slashed requests for the forthcoming 1984 fiscal year. As well, the $60 million reprogramming bid was in trouble in the House Appropriations Committee. The unlikely guerrilla leader of the congressional rebels was 74-year-old Representative Clarence "Doc" Long of Maryland, a heretofore mild mannered, twenty-two-year veteran of the House. "We made a mistake by becoming involved," said Long, "but we are involved and it would be a mistake to pull out." Nonetheless, Long wasn't planning to sign over any more money until the White House met his conditions, among them: appointment of a special envoy to El Salvador, review of the still unsolved murders of the American churchwomen, the opening of Salvadoran prisons to Red Cross visits, and the release of Salvadoran prisoners. "First things first," said the crusty Long. "I need something in writing...I want a real down payment to be sure that everybody is acting in good faith, and then we can get on with talking about aid." Just to show he meant business, Long's committee chopped the reprogramming request from $60 million to $30 million, pending White House capitulation.

Up at Bill Clark's office, the strategists of the retreat which inevitably followed the spring offensive, decided to call on their big gun. The president himself would make a foreign policy address to the joint houses of Congress, an event that had occurred only seven previous times in American history. In fact, the last Latin American foreign policy speech to Congress had been made in 1927 by President Reagan's favorite predecessor, "Silent" Cal Coolidge. Meanwhile, as a diversionary sop to Representative Long, the day before the speech it was leaked that a special envoy to El Salvador with ambassadorial rank would be appointed. When the White House was asked why a special envoy was needed when the U.S. already had Ambassador Hinton, a spokesman mumbled, "This appointment will help signify the seriousness of our intentions to seek a political solution to the problems there." Whether Hinton took the news as a hint to buy luggage, it was clearly a sign of things to come.

The president's speech, April 27, 1983, was set for prime-time television. "The national security of all the Americas is at stake in Central America," Reagan declared. "If we cannot defend ourselves there, we cannot expect to prevail elsewhere. Our credibility would collapse, our alliances would crumble, and the safety of our homeland would be put at jeopardy." For those who didn't understand how close the danger was, the president indulged in the administration's new-found enthusiasm for geography. "El Salvador is nearer to Texas than Texas is to Massachusetts. Nicaragua is just as close to Miami, San Antonio, San Diego and Tuscon as those cities are to Washington, where we are gathered tonight." When viewers finished folding up their roadmaps, the president pointed out that the $600 million he wanted for Central America in fiscal 1984 was a drop in the bucket. It was "less than one-tenth of what Americans will spend this year on coin-operated video games," Reagan said, referring to the latest electronic craze sweeping the nation. He called on legislators to set aside "passivity, resignation, defeatism" and come up with some bipartisan unity in facing "this challenge to freedom and security in our hemisphere."

Not everyone was ready to jump on the bipartisan bandwagon. Senator Christopher Dodd, replying to the president's speech on behalf of the Democrats, called the pitch for more money a "formula for failure." Said Dodd, "The American people know that we have been down this road before—and that it only leads to a dark tunnel of endless intervention...It will mean great bloodshed. And, inevitably, the day will come when it will mean a regional conflict in Central America. When that day comes—when the 'dogs of war' are loose in Central America, when the cheering has stopped—we will know where the president's appeal for more American money and a deeper American commitment has taken us.''

Nor were congressional liberals particularly enthused about Reagan's appointment the next day of former Senator Richard Stone as his special envoy. Appropriations Committee chairman Long was known to favor Francis McNeil, currently ambassador to Costa Rica, as being more likely to be able to bridge the gap between the Salvadoran government and the guerrillas than a person too closely identified with administration policy. The Costa Rican ambassador was about to be replaced by Curtin Winsor, a longtime Reagan supporter who had headed the Alliance for Free Enterprise, a pro-business lobby, and was currently a coal company operator. Though McNeil was available for the job, the White House was choosing the conservative Stone. Congressional opponents of Stone were particularly irked by the fact that the former senator had been a registered agent from March 1981 to March 1982 for the murderous Guatemalan government.

Despite the president's speech and the halfhearted concession to Representative Long, the monetary request languished in Congress through most of May. Even the Republican-dominated Senate would at most, of the $110 million requested, offer half the $60 million reprogramming proposal, and $20 million of the additional $50 million sought. This brought total military aid to El Salvador to $75 million, about the level granted the previous year. The House was even more stingy, insisting that any aid be tied to a condition that the Salvadoran government open talks with the guerrillas.

If the spring offensive against Congress had failed, the attack on the State Department was a raging success. Despite Thomas Enders' reputation as a hardliner, William Clark's rap against him was that he was too soft on negotiations with the guerrillas and too hard on the Salvadoran government's human rights abuses. Enders had run afoul of Clark as far back as the previous October when he approved of Ambassador Hinton's toughly worded speech that said the "rightist mafia" was destroying El Salvador "every bit as much as the guerrillas." When Enders made an unannounced trip to Spain in February to see Spanish Prime Minister Felipe Gonzalez, who had sought a role in easing tensions in Central America, Clark decided the State Department's chief Latin policy man had to go. Kirkpatrick agreed, and so did CIA director William Casey. George Shultz was called in. In return for carrying out his part of the deal, the secretary would be given day-to-day control of Central American policymaking.

On May 27, Enders was fired. Hinton was dumped the next day. Bill Clark's choice of a replacement for Enders was Ambassador to Brazil Langhorne A. Motley, whose unwieldy moniker was reduced to Tony among friends. The 45-year-old Brazilian-born American, the son of an oil executive, was a former air force officer, a veteran of Republican politics in Alaska, a lobbyist against environmental groups trying to put restrictions on the Alaska oil pipeline, and the head of the largest real estate company in America's northernmost state. Shultz docilely agreed with Clark that Tony was the man for the Central American job. Shultz was also prepared to accept Clark's recommendation of retired Admiral Gerald Thomas to replace Hinton, but when senior Foreign Service officers balked, it was agreed that career diplomat Thomas Pickering, currently ambassador to Nigeria, would get the El Salvador posting.

If the musical chairs routine in the State Department was as farcical as the power struggle in the Salvadoran military that saw General Garcia ousted, that same spring a gruesome rift was revealed in the ranks of the FMLN. In early April 1983, one of the leaders of Salvador Carpio's Popular Liberation Forces (FPL), Melida Amaya Montes, known as Commander Ana Maria, was brutally murdered in Managua. A week later, 63-year-old Carpio, allegedly despondent upon discovering that Amaya Montes' assassination had been carried out by a member of his own group, committed suicide. Initially the Nicaraguan government and the guerrillas alleged CIA involvement in the Amaya Montes murder. The Nicaraguans had launched an investigation and soon concluded that FPL central-committee member Rogelio Bazzaglio had organized and executed the slaying. Carpio, who had flown to Nicaragua in the midst of an African trip upon hearing the news, was permitted along with other guerrillas to talk to Bazzaglio in prison and to verify that he had not confessed under duress. According to a rebel source, Bazzaglio not only repeated his confession, but insisted that he had "acted for the good of the revolution."

The story had come out a month later in early May when FDR-FMLN spokesman Salvador Samayoa met the press and said, "We decided to tell the truth" about both killings. "It would have been easier," he said, "for us and for Nicaragua to keep blaming the CIA, but if we covered up rumors we would have caused insecurity and distrust among our people at an important stage in the war." The Nicaraguan government, admitted Samayoa, had also pressed the guerrillas "to tell it straight." A minority faction within the FPL, led by Bazzaglio, had been intransigently opposed to the possibility of a negotiated settlement with the Salvadoran government (even as unlikely as such negotiations were), and further, was also strongly against further integration of the five guerrilla groups who made up the FMLN. It was this doctrinal dispute that had led to the act of fratricide. Those close to Carpio agreed that he had been suffering from asthma and exhaustion, and had been deeply affected by the recent death in the field of a close friend. The murder of Commander Ana Maria had been the final blow. Referring to him by his nom de guerre, Marcial, a friend told American reporters, "We had painted a Marcial of steel, but behind this facade there was a sensitive and ailing man." It was a grim episode that only proved, if proof were needed, that the guerrillas were as human as anyone else, and on occasion, as inhumane.

Although the Reagan administration had spent about a billion dollars to educate Salvadorans in the ways of democracy, they were having a harder time educating the folks at home about whose side the U.S. was on. Notwithstanding the president's April speech to Congress, a July 1983 poll trying to find out if Americans supported Reagan's Central American policies, was startled to discover that Americans didn't know what they were. Only 25 percent of those surveyed knew that the administration supported the government in El Salvador, only 13 percent knew it sided with the counter-revolutionaries in Nicaragua, and a mere 8 percent knew of both alignments. Whether they were knowledgeable or know-nothings, two-thirds of all respondents knew they didn't want American troops sent to El Salvador. As it turned out, the administration could well conclude that, despite the ignorance, perhaps they ought to leave well enough alone. According to the New York *Times*/CBS survey, the more people knew, the more likely they were to be opposed to Reagan's policies.

That month, the president decided to try once again. Speaking to a longshoremen's convention in Florida, Reagan said, "Some people throw up their hands and say there's not much we can do down there. I say baloney, and I think we'd all say something stronger down on the docks." What Reagan was going to do, he told the dockers, was to appoint former Secretary of State Henry Kissinger to head a "bipartisan" presidential commission to "lay the foundation for a long-term unified national aproach" to Central American problems. Since the president wasn't finding much bipartisan support in Congress, perhaps he could invent some. Henry Kissinger had been around American politics so long, he almost seemed to be bipartisan, notwithstanding his fervent anti-communism, his role in the Vietnam War, and his successful efforts to overthrow the democratically elected government of Chile.

At Foggy Bottom in Washington, the State Department's loss of clout on Central American policy was evident in the Kissinger appointment. "Well, so much for Shultz being in charge," said one of George's staffers. Said another, "We find out about our policy options in the morning paper." Complained a third, "We are suddenly out of the information loop on a lot of stuff."

6   Born-Again Brutality

> *We have no scorched earth policy. We have a policy of scorched Communists.*
> —General Efrain Rios Montt,
> December 1982

When the call for General Jose Efrain Rios Montt went out over Guatemalan radio on Tuesday morning, March 23, 1982, urging him to join rebel soldiers in the process of carrying out a coup at the National Palace, the semi-retired brigadier general and former Christian Democratic presidential candidate was to be found in a most unmilitary setting.

Rios Montt was presiding over a parent-teacher conference at a school run by the Christian Church of the Word, a California-based, born-again sect with a branch in Guatemala City. Since his political career went into eclipse after Guatemala's fraudulent 1974 election, the general had received a call of a different kind from those emanating from the barracks. The former Roman Catholic was drawn to the "charismatic" movement, whose followers believed that God gave them the power to heal, prophesy and speak in tongues.

After getting word of the radio appeal for him to join the leaders of the coup, he consulted the church's elders. Rios Montt clasped hands with them and prayed. The phone rang. As the others listened on an extension, the general spoke to the young officers leading the coup against the government of General Fernando Romeo Lucas Garcia.

Guatemala

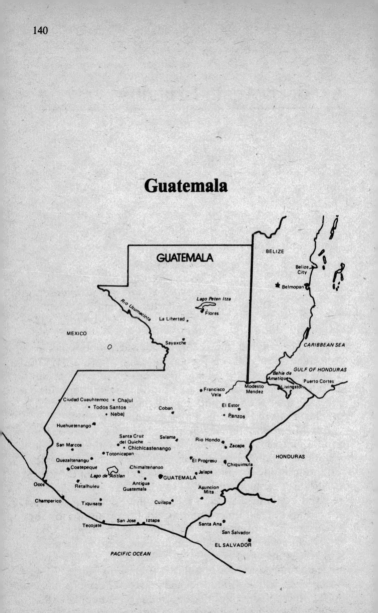

"What do you want of me?" he asked.

"We want to know if we can count on your cooperation and counsel," they said. "We want to talk to you." The military men explained that they had staged the coup to clean up political corruption and wanted to hold elections that would turn the country over to a civilian leadership.

"I'll call you back in ten minutes," Rios Montt told them. Then he conferred with church leaders again. As the born-again general sat with eyes closed and palms uplifted in prayer, the elders laid their hands on his head and shoulders and asked for God's blessing.

Said Carlos, a governing elder of the church, "We feel a great door has opened. We don't understand what is going to happen, but he will be operating with a power that is not like men's corrupt power. He is going to have an anointing from God."

Despite the Reagan administration's desire for electoral uniformity, the four elections held in Central America between November 1981 and March 1982 each had a different outcome. In Costa Rica, social democratic opposition leader Luis Monge, as widely predicted, succeeded the incumbent governing party in a routinely democratic transfer of power. In Honduras, a civilian figurehead president was elected to replace a general but, as everyone knew, power remained with the military. In Salvador a few days hence, the U.S.-sponsored Constituent Assembly elections would produce a surprise victory for Roberto D'Aubuisson's extreme-rightwing ARENA party. In neighboring Guatemala, where a civil war as savage but less publicized than that of El Salvador had claimed 11,000 victims in 1981, the generals were planning business as usual for their coffee-growing mineral-rich country of 7.2 million inhabitants in the upcoming March 7 presidential election.

The war against the nation's Mayan-descended Indians, who comprised half the population of Guatemala, was being run by the president's brother, General Benedicto Lucas Garcia. He was a graduate of France's St. Cyr military academy during the era of the Algerian War, and had learned a good deal about scorched-earth counterinsurgency techniques. The general, known as Benny, had a penchant for riding in helicopters and, according to reporters who hitched a ride with him in January 1982, for cheering on his gunners as they blasted away with M-60 machine guns at the trails below, hammering 30-calibre bullets into fire-scarred Indian settlements and small plots with broken cornstalks. *"Dales! Dales! Give it to them!"* General Benny shouted over the din of the chopper and the crackle of bullets.

Since taking command in autumn 1981, Benedicto Lucas had transformed the army's tactics, sending the troops on a major drive through Chimaltenango province, just west of the capital. Benny's elite corps, called *Kaibiles* in honor of Kaibil, the Mayan god of war, undertook mountain patrols and, unlike El Salvador's nine-to-five army, often worked at night. Chimaltenango was soon "totally pacified," the general claimed. The bulk of his 22,000-man force, considered the best trained, best equipped and most professional among Central American dictatorships, had now moved on to El Quiche.

The problem, Benny explained to the press, was that the guerrillas involved the entire family in the fight—husband, wife, and even the children all had roles. "Then there are irregular local forces that also aid the guerrillas and warn them of the army's arrival," he continued. "Of course, these people are difficult to distinguish from most of the rest of the local population, but these organizational bases have to be won over or wiped out. Because of that, well, the population suffers," shrugged Benny. He left it to his interviewers' imaginations to picture the ultimate solution to these problems of identification.

Despite General Lucas' pacification strategy, the guerrillas continued to periodically overrun towns. The provinces of Quiche, Hueheutenango and San Marcos in the northwestern portion of the country could "practically be considered liberated zones," according to diplomats. While the military reported the deaths of about fifty soldiers a month during 1981, independent estimates put the army's death toll at closer to 2,500. More important, after years of differences, the revolutionaries, as in El Salvador, had reached a new level of unity. Displaying considerable sophistication, the rebels cut into several commercial radio stations' wavelengths in January 1982 to announce the formation of Guatemalan National Revolutionary Unity (URNG), bringing together the Guerrilla Army of the Poor, the Organization of People in Arms, the Rebel Armed Forces, and a segment of the

Guatemalan Workers party. The first response to the guerrillas' appeal for unity came the following month in Mexico City when two dozen prominent Guatemalan exiles, headed by 80-year-old Luis Cardoza y Aragon, announced the creation of a Committee of Patriotic Unity to mobilize foreign support. Although not directly linked to the guerrillas, the committee endorsed the "popular revolutionary war" as the "only path" left open to Guatemalans, and denounced the forthcoming "electoral farce" in March.

It was a foregone conclusion that the winner of the election, no matter how Guatemala's 2.3 million registered voters cast their ballots, would be General Angel Guevara, President Romeo Lucas Garcia's defense minister, and candidate of the official ruling party and the army. The election also offered three not particularly distinguishable alternatives: Mario Sandoval Alarcon, of the misnamed National Liberation Movement, an extreme-rightwing formation upon which Roberto D'Aubuisson had modelled ARENA in El Salvador; Gustavo Anzueto, candidate of the Authentic Nationalist party, a creation of General Carlos Arana, the man whose counterinsurgency campaign in the 1960s had won him the title of "Butcher of Zacapa" as well as the presidency from 1970 to 1974; and finally Alejandro Maldonado, standard bearer of a Christian Democratic party whose ranks had been decimated by the murder of 130 party figures in the past two years. It was expected that, despite obligatory voting laws, the abstention rate might run even higher than the 60 percent recorded in 1978.

Nonetheless, on election day, Sunday, March 7, there were lengthy and patient voter line-ups in Guatemala City; unlike the Salvadoran electoral demonstration three weeks hence, it was not participant enthusiasm but polling inefficiency which accounted for the display. Unsurprisingly, official candidate Guevara, the latest in a line of beefy generals behind sunglasses, took an early lead in the next day's counting with 35 percent of the million or so votes cast (less than 45 percent of those registered; in addition, about 10 percent of cast ballots were blank). According to the official tally, extreme rightist Sandoval was second with 26 percent, followed by Christian Democrat Maldonado with 20 percent, and Anzueto, reportedly the favorite of the American embassy for his supply-side economic policies, bringing up the rear with 9 percent. Since none of the candidates had a majority, Guevara would be elected by the Congress, which was under the control of the current ruling party coalition.

What wasn't in the script was the protest of the losers. "This is the most scandalous fraud in Guatemala's history," said Lionel Sisniega, vice-presidential candidate and spokesman for the National Liberation Movement, as he stood next to party leader Sandoval (whose throat cancer operation several years before limited his verbal pronouncements on behalf of the "party of organized violence," as his wing of the mafia-like structure of Guatemalan politics was known). In charging "they are manipulating the results" to give victory to the official Popular Democratic Front, Sisniega, oddly enough, wasn't claiming anything on his own party's behalf. According to him, candidate Maldonado, the relative moderate of the lot, held a commanding lead over General Guevara, with his own National Liberation Movement running a tight third. General Guevara would have none of it. "I am going to defend my triumph in the streets, if necessary," he growled.

Cameramen, perhaps warming up for the forthcoming Salvadoran spectacle, provided American television viewers with a rare glimpse of Guatemala the next day. It was a made-for-TV stereotype: staccato bursts of gunfire echoed through the streets, clouds of tear gas hung in the air, and a phalanx of blue-shirted policemen, equipped with gas masks and steel helmets, blocked the avenue in downtown Guatemala City. They trained their rifles on six unarmed men who were advancing like prisoners of war, with arms held high, one of them clutching a manila folder containing the letter to outgoing President Lucas Garcia charging electoral fraud. "We have come peacefully, without arms," protested one of the group, made up of defeated presidential candidates and their running mates. The police officer brandishing a .45 was unmoved; instead of being allowed to proceed to the Presidential Palace to make their gesture, they were herded off to the local police station as a tear gas canister clattered into the street. Taking no chances, Lucas Garcia hastily summoned his lameduck Congress several days earlier than scheduled to put the pro forma rubberstamp on Guevara's election. As a local businessman summed it up: "You now have the government with no popular support and the rest of the

Ronald Reagan's White House troika of aides: Chief of Staff James Baker, Presidential Counselor Edwin Meese and Deputy Chief of Staff Michael Deaver.

CIA director
William Casey

Honduran Ambassador
John Negroponte

Judge William Clark,
National Security
Council advisor

Former Bechtel executive George Shultz took over as sectretary of state in the wake of Al Haig's departure

U.S. Ambassador to the U.N. Jeane Kirkpatrick, the brains behind Reagan's Central American policy

Nicaraguan leader
Daniel Ortega

Born-again dictator
Rios Montt appears in
freshly pressed
camoflauge fatigues
to take over Guatemala

Salvadoran rightist
Roberto D'Aubuisson

Salvadoran President
Jose Napoleon Duarte

Ronald Reagan and flag

Eden Pastora,
former Nicaraguan
commander turned
contra

U.S. military advisor trains Honduran troops

CIA-financed *contras* in the field against Sandinista soldiers

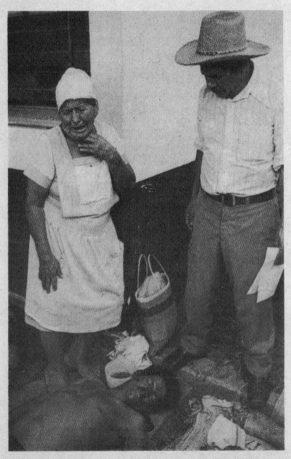

In San Salvador, despite President Reagan's certifications of human rights progress, death-squad violence continued to be a fact of daily life.

parties breaking away from the government."

From there it was only a short step to the barracks. The coup's chief planner was Captain Carlos Munoz Pilona, head of a group of young reformist officers who had only the scraps of a plan for setting up a new government, but whose simple goals included free elections, no military candidates, and a clean-up of the corruption-riddled structure. At dawn on March 23, a week after the Congress confirmed Guevara's election, a dozen or so junior officers stalked into the barracks at the Mariscal Zavala Brigade headquarters, on the outskirts of Guatemala City. Heavily armed and dressed in camoflauge battle fatigues, they announced to their comrades in arms, "The coup is on. Are you with us or against us?" The same scene was played out at barracks across the country and, with few exceptions, junior officers closed ranks behind the insurgents. In short order, tanks, armored personnel carriers and 105-mm. howitzers appeared in the plaza before the colonnaded National Palace. As some 500 infantry troops encircled the area, Captain Munoz Pilona set up his field headquarters in an arcade of shops on the far side of the square.

The first task was to clear out Lucas Garcia and his accomplices. That morning the president's brother, Benny, was in a helicopter flying toward a northern battle zone. His pilot told him they had to turn back because of mechanical problems. When the chopper landed, the military commander was escorted to his office at the airstrip, and invited to negotiate his brother's surrender. Benny defiantly refused, instead choosing house arrest at his *hacienda*. Back at the plaza, the besieged Lucas Garcia sent out aides to negotiate with Captain Munoz. The coup leader's conditions were straightforward: turn over the government and clear out of the palace by 3 p.m. or be fired upon. The next move was the radio appeal to Rios Montt and National Liberation Movement leader Sisniega. The ultra-right politician had been in on the planning from the beginning and expected a prominent role for his party in the subsequent junta; although the later scriptural version denied that Rios Montt had any prior contact with rebel officers, heretical reports circulated that he, too, had previously been consulted by the coup leaders.

Rios Montt arrived at coup headquarters, accompanied by

church elders and wearing civilian clothes, at 1 p.m., and he talked to the young officers in charge. It was unclear whether the born-again general had been brought in to negotiate Lucas Garcia's surrender or to serve as a temporary respectable figurehead for the junta; in any case, he would turn out to have his own plans. At 4 p.m., a Lucas Garcia aide came to the plaza and informed Munoz that the palace was ready for them. The president had exited by a side door and was on his way to join brother Benny at the family plantation. (President-designate Guevara had also been picked up during the day and was under house arrest.) Led by Rios Montt, the coup leadership entered the empty palace.

Sometime between their late afternoon takeover of the government and the 9 p.m. nationally televised appearance of the new junta, the coup got away from the junior officers and Sisniega-led branch of the far right. There was a confused radio announcement in early evening of the makeup of the new junta including some of the junior officers. But by 9 p.m., as the TV lights went on, Rios Montt, now garbed in freshly pressed camoflauge battle fatigues, was flanked by two plump military veterans: General Horacio Maldonado, an officer connected to the Sisniega group; and Colonel Francisco Gordillo.

Rios Montt discarded the speech prepared for him by the junior officers and improvised a fire-and-brimstone sermon of his own. Said the evangelical general, "Above all, I am trusting my Lord and my King, that he shall guide me. Because only he gives and takes away authority." At the end of the rambling, emotional diatribe punctuated with dramatic gestures, some Guatemalans quickly dubbed their fervent new leader "Ayatollah" Rios Montt, after the fundamentalist in charge of Iran. Instead of any mention of new elections or political pluralism, Rios Montt recommended "prayer to God our Father" as the solution to the country's problems. As one official connected to the coup put it, "General Rios Montt has temporarily stopped being a figurehead and has assumed control. We are waiting for the other shoe to drop." The next morning the junta suspended the constitution and banned the activities of all political parties. The March 8 vote was formally annulled the day after. Guatemala was now in the hands of a humble megalomaniacal mystic of the sort not seen in Central America since the days of the Witch Doctor of El

Salvador, General Maximiliano Hernandez Martinez, author of the Salvadoran *matanza*.

Just as the 1932 massacre of some 30,000 peasants was the traumatic event at the heart of Salvadoran politics, in Guatemala the formative cataclysm in the country's modern history was the U.S.-directed overthrow of a democratically elected government in 1954, marking the enforced end of the nation's decade-long experiment in social revolution.

At the end of World War II, after seventy years of dependence on agricultural exports, mainly coffee and bananas, the Guatemalan dictatorship of Jorge Ubico, in power since 1931, was in economic and political trouble. Responding to the coffee-grower social base of the regime, Ubico had protected their interests, particularly with legislation facilitating the exploitation of Indian plantation workers, including repressive anti-vagrancy laws. While other Latin American countries took advantage of the slowdown in foreign investment during the 1930s depression to diversify production and reduce their dependence on manufactured imports, Ubico reinforced the status quo. He not only failed to establish national control over key sectors of the economy in the face of capital outflow (or disinvestment), but instead granted contracts extending the privileges of U.S. monopolies, especially the United Fruit Company (UFCO) and its affiliate, International Railways of Central America which dominated Guatemalan transportation.

The same forces that ousted the Salvadoran dictatorship in 1944 and that would produce a liberal revolution in Costa Rica were also at work in Guatemala. What began as a student strike in June 1944 mushroomed into a general strike in Guatemala City; within weeks this middle class revolution, led by intellectuals and young army officers, forced Ubico's resignation. After several months of skirmishing with Ubico's followers, the decisive break occurred in October; the last of the *Ubiquistas* was ousted and an interim junta headed by two army officers, Francisco Arana and Jacobo Arbenz, set the stage for the country's first democratic elections, held in March 1945.

The winner was 40-year-old author and educator, Juan Arevalo, who described himself as a "spiritual socialist," disavowing both Marxism and individualistic capitalism.

Though possessing neither a systematic ideology nor a formal program, the ad hoc series of reforms initiated under Arevalo put Guatemala on the road to constitutional democracy. Among the reforms: a new constitution that granted so-called "universal suffrage" (in fact, illiterate women were excluded from the vote) and freely functioning political parties except for the communists; a budget that devoted one-third of state expenditures to an ambitious social welfare and literacy program; and for the first time in Guatemalan history, legislation designed to improve conditions for labor, rather than to further exploit it. The vagrancy laws and all forms of forced labor were abolished. In 1947, a labor code defined basic rights for workers; inevitably, urban, banana and railroad workers began to organize, leading to the formation of various labor confederations. Progress in the countryside was considerably slower, although the 1949 Law of Forced Rental obliged oligarchs to lease uncultivated lands to peasants at regulated rates. Finally, foreign investment was left intact, but there were initial attempts to regulate the operations of foreign firms in accordance with national interests. All in all, Arevalo's program consisted of moderate reforms; as one American observer noted, they were "not as radical as those of the New Deal in the U.S. or the Labor government in Britain."

Although there has been a mild scholarly controversy over the role of Guatemalan communists in the Arevalo regime, the consensus among historians is that the banned Guatemalan Workers party exercised no more than a moderate influence on the course of events, having their greatest impact on trade union organizing where they rose to the leadership of the main labor central, the Confederacion General de Trabajadores (CGT). They were, in any case, clearly an indigenous force within the nation's political framework. This didn't stop U.S. Ambassador Richard Patterson from demanding in 1949 that Arevalo fire seventeen government officials (among them, three of the four GWP members) whom Patterson considered too radical. The Guatemalans responded by quietly demanding, and obtaining, the ambassador's recall to Washington.

Subsequently, Patterson became outspoken about the communist danger in Guatemala, and in lecture-circuit speeches around the U.S. in the early 1950s he devised the inflammatory "duck test." "Many times it is impossible to prove legally that a certain individual is a communist,'' admitted Patterson, ''but for cases of this sort I recommend a practical method of detection—the duck test.'' Naturally, there was no ''test,'' but rather a folksy rhetorical device entirely consistant with the comic book anticommunism of the period which would be remembered for Senator Joe McCarthy's witchhunt for ''subversives.'' ''Suppose you see a bird walking around in a farmyard. This bird wears no label that says 'duck.' But the bird certainly looks like a duck. Also he goes to the pond and you notice he swims like a duck. Then he opens his beak and quacks like a duck. Well, by this time you have probably reached the conclusion that the bird is a duck, whether he's wearing a label or not.'' That this sort of thing went down quite well with audiences who couldn't tell a duck from a seagull was harmless enough; that it should form the basis of U.S. policy during the presidency of General Dwight Eisenhower was another matter.

In the contest to succeed Arevalo in 1950, Colonel Francisco Arana, head of the armed forces, and Defense Minister Colonel Jacobo Arbenz emerged as leading candidates. Arana, seen by the rightwing opposition as its last hope of turning back the social revolution, was gunned down in July 1949. Though his killers were never found, both then and subsequently there was an attempt to implicate Arbenz in the assassination; more immediately, Arana's death touched off a brief military uprising put down by a voluntary militia of students and workers armed by the Arevalo government. Arbenz, backed by organized labor, the peasantry and radical groups within the middle class, was challenged by a candidate supported by more moderate elements among the reformers and by Miguel Ydigoras Fuentes, an old *Ubiquista*, now running as the standard bearer of the opponents of the Arevalo reforms. In an election universally acknowledged to be honest, Arbenz won in a landslide, capturing 63 percent of the total vote (including 77 percent of ballots cast by illiterate males, who were voting for the first time). Insofar as elections provide a measure of popular support (an issue that would eventually be of concern to U.S. policy makers), the preceding five years of democratic reform had been overwhelmingly ratified by the Guatemalan populace.

Upon taking power in 1951, Arbenz envisioned what political scientists would describe as a modest social democratic program. His goals were "first, to convert Guatemala from a dependent nation with a semi-colonial economy to an economically independent country; second, to transform our nation from a backward nation with a predominantly feudal economy to a modern capitalist country." In short, Arbenz sought a national and independent capitalism, a break from the dependent forms (which he called "feudalism") of the past, and some redistribution of income, primarily through aid to peasants and Indians. From the American point of view this program appeared radical or worse, especially when Arbenz obtained passage of an Agrarian Reform Law in 1952.

The need in Guatemala, as elsewhere in Central America, was obvious. Less than 2 percent of the population owned 72 percent of the farmland; on the other side, about half the agricultural population was supposed to make do with 4 percent of the available arable land. In more human terms, it meant that per capita income in rural areas amounted to $89 a year. Malnutrition was rampant, and worsening as banana and coffee plantations spread over areas that once grew staple crops such as beans and corn. In macroeconomic terms, land reform was a precondition for expanding the domestic market and creating mass consumer purchasing power, which in turn would provide a basis for national industrialization.

The law had far-reaching effects on Guatemalan society. It provided for the expropriation, with compensation, of plantations larger than 223 acres—particularly idle agricultural acreage—and their transfer to *campesinos* in 42 acre plots; estates with lands fully in production were exempted from the law. Compensation for landowners was based on their own grossly undervalued tax declarations, a table-turning move that, naturally enough, enraged the oligarchy. Politically, the law was equally revolutionary. It was to be administered by peasants at the local level, rather than run from the capital.

As of mid-1954, at least 100,000 families had received land as well as bank credit and technical assistance. By most measurements, the program was a success. Guatemalan agricultural exports rose (in 1954, the country enjoyed a favorable balance of payments), the notion that land reform meant reduced productivity was dispelled, and peasants were not only able to once again grow their own food, but also to participate in the political system for the first time in the country's history. Although conceptually the plan was similar to subsequent schemes, such as the Salvadoran reform of 1980, the one marked difference between it and other programs was that it was actually implemented, rather than merely advertised for cosmetic political purposes.

Naturally, as the country's largest landowner, United Fruit Company was also subject to the law. Of the company's three million-acre holdings (over 40 percent of available farmland), only 139,000 acres were actually planted in bananas when Arbenz announced that Guatemala was expropriating 234,000 acres of UFCO territory. In Washington, the Arbenz government had just passed the "duck test." Not only did the government move to take over UFCO land, it planned a new electrical generating station that would make Guatemala City independent of the UFCO-owned utility, and it drew up blueprints for roads and railways that threatened the company's monopoly on the nation's transportation.

What followed was an intervention scenario that fixed the mold for post-World War II American strategy in Latin America. Economic aid was cut off; a series of State Department White Papers traced "the ascending curve of Communist influence" under Arbenz; Secretary of State John Foster Dulles spoke of "drawing the line" against the Kremlin.

United Fruit's enviable connections to the Eisenhower administration could probably be described in strict legal terms as conspiratorial. Secretary of State John Foster Dulles and his Wall Street law firm, Sullivan and Cromwell, had represented UFCO for a quarter century. His brother, Allen Dulles, head of the CIA, had served on UFCO's board of trustees. Eisenhower's National Security Adviser Robert Cutler was formerly the president of Old Colony Trust, one of the major banks associated with United Fruit. The company's top public relations officer, Ed Whitman (best known for a Cold War propaganda film entitled "Why the Kremlin Hates Bananas"), was the husband of Ann Whitman, Eisenhower's private secretary.

The fruit firm's success in linking the taking of its land to the evils of international communism was later described by a UFCO executive as "the Disney version of the episode." Although plans for the overthrow of Arbenz were in the works as early as the beginning of 1953, it was not until the following year that General "Ike" gave the order to the CIA to launch a counter-revolution. Some $7 million was budgeted for the CIA to recruit and train several hundred Guatemalans on a UFCO plantation in Honduras. After interviewing several prospective candidates, including defeated presidential aspirant Ydigoras Fuentes, the CIA settled on Colonel Carlos Castillo Armas to lead the attack. In November 1953, John Peurifoy was named ambassador to Guatemala to coordinate the operation on the ground. At the same time, Secretary of State Dulles launched an international propaganda offensive that included the formality of obtaining a resolution from the Organization of American States meeting in Caracas in March 1954 condemning communism in the hemisphere. Subservient as the OAS was, it insisted on appending a phrase stressing "dangers originating outside the hemisphere." Notwithstanding the sale of arms to Arbenz by Czechoslavakia in May 1954, and the presence of four communists out of fifty-six members of the Guatemalan Congress, there was, of course, no "outside" danger.

Diplomatic niceties aside, on June 18, 1954, Castillo Armas crossed the Honduran border into Guatemala with 150 men. As counter-revolutionary warfare, the operation was hardly distinguished. The initial skirmishes produced no triumphs and Castillo Armas was soon bogged down. CIA-produced radio broadcasts nonetheless declared the "liberators" were driving on the capital and called for a popular uprising; nothing happened. At which point, Eisenhower and Ambassador Peurifoy stepped in with airpower provided by special State Department adviser William Pawley. A Miami-based millionaire, Pawley owned a piece of the quasi-official "Flying Tigers" airlines which did substantial covert work for the CIA (another part-owner of this cosy operation was U.S. Ambassador to Honduras Whiting Willauer). Strafing Guatemala City and bombing other towns, the covert "air rescue" put Arbenz on the defensive. When he attempted to supply the worker-peasant militia with weapons, the previously neutral military leadership defected. Arbenz promptly resigned, leaving the government in the hands of a liberal army colonel. Ambassador Peurifoy, with a pistol conspicuous in a shoulder holster, appeared at the colonel's door and power was quickly transferred to Castillo Armas, who made a triumphal entry into Guatemala City. Peurifoy later bragged that the counter-revolution had been brought in only "forty-five minutes off schedule." In the U.S., the intervention was capped by the appearance of John Foster Dulles on American television to abhor "the evil purpose of the Kremlin to destroy the inter-American system," and to congratulate the people of Guatemala because "the situation is being cured by the Guatemalans themselves."

Guatemala was once again under control. Castillo Armas was assassinated by one of his own presidential guard three years later, only to be replaced in a highly fraudulent election by the patient General Ydigoras Fuentes, whose inept regime, combined with falling world coffee prices, gave rise to mass unrest and the beginnings of a Guatemalan guerrilla movement. For the next quarter century a succession of generals donned the presidential sash and, aided by U.S. military hardware and on occasion by American counter-insurgency advisers, sent the troops out to slaughter hard-to-distinguish guerrillas and peasants. The only institutional feature that distinguished the Guatemalan military from its Salvadoran or pre-Sandinista Nicaraguan counterparts was the establishment of the Bank of the Army which permitted senior officers to expropriate or buy up peasant land at giveaway prices. By the time of Rios Montt's ascension to power in 1982, the Guatemalan military, unlike most other Latin American armed forces who were basically the elite's hired help, occupied the position of full-fledged members of the upper class, a fact that perhaps explained the army's resistance to land reform and to observance of human rights standards.

Each Sunday evening at 9 p.m., the TV show opened with a picture of a sunset over famed Lake Atitlan, followed by the appearance of General Rios Montt in civilian clothes standing in a garden filled with trees and chirping birds. "Good evening," said the star of the one-man show. "I sincerely thank you for the opportunity that you give me to be with you tonight. It cannot be any other way." While the well-to-do regarded the general's nationally televised weekly spiritual talk as an embarrassing vulgarity, others called their president "the maid" because, like household domestics, he came out on Sundays.

The proselytizing Rios Montt made no converts among the guerrillas. As URNG representative Silvia Suarez told reporters in Mexico City the weekend after the coup, "It was necessary to change the facade of the government for international consumption, so that economic, political and military aid could continue." Despite the promises, however, "no real reforms are possible without revolutionary changes because, otherwise, they would affect the interests of the oligarchy and the dominating classes." By April, military casualties were again being reported. And just as it had been before the departure of Benny Lucas Garcia and his brother, the peasant population was suffering. "The army is going around killing people," reported an Indian *campesino* who had fled from the border village of Chaca to La Sombra, one of a number of refugee camps along the Mexican border which provided shelter for upwards of 30,000 homeless Guatemalans. "We have seen corpses floating in the river. Before, there were 300 people in Chaca. Now only eight families are left."

That's not the way the Reagan administration saw it. Indiscriminate violence "has been brought virtually to an end," the State Department reported to Congress in late April 1982. A few days later, the administration said it was about to approve the sale of $4 million in spare parts for U.S.-built helicopters, to add $50,000 to the quarter-million dollars already requested for military training funds, as well as to resume support for Guatemalan loans through the Inter-American Development Bank. Assistant Secretary of State Thomas Enders called the Rios Montt regime "a promising evolution." U.S. Ambassador Frederic Chapin was pressing for a $50 million economic aid package for fiscal 1983.

However, Guatemala had no need of U.S. government aid, declared Rios Montt the following month, in mid-May, to the consternation of his would-be benefactors. Apparently, God would provide, or at least, said the general, U.S. Christian fundamentalists who had pledged millions for helicopters and other such necessities. "The only solution" to civil strife "is love," Rios Montt told reporters as he sat behind a table in his mahagony-paneled office piled with blue-covered New Testaments in Spanish and in a half-dozen of the country's twenty-two Indian dialects.

"Sometimes he speaks in parables," explained church elder Francisco Bianci to those who wondered whether the fundamentalist millions were real. "It is difficult to understand." But there was no misunderstanding Rios Montt when on June 9 he fired the other two members of the junta and proclaimed himself president. "Thank you, God, for giving me this opportunity to govern Guatemala," said the general in a fiery speech to the nation. "In this transcendental moment for Guatemala, I assume the weight of government only on my shoulders." According to church elder James Degolyer, Rios Montt would also get a little help from scriptures. "There is an amazing amount of guidance that the Bible gives kings, heads of state, in how they should rule," said Degolyer, a former hippie in San Francisco's Haight-Ashbury district before being "saved." Explained the true believer: "We pray for Efrain and the brothers. Thousands of people are praying for them in the U.S. too. We have twenty-four-hour prayer chains in the church for them. We believe that prayer coverage is very important."

But it was not half as important as the army believed air coverage to be. Beneath the "prayer chains," spiritual guidance, and avowals of transcendental love, there was a rather more materialist policy of "bullets and beans" (*fusiles y frijoles*). Hidden from public scrutiny, the army had drawn up a political-military scheme (the National Plan for Security and Development) approved by Rios Montt on April 1, 1982, only a week after the coup. The born-again general's precise connection with the operation proposed in the scheme remains unknown. In fact, the story of this savage and largely successful counterinsurgency campaign, which lasted through 1982 and into the next year, went all but unreported in the North American press. True, from time to time, while noting that death-squad violence in Guatemala City had declined markedly, there were accounts of massacres of Indian peasants, including claims by peasants' unions that more than 3,000 *campesinos* had been killed by the government in the first six weeks after the coup. But the systematic nature of the counterinsurgency campaign was recounted only in such publications as the Americas Watch May 1983 report entitled *Creating A Desolation and Calling It Peace*, in bulletins published by the network of U.S. solidarity support committees, and in subsequent reconstructions such as Richard White's *The Morass*. Most Americans, even those taking some interest in foreign affairs, remained totally unaware of the Guatemalan military operation that claimed some 10,000 civilian lives.

What differentiated the Guatemalan army's strategy from classic counterinsurgency methods was that it avoided direct confrontation with the guerrillas; it focussed instead on eliminating the insurgents' popular base by massacring whole communities of suspected sympathizers. Whereas standard counterinsurgency operations attacked the guerrillas and their infrastructure, with the killing of non-combatant civilians being only a collateral activity, in Guatemala, as Amnesty International reported in July 1982, the "security forces continue to attempt to control opposition, both violent and nonviolent, through widespread killings including the extrajudicial executions of large numbers of rural noncombatants." Those who survived were forced to become refugees, once again upsetting Jeane Kirkpatrick's thesis about the absence of displaced persons in traditional authoritarian regimes. In fact, in addition to some 70,000 to 100,000 people who sought refuge in neighboring Mexico, it was estimated by 1983 that the continuing persecution had created as many as one million internal refugees—that is, one out of every seven Guatemalans.

Despite pro forma denials by the military, there was little doubt of a staggering escalation of massacres. In 1979, there were two such instances documented; in 1980 three; in 1981, the last year of Lucas Garcia's reign, the mass killings increased to at least two dozen. However, as shocking as the magnitude of the 1981 killings was, it paled in comparison to what occurred under Rios Montt. In the first nine months of the year, as the army created a *cordon sanitaire* along the Mexican border, several hundred massacres were documented; moreover, the number of those killed in each instance increased dramatically over previous atrocities. Reliable sources recorded at least 500 murders per month. Between the coup in late March and the last week of June, Amnesty International produced a partial listing of 2,186 extrajudicial executions in rural Guatemala.

Rios Montt, who declared a state of siege on July 1, admitted, with no sense of irony, that he had done so "so we could kill legally." When asked about army killings of unarmed civilians, the evangelist came down to earth as a practical-minded general: "Look, the problem of the war is not just a question of who is shooting; for each one that is shooting there are ten working behind him." Rios Montt's press secretary, church elder Francisco Bianchi, put it even more candidly. "The guerrillas won over many Indian collaborators," he explained. "Therefore, the Indians were subversives, right? And how do you fight subversion? Clearly, you had to kill Indians because they were collaborating with subversion. And then they would say, you are massacring innocent people. But they weren't innocent. They had sold out to subversion."

The military was concerned not only with eliminating guerrilla collaborators, but with creating its own collaborators as part of the "pacification" program. To the latter end, an important aspect of the National Plan was the establishment of the Civil Defense Corps, a euphemistic renaming of civilian collaborators. In the subsidiary war on language, even the word "counterinsurgency" disappeared from the official vocabulary. As a senior U.S. military adviser in the area haltingly tried to explain, counterinsurgency was now called "low intensity conflict...Counterinsurgency no longer being, ah, having conjured up memories of Vietnam and evidently people no longer, ah, don't want to stay worrying about it." Whatever they were called, Americas Watch reported in 1983 that "there is growing evidence that civilian males, including teenagers, are being conscripted under threat of death into 'civil patrols' which are controlled by local army commanders. A principal function of the civil patrol is to kill other civilians suspected of being 'subversive' or otherwise objectionable."

The Guatemalan army, said Americas Watch, "tended to view the willingness of a particular village to form a civil patrol as a test of 'political sympathies.' Villages that form such patrols are considered by the army 'white' villages, under its 'protection'; those not doing so are considered 'red' villages and are targets for military attack." In terms of the "beans and bullets" policy, the red villages got the bullets and the white villages got the beans while groups of internal refugees were herded into what were called, in yet another echo of Vietnam, "strategic hamlets."

The account of the Parraxut massacre on December 22, 1982, given to Americas Watch investigators the following spring, graphically depicted the diabolical counter-terror. "The Guatemalan army entered the village of Chiul, in the municipality of Cunen, Quiche, on Wednesday, December 22, and ordered all male members of the civil patrol to appear in the town as quickly as possible. Because of the village's size, it required two hours for the nearly 350 men (ranging in age from fifteen to sixty-five) to assemble. The army captain allegedly ordered the men to march to the nearby village of Parraxut, where, he told them, they must be prepared to demonstrate their masculinity to him.

"While the 350 civil patrol members were marching the hour and a half to Parraxut, a similar number of soldiers drove by truck to that village and rounded up all available men, women and children...According to the accounts we heard, the captain then ordered the members of the Chiul civil patrol to prove their masculinity by killing all the men from Parraxut, using guns given them by the soldiers who surrounded the patrol members.

"After the men had been murdered, the women were allegedly separated into subgroups: the young and the old. The civil patrol was then directed, under threat of death, to kill the older women, while the younger women were divided among the soldiers to be raped that night. The following morning, the Chiul civil patrol, we were told, was directed to murder the surviving younger women, except for two who were particularly attractive. One was carted off under the captain's instructions; the other was shot by the captain after she begged him to end her life." On the march back to Chiul, the patrolmen, according to an eyewitness, "didn't say a word; they walked in complete silence and when they reached their homes, they broke down in tears. They cried for several hours." Some, overcome by remorse, returned to Parraxut to try to help the surviving children, many of whom had escaped during the night of terror, but seeing the men who had killed their parents, they hid by running off into the jungle.

There was a final irony to the Parraxut atrocity. When news of the killings reached the international press a couple of weeks later, several journalists, taking advantage of Rios Montt's standing invitation to investigate any such reports, asked the president about the "Chiul massacre." The general denied that it had occurred, and to prove it, provided the newsmen with a helicopter to visit the village. Upon arrival in Chiul everything seemed normal and the people claimed to know nothing about any massacre. As for the patrols, Colonel Roberto Matta, commander of El Quiche province, declared, "The Civil Defense members are very proud of themselves. They no longer only depend on the army to protect them. Now they feel they are defending themselves against the subversives. This is a commitment because they have actively chosen sides. For the first time in history they have been brought into the national life. This is the true revolution.'' By the time Americas Watch confirmed the massacre in Mexican refugee camps three months later, and its report was reprinted in the liberal New York *Review of Books* in June 1983 (thus achieving its broadest American readership, about 250,000 people), Parraxut was but one more barbaric tale from a distant, violent land, lost in the more immediate reportage from El Salvador and Nicaragua.

Insofar as Guatemala was noticed at all, the comic opera character of the Rios Montt regime tended to make observers impervious to the bloodbath. Nonetheless, in May 1983, Americas Watch arrived at the "inescapable conclusion that the government of Guatemala is engaged in the most profound violations of fundamental human rights—above all, the right to life—and that these violations are occurring on a scale and with a degree of brutality that amount, for all practical purposes, to a policy of extermination of a significant portion of Guatemala's Indian population." Or as Richard White succinctly put it: "It is not an exaggeration to state that the armed forces and their paramilitary units have unleashed a campaign of generalized terror, which must be recognized as genocide."

Genocide was not something Ronald Reagan was likely to recognize. When the evangelical Guatemalan dictator met the U.S. president who wanted to reinstate classroom prayers in American schools, there was bound to be a meeting of souls. The president, concluding a five-day, 11,000-mile Latin American tour in December 1982, arranged a get-together with Rios Montt in Honduras. The two promptly hit it off.

Flying home to Washington that night on Air Force One, the president decided that charges of widespread human rights abuses in Guatemala were "a bum rap." "I very frankly think that they've been getting a bad deal," said Reagan. Rios Montt "is totally dedicated to democracy," he added. The U.S., Reagan acknowledged, was leaning toward providing military assistance to Guatemala, which was "confronting a brutal challenge from guerrillas armed and supported by others outside Guatemala." A month later, in January 1983,

Reagan approved the sale of $6.4 million in helicopter spare parts.

Rios Montt emerged from his meeting with Reagan a born-again believer in democracy. He promised to end death squads and to announce electoral plans by March 1983, the first anniversary of his coup. When reporters pestered him about reports of his army pursuing a scorched-earth policy, the general replied, "We have no scorched-earth policy. We have a policy of scorched communists." Having confidently predicted victory over the guerrillas by December, Rios Montt returned to Guatemala City from his rendezvous with Reagan to announce that "the war against the subversives is already over." The government's "beans and bullets" program would give way to one of *techo, trabajo y tortillas*—roofs, work and tortillas. Despite the general's on-deadline assertion of victory in December, in March 1983, Americas Watch was recording the testimony of hundreds of refugees who had fled Guatemala between December 1982 and spring 1983. There was a common theme to the refugees' accounts: "They had fled because the Guatemalan army had tried to kill them with bullets and by starvation...Attacks against the Indian population, their property, and their food supply had become virtually indiscriminate. We were repeatedly told of children being picked up by the feet and having their heads smashed against the walls, choked to death by hand or with ropes, or killed with machetes or bayonets."

At the same time that investigators were collecting evidence of the army's continuing war against Guatemala's Indian peasantry, Rios Montt was gearing up for ecclesiastical conflict. His opponent was Pope John Paul II, who was making a pastoral tour of Central America the first week of March 1983. The Guatemalan president had already offended the country's Catholics by his sermonizing and the prominent place given to his Protestant fellow sect-members. A few months earlier, when 200,000 Protestants had gathered for a religious service, Rios Montt couldn't resist setting Catholic nerves on edge by wondering aloud whether the Pope would be able to draw such a large crowd. When he turned down the Vatican's request to provide a bulletproof "Popemobile" for the pontiff's visit, Catholics were further incensed. The visit was shaping up, in the words of a local Christian Democratic politician, as "a rallying point against Rios Montt."

A final sore point between the competing churches concerned a Vatican request for mercy. Despite the announcement of victory on the war front, there were apparently a few subversives still around. The Rios Montt government had devised an unorthodox method of disposing of them: trial by secret tribunal. "Secret" meant something far more bizarre than merely holding the proceedings in unannounced venues. The tribunals didn't permit the defense lawyer or the accused to see the judge, the prosecutor, the evidence or the witnesses. The defense attorney was allowed, but not without difficulty, to see the defendent; however, one attorney explained, "He is the only person we see." The procedure, he said, was "like something out of Kafka." The verdict was delivered either by mail, or by a telephone call from a person who didn't give a name.

A half-dozen men were slated for execution shortly before John Paul's arrival. In one of those protocols which are traditional between messengers of mercy and God-fearing potentates, the Pope begged for a stay of execution. It was the sort of request that dictators seeking to display human rights progress usually routinely granted, scoring points with their political patrons for the display of largesse. Four days before Pope John Paul's appearance, however, Rios Montt sent the condemned to the firing squad, an event duly noted in headlines around the world. The U.S. jerked Ambassador Chapin home for a couple of days as a sign of the Reagan administration's displeasure.

Once in Guatemala, the Pope easily won a numbers game he was perhaps unaware of, drawing 350,000 people to an open-air mass where he circumspectly chastised the born-again government of the day. Referring obliquely to the recent executions, John Paul cited a passage in Ezekial reminding the faithful that God "does not desire the death of the sinner, but that he be converted and live."

The erratic Rios Montt appeared to be momentarily repentent. "We have sinned, we have abused power, and we want to reconcile ourselves with the people," he declared in contrite tones. A week later, though, the firing squad dispatched five more victims of the secret tribunals. Said Ambassador Chapin wearily, "We think that public courts are better than closed or secret courts."

The U.S. representative wasn't the only one growing tired

of the president in the pulpit. Rios Montt's announcement on March 23 that he would turn power over to an elected civilian government was hardly reassuring, since he neglected to say when it would happen. The far right called it a maneuver to keep Rios Montt in power "an indefinite time." The Christian Democrats found the vague pledge "not sufficient." The religious fanaticism of Rios Montt was not the only cause for criticism of his regime; as the summer of 1983 wore on, the increasing hostility on the part of the nation's elite amounted to much more than spiritual disputations.

Businessmen might be willing to sit still while the moralizing Rios Montt admonished them to give up their mistresses, but when the Gross Domestic Product fell from a 1 percent growth rate in 1981 to minus 3.3 percent in 1982, there was cause for grave concern. The final straw was the general's announcement of a 10 percent sales tax, effective August 1983, to offset the extraordinary costs of the counterinsurgency campaign. "You can strangle a country to death by raising taxes beyond a certain point," complained prominent industrialist Manuel Ayau. Already suffering the effects of world recession, as well as a precipitous decline in the lucrative tourist industry due to the turmoil, the industrial-commercial sector was ready to see a change in dictators.

Nor had Rios Montt's frequent references to land reform, even though nothing ever came of them, endeared him to the landed oligarchy, many of whom were senior military officers. Moreover, his reliance upon, and promotion of, a small group of junior officers, along with an ambitious campaign to root out corruption in the armed forces, provided reason enough for the top echelons of the military to worry about their own positions. Finally, his stalling on an election date—a July 1984 vote for a constitutional assembly wasn't set until the end of June 1983—put him at odds with the country's political parties.

However, in an interview on August 5 with foreign reporters, he laughed out loud while dismissing reports of serious problems in his regime as being "hairs in the soup." For a man whose beliefs purportedly bestowed on him the gift of prophesy, Rios Montt seemed unperturbed when Defense Minister General Oscar Mejia Victores, a 52-year-old paratrooper, flew off the next day to the U.S. aircraft carrier *Ranger* for a "courtesy call." On the way home the following day, General Mejia stopped off in Honduras where he conferred with his counterparts—the defense ministers of El Salvador and Honduras—as well as with General Paul Gorman of the U.S. Southern Command in Panama. The State Department would later dismiss as "ridiculous" the notion that Mejia Victores' weekend activities were a plotting session.

On Monday morning, August 8, 1983, the commanders of most of the country's armed forces gathered at the Guatemala City barracks of the elite Guardia de Honor. Rios Montt was asked to stop by. When the president entered the hall he was informed that he was once more a preacher. After a twenty-minute discussion Rios Montt agreed to quit, but asked to return to the presidential mansion to tidy up his affairs. Once there, however, he began calling military units he thought were still loyal to him. The rebellious officers decided to be a bit more persuasive. Planes and helicopters buzzed the Presidential Palace, and soldiers surrounding the building exchanged gunfire with the presidential guard. After a two-hour standoff, Rios Montt realized it was over, thus ending the oddest "parenthesis" (as he once called his reign) in the history of Guatemalan military dictatorships.

That night it was back to business, minus the evangelism. In his first statement as president, General Mejia, the man who had supervised the savage and largely successful counter-insurgency campaign, pledged to "fight by any means to eradicate Leninist-Communist subversion, which threatens Guatemala's liberty and sovereignty." Washington hailed Mejia Victores' "positive steps." Born-again brutality had given way to the old-fashioned kind.

Nicaragua

7   The Not-So-Secret War

*No comment, no comment, and a big
fat no comment.*
　　　—Ambassador John Negroponte,
　　　　　　　　　　October 1982

U.N. Ambassador Jeane Kirkpatrick decided that Sandinista
commander Daniel Ortega was in need of psychoanalysis. The
Nicaraguan leader had traveled to the United Nations on
March 25, 1982, to persuade the international body that the
U.S. was waging a covert war against his country's not-quite-
three-year-old revolution.

Just two weeks before Ortega leveled his charges, an expose
in the Washington *Post* revealed that three months earlier, in
December 1981, President Reagan had approved and signed a
ten-point plan authorizing clandestine CIA operations in
Central America, including $19 million in funding to create a
500-man force to conduct paramilitary activities in Nicaragua.
If the allegations were true, the U.S. could find itself in
violation of Articles 2 and 33 of the Charter of the United
Nations, Articles 3, 14, 18, 19 and 21 of the Charter of the
Organization of American States, Articles 1 and 2 of the Inter-
American Treaty of Reciprocal Assistance, and a venerable
1794 piece of U.S. law called the Neutrality Act. Thus, it
might have been thought that the initial disclosure of what
would turn out to be the worst-kept secret in the history of the
CIA would excite considerable interest.

In an earlier story in mid-February that should have whetted readers' appetites, the *Post* hinted at these nefarious doings enough that a reporter at Reagan's February 18 news conference was able to ask straight out, "Mr. President, have you approved of covert activity to destabilize the present government of Nicaragua?"

The Great Communicator had been busy fielding various hot potatoes, ranging from a query on whether he would send U.S. combat troops to El Salvador (he wouldn't) to a question about whether his recent appointee to the Civil Rights Commission—a fundamentalist preacher opposed to equal rights for women and minorities—was a bigot (he wasn't). It was understandable, therefore, that he might get a bit flummoxed trying to keep these tiny Central American countries straight. "Well, no, we're supporting them," Reagan began. "Oh, wait a minute, wait a minute, I'm sorry, I was thinking El Salvador, because of the previous—when you said Nicaragua." Having unscrambled the geography, if not the grammar, the president gave a firm blast from the fog machine. "This is something upon which with national security interests, I just—I will not comment," said Reagan.

As it turned out, the *Post*'s exclusive made barely a ripple. It came in the midst of Secretary of State Alexander Haig's 1982 pre-spring offensive against Central America. The secretary briskly turned away from the secret-war question with a formula that would become standard for American officials: "It is inappropriate to comment on covert activities...whether or not such exist." The day the story appeared, March 9, most of the media were busily ogling CIA spy photos of the "Cuban-style" barracks and "Soviet-style" obstacle courses that purportedly depicted a Nicaraguan military buildup of ominous proportions. As Secretary Haig's butterfingered operatives staggered from one "smoking Sandinista" to another, and the propaganda offensive fell to pieces, the press corps was too busy over the next few days chasing down loose ends or being convulsed in laughter to pay much attention to the charges of covert war. But the oversight was temporary. The revelation of America's secret war against Nicaragua would be revealed again and again over the next two years, each time in more disturbing detail, each time necessitating a rewrite of recent American history.

Nor did Commander Ortega get much attention outside of

U.N. chambers. By the time he reached the podium, the American focus had shifted to El Salvador where the U.S.-sponsored Constituent Assembly elections were to be held that weekend. There had even been some doubt as to whether Nicaragua would be allowed to present its case. At a Managua news conference on March 19, Nicaraguan Foreign Minister Reverend Miguel D'Escoto called for an urgent meeting of the U.N. Security Council to head off what he described as "imminent" invasion of his country. Less than a week before, the Sandinista government had declared a thirty-day state of emergency in the wake of the bombing of two bridges near its Honduran border that had all the fingerprints of a CIA operation. "We no longer say an invasion is possible, nor even probable," said D'Escoto. "Rather, we're convinced that the decision has been taken and they're just awaiting a propitious moment."

In Washington, the State Department called the Nicaraguan charges "nonsense." More importantly, Secretary Haig said that the U.N. had no role to play in the Caribbean crisis, a possible hint that the U.S. would lobby to prevent Nicaragua from securing the necessary ten out of fifteen votes which the Security Council required to get an item on the agenda. The Americans preferred to keep their "backyard" squabbles confined to the friendlier precincts of the Organization of American States. The next day, however, Jeane Kirkpatrick, taking her turn as Security Council president that month, said that it was her "clear and firm intention to proceed fairly and expeditiously" with Managua's request. Once more, apparently, Kirkpatrick and Haig, between whom there was no love lost (by this time, the plan to ease Haig out was well advanced), had gotten their signals crossed. Kirkpatrick had the final word.

The 36-year-old coordinator of the Nicaraguan junta, who had come to the U.N. to lay out his country's grievances against the U.S., was a solemn mustachioed man dressed in army olive drab. Born to a family of middle class intellectuals in the provincial town of La Libertad, Ortega had dropped out of law school at age seventeen in 1963 to join the newly formed Sandinista National Liberation Front (FSLN). His entire family had been longtime opponents of the Somoza regime. "My father was in the struggle with Sandino at different times, different places," Ortega recounted in a later interview. "Once, he was taken prisoner in the mountains in the north of Nicaragua." Ortega's grandfather had interceded with the first of a line of Somoza dictators to get his son released. "Somoza personally scolded my father and said the only reason he wasn't killed was my grandfather's intervention. Then Somoza gave my father a sealed envelope. When my father got home, he opened the envelope and found money inside. He immediately returned it. So Somoza responded by sending him a telegram with the words: 'Eat shit!' When I was a child, my father would often show me and my brothers that telegram."

Four years after joining the FSLN, Ortega was captured and sentenced to twelve years in prison. He served seven of them. His freedom came in December 1974 when the Sandinistas seized a group of prominent Somoza backers and exchanged them for political prisoners, Ortega among them, who were flown to Cuba. "Finding ourselves free in Havana was a tremendous experience," Ortega recalled. "After seven years of imprisonment, it seemed unreal." Soon he was back in Nicaragua where he and his brothers, Humberto and Camilo, formed a powerful family group within the FSLN. The triumph in Managua came on July 19, 1979, but what Ortega recalled was the evening before, the last night of the old regime. "There we were, resting up for the next day's march, watching television in Leon. And on that night, for the first time, I saw some old film footage of Sandino being broadcast. During all the years of Somoza, we had never seen any film of him... But there he actually *was*, waving his hat. And that was the thing that impressed me most: to see Sandino waving his hat on TV."

Now, almost three years later, Ortega was detailing the U.S. "policy of aggressions, threats, interventions, covert operations and invasions against our homeland and the region." There were Somocista training camps in the U.S. (Ortega noted the possible violation of the Neutrality Act); 2,000 counter-revolutionaries along the Honduran border had been "brought together, trained, supplied and armed" by the CIA; the U.S. was building massive air and naval bases in Honduras; Nicaraguan air space had been violated forty times in the past nine months; finally, when the Washington *Post*, of which Ortega was apparently a more careful reader than most, published accounts of U.S. covert war plans, "not a single spokesman of the U.S. government has denied such reports. On the contrary, those who have referred to them have wrapped them in doubt or given them an affirmative character.'' The Nicaraguans were not seeking condemnation of U.S. aggression, said Ortega, but "direct and frank conversations with the U.S., even in a mutually agreeable third country, with the objective of reaching concrete results through such negotiations."

Ortega could hardly have expected that, in the response to his charges, he would be confronted with Lucy, the *Peanuts* comic strip character who dispensed psychiatric advice for a nickel from a converted lemonade stand. Ambassador Kirkpatrick was concerned with Nicaragua's state of mental health. "These charges—as extravagant as they are baseless," Dr. Kirkpatrick pointed out in her best couch-side manner, "are an interesting example of projection, a psychological operation in which one's own feelings and intentions are simultaneously denied and attributed—that is, projected on—to someone else." All that was missing from this stock scene was a goateed colleague to judiciously nod and murmer, "Ah, ver-ry interesting, doctor." Kirkpatrick proceeded with the diagnosis: "Hostility is the dominant emotion and projection the key mechanism of the paranoid style of politics, a style which, much to our regret, has characterized the political behavior of the Sandinista leadership since its arrival in power. The principal object of Sandinista hostility, I further regret, is the government and people of the United States."

Ortega didn't stay to hear the prescription. Nor was the rest of the Security Council persuaded by Kirkpatrick's account of who was crazy. The resolution on Nicaragua, proposed a week later on April 2, named no names and made no charges, but simply repeated U.N. Charter principles opposing intervention in the affairs of other countries and the use of force. It also contained a clause requesting U.N. Secretary General Javier Perez de Cuellar to keep the Council informed of the crisis in Central America. That was enough to bring on an American attack of paranoia. While twelve council members voted for the resolution, with Britain and Zaire abstaining, Kirkpatrick exercised the American veto to quash the measure, insisting that the OAS was the proper forum for Managua's complaint.

In the spring of 1982, U.S. television viewers became

accustomed to the sight of Exocet missiles slamming into naval vessels and a shuttling Alexander Haig appearing in various world airports as he attempted to mediate the British-Argentine Falklands War. The CIA's covert operations receded to the mountainous jungle terrain of northern Nicaragua. Only in one dim corner of the American governmental labyrinth did the secret war stir suspicions.

When CIA director William Casey first unveiled the Nicaraguan operation to the congressional oversight committees that monitored the intelligence agency, he stressed that the *contras*, as the counter-revolutionaries were quickly dubbed, would be carefully limited in their numbers and the scope of their activities; no mercenaries or former Somocista National Guardsmen were to be involved; and the primary mission of the 500-man force would be to stop the arms flow from Managua to rebels in El Salvador.

During a follow-up briefing to Congress in February 1982, the CIA's Latin American director, Dewey Clarridge, aroused committee members from their torpor by casually mentioning that the number of *contra* commandos stood at 1,000 troops. When pressed to explain the increase, CIA officials insisted that there was none, nor had they lied in previous testimony; all along, they claimed, the committees had been informed that the 500-man task force would be augmented by dissident Miskito Indians.

The law required the CIA to report the full plans of covert operations to the oversight committees; however, the next step in Congress' growing inklings that the administration's secret war was being kept secret even from the legislators, came in summer 1982. While most people were following the progress of the Israeli invasion of Lebanon, Congress was learning from fresh CIA briefings that the U.S.-financed *contras* had, as Daniel Ortega had suggested to the U.N., blown up two major bridges inside Nicaragua in March, and moreover, the "carefully limited" commando forces had grown to 1,500 soldiers who were preparing to move some of their camps into northern Nicaragua. Perturbed about the legality of those activities and the growing danger of setting off a war between Honduras and its neighbor, in August 1982 both oversight committees drafted amendments to the secret intelligence bill to limit the zealousness of U.S. covert operations in Central America.

While the congressmen nursed their doubts about the innocent enthusiasm of the CIA, the Nicaraguans were displaying an interest in peace negotiations that hardly accorded with the State Department-sponsored image of them as an incipient regional "superpower" bent on the export of revolution. On March 18, a week before Ortega's U.N. appearance, Nicaraguan junta member Sergio Ramirez said that his government was prepared to hold negotiations with the U.S. on all issues, including assertions of Sandinista arms shipments to Salvadoran rebels. "We have never accepted the U.S. charge of an arms flow through here," Ramirez said, "but this does not mean that we're unwilling to discuss the point." Sandinista Interior Minister Tomas Borge was even more inviting. "If the wise men of the CIA know where it's happening, why don't they tell us so we can stop it?" he asked.

The Nicaraguans were following up on a renewed Mexican bid to work out a regional peace plan. The day after Ortega appealed for negotiations from the rostrum of the U.N., the Mexican delegate to the international body disclosed that high-level meetings between the Sandinistas and U.S. Assistant Secretary for Inter-American Affairs Thomas Enders would be held in Mexico City the following month. Unfortunately, far less was going on than met the eye. The U.S. State Department quickly denied that the meeting was on and called the Mexican announcement "premature."

It became apparent that the announcement would always be premature. In mid-April, the Nicaraguans accepted an eight-plank U.S. proposal to establish the basis for talks and they promptly shipped Washington their own list of agenda items. Ten days later, the U.S. was hedging. The State Department would send an "early reply" to Managua's latest offer, but was not yet ready to hold formal talks. "We want to make sure they're serious," said an American spokesman. In any case, Mexico City was out as a venue. "I think that they want a big propaganda show with small, poor Nicaragua taking on the big United States to the cheers of the Mexicans," was the slightly paranoid explanation from Foggy Bottom. Six weeks later, in early July, though conceding that "the ball is in our court," there was still no word from the Reagan administration. The Nicaraguans were getting the idea that Washington was stringing them along.

Meanwhile, on the ground, beneath the high-flown rhetoric about the need for negotiation, and the lofty declarations of international bodies, the hit-and-run skirmishes along the Nicaraguan-Honduran border were turning into a war. Jeane Kirkpatrick might claim that Daniel Ortega was imagining things, but the French government didn't think so. At the beginning of 1982, France announced that it would sell $17 million worth of military equipment to the Sandinistas, much to the displeasure of Secretaries Haig and Weinberger. It looked like the Nicaraguans would need all the help they could get. In mid-January reporters stumbled upon former Somocista National Guardsmen limbering up in San Bernadino county, California. Thomas Enders explained that it was all perfectly legal "as long as they don't hurt anybody and as long as they don't actually conspire to invade in a specific way." Of course, the same could be said of the rattle-snakes in the California desert.

With each month, the noose tightened. In February, there were skirmishes with Miskito Indians who had joined the *contras*, and a U.S. spy ship was sighted off the Pacific Coast, gathering information for the State Department's spring slide show of the Nicaraguan military buildup. When *contras* blew up the two bridges in March, Nicaragua placed its armed forces on full alert and Commander Ortega headed for the U.N. to complain.

The following month in Costa Rica, a potentially serious political problem for the Sandinistas surfaced in the form of Eden Pastora, a former revolutionary hero who had left the country in mid-1981. For months, the CIA had been looking for a credible Nicaraguan leader who could lend their covert operation the appearance of being more than a shady conspiracy led by a gang of thugs. Commander Zero, as Pastora had been known during the war against Somoza, looked like he might be the right man for the job. For the moment, however, he contented himself with denouncing his ex-comrades-in-arms and calling for their overthrow.

By mid-1982, *contra* raids reached Matagalpa province, 125 kilometers north of Managua. In mid-July, days before the third anniversary of the revolution, a thousand *contras* poured over the Honduran border with heavy artillery. "Nicaragua is undergoing a silent, yet bloody invasion," Daniel Ortega told a July 19 rally in Masaya, a town thirty kilometers southeast of the capital. Since the beginning of the month, he said, the counter-revolutionaries had staged more than twenty raids on Nicaraguan territory and killed at least fifty government troops. "This is not a figment of our imagination," Ortega declared for the benefit of amateur psychologist Kirkpatrick.

The reality of the war received confirmation at the end of August from a senior Honduran military officer; Colonel Leonides Torres warned that the country's strongman, General Gustavo Alvarez, was leading them toward a military confrontation with Nicaragua, an "adventure of madness" that Honduras could not win. By early September, Nicaragua was bracing for an invasion as the CIA-trained commandos conducted sabotage attacks, mortar shellings and raids on Nicaraguan border villages. In October, as President Reagan was trying to sell his policies in Peoria for the upcoming mid-term congressional elections, Honduras and Nicaragua were exchanging angry diplomatic notes as well as accusations at the U.N. General Assembly.

Newsweek's cover story of November 8, 1982, began with a nostalgic nod to Rick's Cafe, the setting of the Humphrey Bogart and Ingrid Bergman screen classic, *Casablanca*. "The smoky bar in Tegucigalpa was a cousin to Rick's cafe, a nightly gathering place for the dangerous and the desperate in Honduras." The special report, entitled "America's Secret War—Target: Nicaragua," blew the cover off the CIA's biggest undercover operation in a decade.

Four Argentine military advisers were nestled in one corner. At the bar a half-dozen Americans were drinking beer and "talking too loudly about guns." A clutch of men at a table in the center of the room were belting back rum. The one with a gold earring explained that all of them were Nicaraguan exiles who belonged to various factions of *la contra*. They were ready to hit the jungle trail toward Managua. "We just need to hear from The Boss that it's time to go." Who was The Boss? The man with the earring was impatient with the gringo journalist's evident naivete. "He's the man you call Mr. Ambassador."

Having established the atmosphere, *Newsweek* got down to business. The envoy in question was John Negroponte, American ambassador to Honduras. The caper he was running out of the U.S. embassy, far from being a carefully limited exercise to interdict the arms flow to Salvadoran rebels, was designed to harass and undermine the government of Nicaragua and, as far as the 4,000 troops assembled along the Honduran border were concerned, ultimately to topple the Sandinistas. Negroponte, who had been handpicked for the job by Thomas Enders, was, like his Washington superior, an old Vietnam hand and a former Henry Kissinger staff member. Helping him out were fifty CIA agents, the largest American spy assembly in Latin America. They were supplemented by dozens of operatives, various retired military and intelligence officers, and assorted Argentines.

Having watched the covert operation grow like Topsy into the invasion-sized force which the "paranoid" Nicaraguans had been complaining about for months, some slightly less cold-blooded American officials were having second thoughts. "This operation's just about out of control and people are getting panicky," one source told *Newsweek*. Said another, "This is the big fiasco of this administration. This is our Bay of Pigs," he added, referring to the disastrous CIA-sponsored bid to overthrow the Cuban government two decades earlier. Secretary of State George Shultz, who had inherited the madcap scheme from Al Haig, was said to be "fuming." But George wasn't doing it. Negroponte was.

"Negroponte is the spearhead," said a Washington insider. "He was sent down there by Haig and Enders to carry out the operation without any qualms of conscience." Since his installation in late 1981, the ambassador had acted with typical "Ugly American" imperiousness. At the inauguration of Honduran President Suazo Cordova, the first civilian president in a decade, a messenger handed the new leader a four-page letter from the U.S. embassy. In it Negroponte instructed Honduras to take a dozen specific actions, such as reducing taxes on mining and lifting some price controls. The Hondurans dutifully complied. "I'm not saying that the guy who gives all the orders here, even for covert ops, is Negroponte," said a *Newsweek* source. "But that guy wears Negroponte's suits and eats his breakfasts. Do you get the picture?"

The proconsul wearing Negroponte's suits was giving most of his orders in fall 1982 to General Gustavo Alvarez. "They discuss what should be done," explained a member of the Honduran military high command, "then Alvarez does what

Negroponte tells him to.'' Alvarez's G2 military intelligence agents were the liaisons to the *contras*, and Alvarez reported directly to Negroponte. The Honduran military was the conduit for arms shipments to the *contras*, which partially explained the rash of joint U.S.-Honduran military exercises, the most recent of which had taken place in August. The massive American buildup of Honduran military equipment freed older equipment to be funnelled to the *contras*. Throughout, Negroponte had been careful to deal with the Somocistas via intermediaries to preserve his own ''deniability,'' as it was called in the diplomatic trade. When *Newsweek* rummaged around, Negroponte denied left and right. ''No comment, no comment, and a big fat no comment,'' he told the nosy newsweekly.

Despite the elaborate chain of command to keep the ambassador ''deniable,'' direct U.S. involvement with the *contras* had inevitably escalated. When *contras*' equipment, such as helicopters and radios, broke down, Americans repaired it. Americans established the guerrillas' training regime. Soon they were treading the thin line between instructing insurgents and plotting the missions they were being trained for. Though Americans were expressly forbidden to go out on operations, one paramilitary operations veteran told *Newsweek*, ''Inevitably that happens...You lose your credibility with the people you're running if you hole up entirely.''

Meanwhile, in the minds of the *contras*, irrespective of the confused intentions of Reagan administration policy, there was *plan numero uno*: to move the *contra* camps remaining in Honduras across the border, then move the Nicaraguan bases south towards Managua, eventually surrounding the Sandinistas. And then? ''Come the counter-revolution, there will be a massacre in Nicaragua,'' promised one *contra* officer. ''We have a lot of scores to settle. There will be bodies from the border to Managua.''

According to CBS newsman George Crile, writing in the New York *Times* about a month after the *Newsweek* story, the CIA had its own *plan numero uno*. Although Crile's account was never fully confirmed, it suggested that there was some genuine madness to the methods of Alexander Haig's March 1982 propaganda offensive with its spectacular spy plane photos, and the government officials scurrying about in search of "smoking Sandinistas." Initially, said Crile, the Reagan administration had gone to great lengths to launder its Nicaraguan operation through Honduras and Argentina. In early 1982, the CIA suddenly pulled a number of its most seasoned operatives and rushed them into Honduras to direct a "quick strike" attack on Managua, which was set for the beginning of March. The plan was built around several hundred elite commandos—at least half trained by the Argentines, with a sizable contingent said to have been trained by Israel, who already had a reputation as one of Latin America's major arms suppliers. The key to the success of the scheme was support from several neighboring countries, such as El Salvador which was harboring more than a thousand former Somocista National Guardsmen in the Salvadoran army, and Guatemala, where several hundred more ex-Guardsmen were serving in the Guatemalan security police. Although the full nature and dimensions of the plan remained murky, it involved a coordinated strike.

"Certainly back in February and March," wrote Crile, "something very big and very risky was being considered." Guatemala's General Benny Lucas told Crile at the time, "For it to begin and for it succeed, there must be a green light from Washington." If Crile's account was close to the truth, then Haig's frenetic propaganda campaign against Nicaragua suddenly made sense. The Nicaraguan preparations to resist invasion also made sense, and were not, as Jeane Kirkpatrick had claimed, a paranoid case of crying wolf.

Suddenly, the rhetoric cooled. Crile didn't have that story. But, in any case, no high risk operation was launched. A month later, with the Argentines embroiled in the Falklands, the CIA had a new problem. Argentine military advisers, as well as legal and banking conduits, were integral to the covert operation. Perhaps Al Haig's desperate bid to mediate the British-Argentine conflict had more to it than the Americans' love of peaceful relations between trans-Atlantic neighbors. Once the U.S. sided with Britain, the Argentines grumpily pulled out of the Nicaraguan operation, and Ambassador Negroponte, presumably, had to squeeze the flesh of Honduran General Alvarez a little more directly. If nothing else, Crile's addenda to the *Newsweek* story suggested how much more was still unknown.

Besides having produced a bona fide journalistic scoop, the

tale *Newsweek* laid out was simply too realistic to ignore. For the preceding nine months, whenever reports of clandestine Central American operations broke in the press, administration officials steadfastly declined to comment. The devastating *Newsweek* documentary, however, put them on the defensive. The day after it appeared the administration broke its coy silence, at least long enough to try to contain the damage. True, the U.S. was supporting small-scale military operations against Nicaragua, but it was not trying to overthrow the Sandinista government. No Americans were directly involved in the operations, claimed an anonymous official mouthpiece, though the CIA was providing money, guns and training to the *contra* units. "We are not waging a secret war, or anything like that," said an administration spokesman.

More important, the not-so-secret war finally had the full attention of Congress. While President Reagan traipsed through Latin America in December 1982, stopping in Honduras (but not Nicaragua; "we are not on the imperial itinerary," junta member Sergio Ramirez drolly remarked), legislators got their teeth into the issue. The covert war was something which liberal American congressmen could understand. Unlike murky El Salvador, this was simple. There was a concept called the "rule of law," and liberals believed in it. As one liberal editorial noted, "The Neutrality Act expressly forbids the raising of secret armies to unseat a regime that the U.S. recognizes as lawful." In short, you're not supposed to make war unless you legally declare you're making war.

The man charged with the responsibility of reminding the Reagan administration of this childlike truth was a septuagenarian thirty-year veteran of the House who could often be found pedaling an exercise bicycle in the legislative gym at 6 a.m. Representative Edward Boland of Massachusetts, chairman of the House Intelligence Committee, was hardly a flaming radical. It was Boland's name, however, that was attached to an amendment passed unanimously by the House on December 9. The Boland Amendment prohibited the Pentagon and the CIA from giving weapons or training to anti-Sandinista *contras* "for the purpose of overthrowing the government of Nicaragua." Just in case President Reagan didn't get the message, Congress renewed the order two weeks later.

There was a loophole in the Boland Amendment, however, one big enough to drive an armored personnel carrier through. It had been noticed by other congressmen. In fact, Boland's proposal had been a compromise substitute for one submitted by Iowa Democrat Representative Tom Harkin, which called for a ban on any U.S. help to *contras* "for the purpose of assisting that group in carrying out military activities in or against Nicaragua."

The White House spotted it immediately. "We are complying with the law now and will continue to do so," said a cool Reagan spokesman. The administration wasn't trying to topple the Sandinistas, it was merely attempting to harass them sufficiently to interdict the alleged arms flow to El Salvador. Senate Intelligence Committee vice-chairman Daniel Moynihan admitted it was "difficult to draw the line between harassment activities and a deliberate attempt to destabilize or overthrow a government." As long as the administration retained the power to draw that line, the Boland Amendment, like the earlier certification conditions for Salvadoran aid, would remain a dead letter. Eddie Boland, a man of the "old school," according to colleagues, found it hard to believe that the Reagan administration might be that sneaky. "It's pretty plain and simple," he said. "If there was any effort to use funds for that purpose, the administration would have to justify it, and I don't know how they would."

While congressmen waited for the next set of revelations to persuade them that they'd have to do something more than declare that illegal wars were illegal, the not-so-secret war was also turning out to be a not-so-successful war. As long predicted by Managua, in early December, while Representative Boland fashioned his amendment, *contras* began daily commando raids into Nicaragua's northern border provinces. In mid-month, the first large-scale incursion of approximately a thousand *contras* penetrated Nicaraguan territory. The immediate object of the assault was to quickly secure a portion of one of the northern provinces. They would then declare the area "liberated territory," thus providing the legal basis for U.S. recognition of an anti-Sandinista provisional government, or minimally, a state of belligerency. A month later, the offensive had clearly failed, even in the most promising province of Nueva Segovia, a poor area from which the

National Guard had traditionally drawn a large number of its members, and despite the fact that the Sandinistas did not deploy seasoned veterans, but instead sent half-trained militia units into the fray.

Naturally, the characteristic American "bigger is better" approach was applied to the failure in the field. Sounding more like bank directors boasting to shareholders than like spies, the CIA congressional briefing in February 1983 reported that *contra* forces had grown to 5,500 combatants. That month, the Somocistas began an even more determined offensive, intensifying their incursions until, by late March, somewhere between 2,000 and 4,500 *contras* were engaged in a full-scale invasion, several hundred of them penetrating as far south as Matagalpa province. This time, the Sandinistas called out veteran troops, some of whom had fought and defeated the National Guard during the revolutionary war. Once again, they proved more than a match for the ex-Guardsmen who, by early April, had taken a severe beating and were in full retreat back to their Honduran havens.

The U.S. wasn't having much more success against Nicaragua in international forums than its proxies were having on the battlefield. As it had done a year ago, the Sandinista government went to the U.N. Security Council in March 1983, reporting the Honduran-based invasion and accusing the U.S. of inspiring the assault. Jeane Kirkpatrick replied that it was a "myth that Nicaragua is about to be invaded by the U.S. or Honduras or someone," and again resorted to psychiatric jargon, claiming that Nicaragua "suffers from an obsession concerning the hostility of the U.S."

This time around, however, U.N. members began to wonder if it was not the erstwhile doctor who was deranged rather than the would-be patient. The Americans soon found themselves virtually isolated in their bid to portray the Nicaraguan conflict as an internal affair. U.S. allies such as the Netherlands, Spain and Pakistan discreetly indicated that they did not accept Kirkpatrick's assessment of events. Apparently stung by the air of disbelief, the American representative lashed out at a string of countries from Mexico to China, describing them as either victims or purveyors of "systematic bias, systematic lies, systematic...distortion of key political processes." Not only was the whole world against her, but so was the American press which reported her isolation at the U.N. Not even Kirkpatrick's plaintive cry that the U.N. "enterprise more closely resembles a mugging than either a political debate or an effort at problem solving" disguised the fact that most of the world believed that the U.S. was waging covert war against Nicaragua.

That didn't mean, of course, that the Security Council was prepared to condemn the U.S. for doing so. Despite Kirkpatrick's charges that the behavior in the sedate U.N. chambers was as barbarous as that in the streets of New York, by the time the Security Council got around to fashioning a resolution in late May 1983, it was a mild-mannered document to which even the U.S. could give its assent. Produced after considerable U.S. arm-twisting of old friends and new client states, it merely reaffirmed Nicaragua's right to live in peace "free from outside interference," and urged cooperation with the Contadora Group (a reference to the peace efforts of Colombia, Mexico, Panama and Venezuela, who took their name from the Panamanian island of Contadora where the group first met in January 1983 to explore fresh approaches to the Central American dilemma). Nicaraguan Foreign Minister Reverend D'Escoto recognized that the "resolution is very minimal," but noted that it nonetheless tended to legitimize his country's claim.

Closer to home than the Nicaraguan battlefield or the U.N. bearpit, the Reagan administration was not having notably better luck. With National Security Adviser Clark and U.N. Ambassador Kirkpatrick having successfully wrested control of Central American policy from the State Department, the 1983 pre-spring offensive was underway with loud cries of "crisis." When she wasn't busy fending off Nicaraguans, Kirkpatrick winged down to Washington to lend a hand with recalcitrant legislators; the secretive Judge Clark, who was preoccupied with ditching policy man Enders, Ambassador Hinton and Salvadoran Defense Minister Garcia, occasionally found time to toddle over to Capitol Hill to put forward the administration's case. Notwithstanding the high-priced help or the cries of alarm, Congress was being stubborn and picky about the additional millions in military aid the White House wanted for Central America.

Managua also had its hands full on various fronts during spring 1983. When not dealing with the invasion from the north, it was busy with Commander Zero in the south and

Pope John Paul II behind the lines in Managua. Eden Pastora, the erratic and individualistic revolutionary hero, had quickly emerged as the most prominent of the Sandinista defectors; others included businessman and former junta member Alfonso Robelo, former Central Bank president Arturo Cruz, and Nicaraguan U.S. Ambassador Francisco Fiallos, who had recently broken with the Managua regime calling for a "dramatic change" in the direction of the Sandinista government.

Whatever merit criticisms of his former comrades might have, Pastora's strategy seemed rather utopian, if not downright pretentious. Apparently, he had hoped that his re-emergence in opposition would inspire massive upheaval in the Sandinista army so that he could come to power by means of a relatively peaceful coup. When his defection failed to bring about the collapse of the government, the CIA saw him as a major catch and moved in. However, the ex-revolutionary attempting to establish a second front from Costa Rica proved an elusive prize. In May 1983, having refused to formally ally himself with the CIA-organized Nicaraguan Democratic Front (FDN) in Honduras because of their Somocista ties and the taint of U.S. imperialism, Pastora launched his Revolutionary Democratic Alliance (ARDE) from its southern border bases. A month later, shortly after the northern *contras* attempted another offensive, Pastora temporarily pulled out, disheartened by the absence of any sign of popular support in Nicaragua, and disgruntled with the pushy CIA, whom he both needed and yet wanted to keep at arm's length. For the next year, Pastora's struggle with his would-be covert patrons would occupy as much attention as his sporadic military forays into Nicaraguan territory.

More immediately, the Sandinistas had to cope with a less temporal opponent, John Paul II. Addressing nearly half a million people in an open air mass in Managua on March 4, 1983, the traveling Pope delivered the most conservative sermon of his Central American tour. The Nicaraguan church was riven between the old-line hierarchy, led by Archbishop Miguel Obando y Bravo, increasingly hostile to the Sandinistas, and a grassroots network of "Christian base communities" that identified with the revolution. Speaking in the name of church "unity," the Pope harshly attacked the "People's Church" wing of Nicaraguan Catholicism and demanded obedience to the local church hierarchy, particularly on the part of five priests who were serving in the government, much to John Paul's displeasure.

One of the priests, internationally-known poet Reverend Ernesto Cardenal, Nicaragua's Minister of Culture, had turned up at the airport to greet the pontiff. When Cardenal dropped to his knees to kiss the papal ring, John Paul withheld his hand, and instead wagged an admonitory finger in Cardenal's face, a scene of Biblical rebuke that played on world television that night. The commentators clucked in dismay as they reported that the Pope had been repeatedly interrupted during his sermon by pro-Sandinista cries of "Popular Power!" and "We want peace!" For days afterward, editorialists deplored the sacriligious "insults" to the pontiff, ignoring, as had John Paul, the CIA-sponsored invasion of the country, and the seventeen women who were in the front row, who had buried their Sandinista sons the day before and had been hoping for a word of solace from their spiritual father, instead of a doctrinal decree.

In the midst of an increasingly complex situation, the next set of revelations about the not-so-secret war could hardly be expected to be a blockbuster on the order of the *Newsweek* disclosures. Rather, the unpeeling of this particular onion now took an incremental form, as layer after layer of detail came off.

First, in light of the deluge of press reports from the front, and the undisguisable fact that the *contra* invasion was aimed at toppling the Sandinista government, it became impossible to credibly maintain the fiction that something less malevolent was afoot. Nor was the denial of America's militaristic intentions helped by the large-scale "Big Pine" Honduran-U.S. military maneuvers that began at the beginning of February 1983. Involving 1,600 American troops, 4,000 Hondurans and an array of sophisticated armaments and communications equipment, the war games were staged within twenty-five kilometers of the Nicaraguan border. Inevitably, the media asked if the maneuvers were a dry run of a war with Nicaragua. Nor, finally, did the U.N. debate at the end of March, highlighted by Kirkpatrick's specious reasoning, reflect favorably on American motives.

By April, there were almost daily reports in the U.S. press:

some, thoughtful reflections by troubled columnists and academics inhabiting the op-ed pages; others, bits of confirmatory data from various dark repositories; none spectacular, but all widening the cracks in the covert war's cover. There was a high-ranking Honduran intelligence officer who described how the U.S. provided frequent intelligence reports to the *contras*, and underwater equipment and explosives to Argentine-trained sabotage teams. The story of how the Reagan administration worked out an arrangement with the Argentine junta of General Galtieri was leaked by an anonymous CIA source who noted, "It was convenient to run the operations through the Argentinians." Unannounced plans for the further militarization of Honduras appeared on the front page. The closest thing to an incriminating document was published in the New York *Times* on April 6. The paper had its hands on a year-old secret summary of the National Security Council meeting in April 1982 at which President Reagan decided to prevent a "proliferation of Cuba-model states" in Central America. Among other things, the meeting planned to step up covert operations in Nicaragua, approved the recent Guatemalan coup of General Rios Montt, developed a strategy to keep Mexico "isolated" on regional issues, and schemed to wheedle money out of Congress at the rate of about a billion dollars a year. Separately, none of these disclosures was devastating; together, they amounted to warmongering.

As Washington *Post* columnist Richard Cohen wrote one day in mid-April 1983, putting into words what those Americans paying attention to the mess were thinking: "We are at war." Everybody said so, noted Cohen, from *Newsweek* to the *Christian Science Monitor*. "Only the Reagan administration, coy as Machiavelli's prince, says, not really. Or it is not sure. Or it will not comment." A frustrated Cohen echoed the question in the minds of many. "Americans may ask, what in the world is going on? They will not be told, though. It is not their business. That is even the case for a member of Congress, the more studious of whom can do nothing more than read the press to find out what the government they are supposed to control is actually doing in Central America."

In fact, the more studious members of Congress began doing something more than reading the papers. For starters, they began to wonder aloud. "A growing number of my colleagues," reported Senator Daniel Moynihan at the beginning of April, "question whether the CIA is complying with the law." Republican Senate majority leader Baker said the same thing a week later. Vermont's Senator Patrick Leahy said it on the Senate floor: "If one is to believe the detailed accounts seen in the press in recent days, the administration is actively supporting" a guerrilla movement whose "undisguised aim . . . is to overthrow the present government of Nicaragua." Even the boys in the State Department anonymously voiced their concern that the operation was illegal. Representative Wyche Fowler, a normally tight-lipped member of the House Intelligence Committee, said it was illegal. So did two congressmen just back from Nicaragua. Finally, even Eddie Boland, in mid-April, said the U.S. was breaking the law that bore his name. "The evidence is very strong," he said. Others could be ignored, but not Boland. President Reagan appeared at a news conference the next day to assure all and sundry that "we are not doing anything to try and overthrow the Nicaraguan government."

The House Intelligence Committee was dubious. "We're overtly carrying on a covert operation, which is screwy," said Representative Norman Mineta. Toward the end of April, the committee was prepared to recommend cutting off funds to the *contras*, but agreed to put the vote on hold until President Reagan delivered his April 27 address to a joint session of Congress. The pitch was not persuasive. Two days later, administration officials were lobbying congressmen to head off two cut-off plans under consideration. The more moderate scheme, put forward by Boland and Wisconsin Representative Clement Zablocki, would ban CIA financing for military operations "in or against Nicaragua," but would provide aid to friendly Central American countries, like Honduras, attempting to stop arms shipments through its territory. A more sweeping measure, moved by Representative Michael Barnes, would block all covert operations against Nicaragua. In the end, the Boland-Zablocki measure won out in the intelligence committee. However, its effect promised to be more symbolic than real, since the restriction was attached to a bill which the president was expected to veto. Nonetheless, for the administration it was a political setback sufficient to flush the president out of the foliage.

Abandoning his previous policy of coy non-denials, Reagan called the *contras* "freedom fighters." If Congress was feeling pangs of conscience about being sneaky, well, then they ought to come out of the closet. "If they want to tell us that we can give money, and do the same things we've been doing—money, giving, providing assistance and so forth to these people directly—and making it overt instead of covert, that's all right with me," said the president. Despite this new-found openness, Reagan knew he hadn't lost the congressional battle yet; there was still the Republican-dominated Senate. By mid-May, the Senate Intelligence Committee had approved another $19 million for covert aid, while the House Foreign Relations Committee was bogged down on whether to have a secret or open debate on the issue.

It was unclear whether they actually believed it or were trying to provide an enticement to congressmen, but CIA director Casey and the State Department's Enders (who was just about to be bounced) reportedly predicted to House members that the *contras* would overthrow the Sandinista government by the end of the year. "They were telling us that, in effect, if we cut off assistance to the rebels now we would be responsible for aborting a great chance to reverse communist gains in Central America," said one intelligence committee member. Casey then furiously and flatly denied that he had predicted anything. The media went back to its sources in the face of the denial and confirmed the story. There was no doubt, however, that a variety of administration officials were claiming that the *contras*, now up to 8,000 troop strength, were growing stronger by the day.

Nevertheless, in early June, a second House committee, the one on foreign affairs, also voted to ban covert aid to the *contras*. The administration was now troubled by the prospect of the issue being debated before the entire House. While a House vote might not have much practical effect, it wouldn't look good, and as White House spokesman Larry Speakes admitted in late June, public support for Central American aid was slipping due to the "negative drumbeat" of critics and the media. While Security Adviser Clark and Ambassador Kirkpatrick worked on a more ambitious scheme to rescue Central American policy, one that Kirkpatrick had long urged, White House negotiators met with legislators through early and mid-July in a bid to find a compromise that would keep the *contras* in the field.

President Reagan revealed the Kirkpatrick plan on July 18. Enough of this partisan debate in Congress over niggling amounts of money, he seemed to be saying. What's needed is bipartisan policy. To that end, Henry Kissinger would head a blue-ribbon bipartisan commission to come up with one. In the meantime, hinted Reagan, Congress ought to fork over the money to keep present policies afloat. It might have worked.

However, the same day as the supposedly soothing Kissinger Commission was announced, the media also revealed that the Reagan administration was about to launch two massive naval, air and ground military exercises to show Cuba and Nicaragua who was in charge. Some enthusiasts were even talking about a possible "quarantine," an overt act of war. Another official admitted, "Some might call it gunboat diplomacy."

Indeed, forty-eight hours later, as an eight-ship aircraft carrier battle group armada steamed toward the Pacific coast of Central America, that's exactly what it was being called. By contrast, the Nicaraguans, who were marking the fourth anniversary of their revolution on July 19, 1983, proposed a six-point regional peace plan that was so clearly conciliatory that even the State Department had to grudgingly call it a "positive step."

Later, Bill Clark would be blamed for the fiasco. The ill-timed revelation of the unprecedented six-month-long exercise off both coasts of Nicaragua, involving nineteen American ships and up to 4,000 troops, was not only a surprise to the public, which immediately perceived it as a sabre-rattling sign the administration was pushing for a military solution, but also a shock to Congress. The National Security Council and the Defense Department, as *Time* magazine's autopsy put it, had "shortsightedly failed to brief key congressional leaders about the planned military maneuvers beforehand, then compounded their error by not getting out their side of the story" once it was leaked. The further revelation that CIA director Casey not only wanted to continue *contra* aid, but wanted to double it in fiscal 1984, came on the eve of the full House debate on cutting off aid to the *contras*. It was one more sign that the Clark-run policymaking team was a crew of bumblers.

The scene on the floor of the House of Representatives on

July 28 was just this side of pandemonium. Democrats whooped, whistled and stamped their feet as the vote tallies on the Boland-Zablocki bill went up on the electronic scoreboard. The count was 228 to 195 to cut off covert aid to the counter-revolutionaries. Since the Senate was unlikely to approve a similar bill, the vote would not stop the *contras'* campaign, but nonetheless it was a major rebuke to the administration.

The next day, the White House said it would continue to fund the *contras*. "It requires no modification in our plans," a National Security Council official snapped. For the moment, he was no doubt correct.

Once and for all, the nasty little secret of the not-so-secret war was out in the open. However, it would take a surprisingly long time before the people elected to control the government would actually be able to do so. More worrisome, though, was whether anyone out there in middle America knew or cared about what was going on in distant Nicaragua and its neighboring countries. A July 1983 poll revealed that 52 percent of the populace knew either "very little" or "nothing" about the situation in Central America (only 6 percent reported themselves well informed; another 42 percent had seen it on the news but weren't sure what it meant). It was distressingly possible that not even the inevitable revelation of additional nasty little secrets would shake the Americans from their implacable ignorance.

8 The Last Marine

*We are no more bandits than was
Washington. If the American public
had not become calloused to justice...
it would not so easily forget its own
past when a handful of ragged soldiers
marched through the snow leaving
blood-tracks behind them to win liberty
and independence.*
—Augusto Sandino, February 1928

Carleton Beals, the young American reporter from *The
Nation* who had come to Nicaragua to find Augusto Sandino,
was feverish with flu as he waited for the horses in Danli, a
Honduran border town, on a stormy night in January 1928.
Somewhere on the other side of the Rio Coco was the man the
U.S. government called a "bandit" and whom his compatriots
referred to as the "general of free men." Whoever he was, he
was at the moment successfully holding off 4,000 U.S.
Marines. The rain came down and Beals shivered.

That evening, unobserved except by barking dogs, three
men on horseback clattered out of the small town in the
frontier coffee-growing region under a driving storm. They
rode up over the ridge, flashlights in hand, and down into a
slot of valley. The rain pounded the oilskins covering their
khaki riding habits, and the water ran down inside their
leggings to their chilled feet. At about eleven the rain
slackened and they paused for a slug of whiskey. A half hour
later a sliver of moon was following them over their left
shoulders. It made the *Yanqui* journalist think of a tawny
mountain cat, stalking them through the tangled branches and
clouds. At midnight, the wind came up and the rain began

again. If Americans didn't know about Nicaragua, it wouldn't be for lack of trying on the part of Carleton Beals.

Ten days later, the foreign correspondent was in San Rafael del Norte, Sandino's current headquarters, a small town of adobe walls and red tiles in Jinotega province on the high flank of the Yali Range. After too few hours of sleep, the blast of the bugler brought Beals awake, fumbling for matches and shoes, at the grim hour of 4 a.m. Thirty minutes later, Sandino received him. The general was a small man, not more than five foot five, dressed in a uniform of dark brown with a silk red-and-black handkerchief knotted about his throat and a broad-brimmed Stetson hat pulled low over his forehead.

After describing the American aerial bombing of El Chipote, the mountain redoubt in neighboring Nueva Segovia province from which he had recently withdrawn, Sandino quickly listed the demands which were the goals of his present struggle: first, the evacuation of Nicaraguan territory by U.S. forces; second, the appointment of an impartial civilian president who had never held office; third, supervision of free elections by Latin America. "The day these conditions are carried out," declared Sandino, "I will immediately cease all hostilities and disband my forces. In addition, I shall never accept a government position, elective or otherwise." He left his chair and paced back and forth, emphasizing this point. "Never, never will I accept public office. I am fully capable of gaining a livelihood for myself and my wife. By trade I am a mechanic and if necessary I will return to my trade," said the 35-year-old rebel leader. "We have taken up arms because all other leaders have sold themselves out. We, in our house, are fighting for our inalienable rights. What right have foreign troops to call us outlaws and bandits and to say that we are the aggressors? I repeat that we are in our own house."

Scribbling notes rapidly, Beals was taken with Sandino's fluid, precise, evenly modulated utterance. Not once during the four-and-half-hour interview, as dawn came up in San Rafael, did the rebel leader dodge an issue or hesitate in the presentation of his almost epigrammatically ordered ideas.

"Our one aim is to throw out the foreign invader," Sandino said.

"But since you are not strong enough to do so, does not opposition merely result in the sending of more and more marines, the intensification of intervention?" queried Beals, asking questions that American reporters would echo for the next half century and more.

"We are not protesting against the size of the invasion, but against invasion," Sandino subtly replied. "The U.S. has meddled in Nicaragua for many years. You tell me that the governments of Honduras and El Salvador are hostile to me. Tomorrow they will regret such an attitude. All of Central America is morally obliged to help us in this struggle. Tomorrow each may have the same struggle."

Sandino's mention of neighboring countries prompted Beals to ask about a well-known rumor, one that would be perpetuated to Alexander Haig's day. "Is it true, as has been charged, that most of your army is made up of adventurers from other Central American countries and from Mexico?"

"Quite the contrary. It is true, I have with me men and officers from Costa Rica, Guatemala, El Salvador, Honduras, even one or two from Mexico, but they are in a decided minority. The backbone of my army is Nicaraguan. What we have done has been through our own unaided efforts."

"How about the story," Beals put in, "that two captured American marines taught you how to make bombs?"

"It is comforting to the American ego to think that we were taught what we know by the marines," Sandino said coolly, and then turning to an aide, ordered, "Call in our bomb maker."

An elderly, sparse, smiling man soon appeared, who explained his methods to Beals. A heavy bomb, wrapped in rawhide, was placed in the reporter's hand as the bomb maker described the technique of making dynamite rockets to bring down airplanes.

"What do you consider the motives of the American government?" Beals asked Sandino later.

"The American government desires to 'protect American lives and property,'" Sandino answered with a lurking smile as he ironically quoted the official pretext for intervention. "The truth of the matter is that the American government has made so many arrangements of not too savory a character with the regime now in power that it is afraid of any other government. But if I had been in the shoes of the American government I would have retraced my steps rather than drown a nation in blood."

It was morning in San Rafael. Sandino had been trapped

and surrounded by marines at his mountain fastness, yet he had melted through their lines, leaving them with a piece of rock while his forces marched across coffee *fincas*. Now he would head south. The Americans would not give up their pursuit for another five years.

"Let me repeat," said the Nicaraguan general, "we are no more bandits than was Washington. If the American public had not become calloused to justice and to the elemental rights of mankind, it would not so easily forget its own past when a handful of ragged soldiers marched through the snow leaving blood-tracks behind them to win liberty and independence. If their consciences had not become dulled by their scramble for wealth, Americans would not so easily forget the lesson that, sooner or later, every nation, however weak, achieves freedom, and that every abuse of power hastens the destruction of the one who wields it."

As Beals was leaving, Sandino had a question of his own. "Do you still think us bandits?"

"You are as much a bandit as Mr. Coolidge is a bolshevik," Beals replied, and then set off to Managua to cable the dispatches of the first American correspondent to find Sandino.

Just over a half century after Carleton Beals filed his scoop, on Wednesday, June 20, 1979, another American journalist, ABC correspondent Bill Stewart, crouched in front of a half-dozen Nicaraguan National Guardsmen who were manning a neighborhood checkpoint in Managua. Cameraman Jack Clark, before focussing in on the 37-year-old U.S. reporter, had panned across the almost-bucolic morning scene, lingering on homely details and pausing to record the youthful faces of the government troops.

The guardsmen seemed friendly. One of the soldiers strummed a guitar while the others toyed with their equipment in the hazy sunshine. Stewart, in white pants and short-sleeved blue sportshirt, crouched in front of the soldiers so that they could be attractively framed behind him, and he delivered one of those encomiums about mortality which, after the day's footage was edited, was often used to wrap up a TV dispatch from a distant war. "It is said that in every society," Stewart intoned, "it is the young men who fight the old men's wars, and that is especially true here in Nicaragua, for those who are fighting and dying on both sides are very young indeed." It was a routine sentiment that had been expressed often enough before, naively apportioning responsibility for the carnage in indiscriminate fashion.

That evening, newsman Stewart appeared on the thirty million or so U.S. television screens tuned to the six o'clock news. But this report was different from the usual minute-and-a-half account of seemingly random gunfire or the piteous vignettes of those made homeless by war; for the past three weeks, these had detailed the latest phase in the disintegration of the dictatorial regime of Anastasio Somoza. Nor was this your typical war item, homogeneously sandwiched in between stories which viewers could placidly consume before sitting down to dinner.

The screen showed Stewart among the friendly guardsmen while the voice-over of Al Dale, another ABC correspondent in Managua, explained that the news team had set off that morning to check out reports of deteriorating morale among Somoza's troops. The scene shifted. At first, it was hard for the viewer to make out. Stewart and his crew—cameraman Clark, a soundman, an interpreter and a driver—had moved on. The news van stopped about a dozen meters from another National Guard outpost at the end of a dirt street in the working class neighborhood of Barrio Riguero. Though the vehicle was clearly marked with "Foreign Press" signs, the reporter decided it was best to approach on foot. In one hand, Stewart carried his government-issue press pass; in the other, he held a small white flag. From the back of the van, cameraman Clark began filming. Stewart's interpreter walked several meters ahead, explaining that they meant no harm.

One of the soldiers raised his rifle, and Stewart dropped to his knees. "At the next checkpoint the attitude of the guards was very different," Dale narrated, as one could make out the kneeling figure of Stewart, hands raised, at the end of the road. The guardsman approached the reporter and motioned him to lie face down, and when he did, kicked Stewart sharply in the side. The soldier then ordered Stewart to put his arms behind his head and as he did so, the guardsman stepped back a few paces, calmly took aim, and shot the correspondent in the head.

The body bucked, rose, and then crumpled back into the street. Out of sight, a similar brutal fate was being meted out to Stewart's translator. The camera eye, which had gazed fixedly at the cold-blooded slaying, now went fuzzy and then blank. In the incalculable arithmetic of atrocity, Stewart's demise was only a small addition to the astronomical death toll that had been incurred in Nicaragua's civil war. Yet, however inadequately, for a few days at least, the magnitude of death in Nicaragua became starkly real to ordinary Americans.

Between these two journalistic events that briefly brought Nicaragua to American attention, the country was ruled for half a century by the Somoza family dictatorship. Both before and, for the most part, after these moments of reportorial illumination, the Central American country of 2.5 million people receded into a sort of pre-history on one side, and political mystification on the other.

Nicaragua's recorded history began with the conquest by Cortez' lieutenants in 1523. Bartolome de las Casas' angry history of the destruction of the Indians (written in 1542) observed that the original inhabitants of Nicaragua "suffered as much as possible the tyranny and bondage which the Christians imposed upon them. This tyrant and his companions subjected this people to so much evil, butchery, cruelty, bondage and injustice that no human tongue would be able to describe it. . . The Spanish kill more everyday through the services they exact and the daily, personal oppression they exercise."

The services exacted by the Spanish-descended oligarchy in their *haciendas* during the three centuries that Nicaragua was a colony took the form of forced labor to produce the wood, dried meat, tallow, leather, cocoa and dyestuffs which were exported to the motherland. At the top of the social hierarchy, royal functionaries levied tribute for the crown; at the next level, a provincial aristocracy ruled over huge landed estates, fiercely exploiting the Indian work force; at the base of society, Indian communities on their collective lands struggled to maintain an existence rooted in subsistence farming.

Before Sandino, the modern political history of Nicaragua, beginning with independence in 1821, was one long, violent, unrelenting fued between two regionally based clans. Throughout the nineteenth century and the early part of the twentieth, endemic warfare pitted the "conservatives" of

Grenada, traditional latifundists engaged in cattle raising and regional merchandising, against the modernizing "liberals" of Leon.

Perhaps, though, it would be more accurate to say that modern Nicaraguan political history began in Washington in 1823. That's when U.S. President James Monroe declared that interference by any European power in the newly emerging Latin American republics would be regarded as an unfriendly act toward the United States. The Monroe Doctrine, as this policy of hemispheric imperialism became known, established the right of the U.S. to protect Latin America. Nicaragua, as much as any nation within this "sphere of influence," would be a paradigm of the multiple forms this "protection" would take.

To the defensive paternalism of the Monroe Doctrine was added an aggressive expansionism, rationalized in the politico-theological notion of "manifest destiny," which held that the territorial enlargement of the U.S. was ordained by higher powers. The Mexican-American war of the mid-1840s, deliberately provoked by the U.S., and ultimately costing Mexico nearly half of its territory (Texas, New Mexico and California), was an early expression of this jingoist ideology.

Nicaragua became a focus of American commercial interest as a strategic transportation route during the 1850s when the California gold rush gripped the U.S. Cornelius Vanderbilt's enormously profitable Accessory Transit Company offered the cheapest and quickest passage from the American east coast to fabled California. The route made use of Nicaraguan waterways, transporting as many as 2,000 fortune-seeking migrants each month at $35 a head. Already by 1850, the dream of an inter-ocean waterway across the Central American isthmus had led the U.S. and Britain to divvy up canal rights through Nicaragua in the Clayton-Bulwer Treaty.

The first American troops came as mercenaries, brought in by the feuding Nicaraguan ruling class itself. The political instability caused by the struggle between Liberal and Conservative oligarchs slowly degenerated into a civil war in which both sides were prepared to seek rescue by foreign governmental and private powers. It was the Liberals, defeated in the field, who called on an American adventurer named William Walker. Financed by Accessory Transit, which was eager to secure its hold on the inter-ocean transportation business, Walker raised an American phalanx and in short order took the Conservative capital of Granada in 1855.

Neither the Nicaraguan oligarchs nor the American businessmen anticipated Walker's own ambitions. A southerner and supporter of slavery in the period just before the American Civil War, Walker's megalomaniac dream was to weld the isthmus states into a single white republic that would bolster the claim of U.S. secessionists. He duly had himself elected president of Nicaragua, declared English the official language, reintroduced slavery, and handed over the property of "enemies of the republic" to favored "naturalized Nicaraguans." Although this parody of a government was recognized by U.S. President Franklin Pierce with indecent haste, sundry Central American oligarchs, Accessory Transit, and the British (who still held a chunk of Atlantic coast real estate) became alarmed. An army was raised and Walker ousted in 1857. Four years later, the American privateer made a second Central American incursion; this time he was captured by the British, turned over to the Hondurans and dispatched by firing squad. In the backlash to this bizarre episode, the Conservatives assumed the reins of government for the next three decades.

During the latter half of the nineteenth century, Nicaragua, like other Central American countries, was swept into the world capitalist market as a coffee producer. Given the relations of production necessary to cultivate the labor-intensive crop in Nicaragua, as elsewhere, legislation was promulgated to create a landless peasantry which would be prepared to work on the coffee owners' terms. The most reactionary of such laws, dispossessing Indian communities of their holdings, unleashed a native uprising in 1881 that was ferociously quelled.

By 1893, the rising plantation bourgeoisie had consolidated its power to the extent that it was able to install its own head of state, Liberal General Jose Zelaya, whose sixteen-year dictatorship embarked upon an authoritarian modernization of the country. While a new battery of legislation simply furthered the process of land expropriation and labor discipline, the economic and state infrastructure underwent considerable development, from electrification to the growth of a more sophisticated administrative apparatus. Zelaya ran into trouble, however, when nationalism collided with North American imperialism.

Just as the close of the nineteenth century saw a renewed European surge of imperialism in the scramble for spoils that carved up Africa, in the Western hemisphere the U.S. confidently extended its regional domination. The Spanish-American war of 1898 brought U.S. troops to Cuba for four years; Puerto Rico became an American possession in 1901; Marines landed in Honduras in 1905; and the U.S. government was deeply involved in Panamanian machinations throughout the first decade of the century as the developer of an inter-ocean canal. This combination of the vigorous pursuit of national self-interest and paternalistic racism toward "backward" peoples incapable of providing "stable" government for themselves, found justificatory expression in President Teddy Roosevelt's 1904 Corollary to the Monroe Doctrine. "Chronic wrongdoing or an impotence which results in a general loosening of the ties of civilized society," declared Roosevelt, "may in America, as elsewhere, require intervention by some civilized nation, and in the Western hemisphere the adherance of the United States to the Monroe Doctrine may force the U.S., however reluctantly, in flagrant cases of such wrongdoing or impotence, to the exercise of an international police power." Thus, in addition to protecting Latin America from European colonialists, the U.S. now proposed to protect its hemispheric neighbors from themselves.

Meanwhile, in Nicaragua, incipient nationalism was the natural ideological concomitant of solidifying class power among the agro-export sector. Under Zelaya, the Atlantic coast region came under government control, at last creating a unified national territory. In financing public investment and expenditure, the increasingly independent-minded ruling class sought to strengthen its autonomy by diversifying its foreign credit burden. When Zelaya bypassed New York financiers to contract a major loan with a British banking syndicate, relations between Washington and Managua soured. The U.S. decision to locate a canal in Panama led Zelaya to seek other partners for a rival canal, a threat the Americans were not prepared to tolerate.

When a Conservative revolt was launched against the central government in 1909, the Roosevelt Corollary, "however reluctantly," was invoked. Although the insurrection was led by Conservative politician Juan Estrada, he was advised and financed by Adolfo Diaz, an employee of the Luz and Los Angeles Mining Company, which had recently suffered the indignity of dictator Zelaya's attempt to cancel the company's concession. U.S. Secretary of State Philander Knox, who happened to be the mining firm's legal counsel (a situation that foreshadowed the involvement of the Dulles brothers with United Fruit in Guatemala), broke off diplomatic relations with Nicaragua and gave unreserved support to the rebels. When the revolt sputtered, the first U.S. Marines landed in Nicaragua, saving the beleaguered rebels and carrying Estrada to power. The bill for this rescue operation was delivered by Thomas Dawson, U.S. envoy to Panama, who arrived by U.S. warship at Bluefields on the Atlantic coast. The Dawson Pacts, signed by Estrada, placed the country under de facto U.S. administration, as Nicaragua's customs department, post office, national banks, mines, railways and harbors were put in the hands of its New York creditor banks, W. Seligman and Brown Brothers.

Within three years, the U.S. guardianship provoked a Liberal-led national uprising. Once again, in autumn 1912, a contingent of 2,700 U.S. Marines landed in Nicaragua at the request of strongman Diaz. The revolt was crushed, Estrada was eased out, Diaz' role was legitimized in ersatz elections, and a permanent force of Marines was stationed in the country. As for the small detail of Nicaragua's desire for an inter-ocean canal, the matter was settled in 1914 by the Bryan-Chamorro Treaty, which stipulated that for $3 million, the areas required for the construction of a second canal would be ceded to the U.S. if it decided to proceed (which it had no intention of doing). The sale was ratified by the Nicaraguan Congress while it was surrounded by U.S. Marines and the terms of the sale were read to the Congressmen in English.

After fifteen years of occupation, the U.S. withdrew its troops in 1925, apparently considering Nicaragua sufficiently pacified. A U.S.-trained National Guard was to be put in their place and a deal was arranged between the eternally squabbling oligarchic factions in which a U.S.-supervised election would produce a Conservative president and a Liberal vice-president. The American architects of this solution, however, failed to attend to the distinctions between the right and the far right. Two months after the Marines left,

Conservative General Emiliano Chamorro seized power in a coup d'etat, deposed the Conservative president and drove the Liberals from office. The Marines were turned around, and again disembarked at Nicaraguan ports to reinstate the trusted Adolfo Diaz in office once more. However, the ousted Liberal vice-president, Juan Sacasa, established a government of his own on the Atlantic coast. His troops, commanded by General Jose Moncada, scored a number of swift victories, despite the arrival of additional Marines. The Americans decided that buying out the rebels was cheaper than fighting them. Special envoy Henry Stimson negotiated a deal with Moncada designed to restore peace and eventually make the general Nicaragua's next president. In May 1927, all the Liberal officers accepted the terms of the Stimson-Moncada agreement.

All except one. Augusto Sandino said, "I consider Moncada to be not only a deserter, but a traitor," as he took to the hills with 400 followers to fight the invaders.

The Republican president in the White House appeared before a joint session of the U.S. Congress to address the legislators on the Central American crisis. In words that would be eerily familiar to contemporary Americans if anmesia had not supplanted history, Calvin Coolidge said, "I have the most conclusive evidence that arms and munitions in large quantities have been shipped to the revolutionists...The United States cannot fail to view with deep concern any serious threat to stability and constitutional government... tending toward anarchy and jeopardizing American interests, especially if such a state of affairs is contributed to or brought about by outside influence or by a foreign power." The only minor difference between Coolidge's oration and the speech Ronald Reagan would make more than half a century later was that the alleged "outside influence" in 1927 wasn't the Soviet Union, but the Bolshevik-inspired Mexicans.

On the inaccessible mountain peak of El Chipote, wreathed in cloud and surrounded by ravines, Sandino built a complex of palm-thatched quarters, corrals for horses and munitions workshops. From there, he launched his military operations, the first of which was an assault on the northern garrison of Ocotal in July 1927. After an all-day seige against the bottled up National Guardsmen, the Americans called in air support, not only bombing Sandino's troops, but reducing much of Ocotal to rubble. As the guerrillas extended their control of the north, massive air strikes pounded El Chipote, which was surrounded by the Marines. But when the U.S. forces reached the summit, they did not encounter a trapped Sandino but only a ring of straw dummies wearing the red and black neckerchiefs of the Army in Defense of Nicaraguan Sovereignty (EDSN). By then, Sandino was in San Rafael, where the intrepid Beals found him in February 1928.

Although it became conventional for Americans in the 1980s to wonder aloud whether deepening U.S. involvement in Central America was turning into "another Vietnam," it might be equally pertinent to describe the 1927-33 war that pitted 4,000 U.S. Marines against Sandino's guerrilla columns as America's "first Vietnam." Much of what came to be standard counterinsurgency strategy in Southeast Asia three decades later was first developed in the rugged terrain of northern Nicaragua in the late 1920s.

Certainly, the rhetoric invoked by President Coolidge established the basic pattern of American propaganda, complete with distortions and dubious claims, that would subsequently be applied both to Guatemala in the 1950s and Vietnam in the 1960s: an allegedly independent nation was under threat by an international communist conspiracy (in the Nicaraguan case, Mexico was assigned the role of "outside influence" and arms supplier) which endangered both the subject nation's yearning for democracy and U.S. security interests.

As in Vietnam years later, enormous destruction was wrought on a small country by sophisticated military technology. The aerial bombing of civilian populations by the latest Curtiss aircraft predated its more publicized use in the Spanish Civil War of the mid-1930s. There was an effort to "Nicaraguanize" the war by developing the capacity of the National Guard. Similarly, the rural pacification strategy used in Vietnam was foreshadowed by a Nicaraguan program to create what were later called "strategic hamlets": forced evacuations of peasants were widespread in the provinces of Nueva Segovia and Jinotega where Sandino enjoyed massive support. During the six years of guerrilla war, farms were burned down, crops destroyed, and peasants relocated into what were essentially concentration camps while the Marines created "free fire zones" as they were eventually known in Asia.

With Sandino, a new political force, and heretofore invisible social classes, hostile to both factions of the Nicaraguan oligarchy, made their appearance on the Nicaraguan historical stage. Sandinism was primarily a nationalist ideology, tinged with utopian socialist and spiritual notions, which grew increasingly radical in the course of the six-year war. Forced by the respective strengths of the opposing armies and by the imbalance of technologies to abandon the conventional tactics of a regular army, Sandino invented a new kind of warfare, one that was simultaneously being developed halfway across the world by another rebel leader, Mao Tse-tung in China. Thoroughly reliant on the support of the local population, the Nicaraguan guerrillas could hardly avoid taking up the central social questions of the country's life.

At the height of the war, in 1932, the year Farabundo Marti and his comrades were being slaughtered in the Salvadoran *matanza*, the zone of Sandino's guerrilla operations covered ten of Nicaragua's sixteen provinces. Though Sandino was no political theorist, within the "liberated zones," as such territory would be known in later guerrilla wars, the rough model of a provisional government took shape: at its heart was a land reform program that encouraged agricultural cooperatives; in addition, Sandino's state-within-a-state conducted basic literacy classes for peasants and soldiers, minted its own currency from local gold mines, established tax collection procedures, and ran an independent communications network with telephone and radio equipment captured from American troops.

A final parallel between America's six years in Nicaragua and the later Vietnamese quagmire was the development of a powerful anti-war movement in the U.S. Opposition to intervention took various forms: hostility from the public to the cost of defending Wall Street's interests in the midst of the capitalist Depression; antagonism to the pointless loss of the lives of American "boys"; the work of journalists like Carleton Beals; and ultimately, open conflict within the U.S. Congress. One indicator of the extent of popular sentiment was the decision of the 1928 Democratic party to include a plank in its election platform opposing intervention in

Nicaragua (a position that would be echoed fifty-six years later by the same party facing the same issue in 1984). As Montana Senator Burton Wheeler summed up the dubious morality of the American role: "Reduced to its simplest terms, the Coolidge policy has led to armed intervention on behalf of an American-made puppet president foisted upon the people against their own will for the simple reason that he is ready to serve the New York bankers who are mercilessly exploiting Nicaragua under the aegis of the State Department."

It was a war America was not winning. By 1930, Washington began looking for a way out. The following year, the State Department opted for a plan—one that would be seen again in Vietnam—to completely withdraw the Marines and Nicaraguanize the conflict. To preserve an image of "peace with honor," as a similar strategy was described in Vietnam, the retreat was arranged to take place in the wake of the 1932 Nicaraguan presidential elections in which former Liberal rebel Juan Sacasa inherited the figurehead post. On January 1, 1933, the month of Franklin Delano Roosevelt's inauguration in the U.S., American forces withdrew, having appointed Anastasio "Tacho" Somoza, a Liberal general who had succeeded in ingratiating himself with the U.S. ambassador, to head the Nicaraguan National Guard. A month later Sandino, as promised, accepted a ceasefire and the disarmament of his intact and undefeated army. He withdrew to the peasant cooperatives in the Rio Coco region, fulfilling the pledge reported by Beals that he would not seek the spoils of public office.

The political ambitions of National Guard chief Somoza soon provided justifiable cause for alarm to President Sacasa, who increasingly had to rely on the mere presence of Sandino as a possible counterweight to the resumption of dictatorship. Somoza also regarded the revered peasant leader as a key to the political situation. Throughout 1933, Somoza's Guard continually harrassed the Rio Coco cooperatives. Three times Sandino traveled to Managua for talks with the Sacasa administration, denouncing the National Guard as an unconstitutional force. On February 21, 1934, Somoza arranged for Sandino to attend a banquet at the presidential palace. That day, the National Guard director held a series of meetings with recently appointed U.S. Ambassador Arthur Lane, who was undoubtedly complicit in what followed. That night, as the guerrilla leader and his colleagues were leaving the dinner, they were ambushed by a Guard patrol and summarily executed. The next day, Somoza's forces attacked Sandino's base camp in the north, killing 300 Sandinistas. A terrorist "Pacification of Las Segovias" campaign continued for the next three years, wiping out the fragile agricultural community and destroying every remnant of possible guerrilla resistance.

The founder of the family dynasty that would rule Nicaragua for the next four and a half decades was a man of dubious but perhaps appropriate talents. Educated at a Philadelphia business school, he became an unsuccessful automobile dealer in Nicaragua, followed by a brief stint as a health officer for the Rockefeller Foundation, and a shadowy career as a counterfeiter that would have landed him in jail but for the influence of the Sacasa family to which he was related by marriage. Intuitively obsequious to the American plenipotentiaries, he rose to power during the war against Sandino. By the mid-1930s, as Sacasa's term wound down, Anastasio Somoza was positioned to carry out a legal coup in the form of presidential elections. With the National Guard counting the vote, the 40-year-old Tacho began his reign.

The former counterfeiting suspect was now in charge of the treasury and all other lootable agencies of the state. Behind the guns of the National Guard he bought *haciendas* from political opponents at cut-rate prices. The country's public works program consisted of improving his properties and building roads to them. Within three years of assuming office, his fortune amounted to $3 million, a sizeable sum in the midst of the Depression. In 1939, Somoza revised the constitution to permit himself to serve a second term of eight years. One of the highlights of the renewal of his dictatorship was the receipt of a long-sought invitation for an official Washington visit. He was delighted by the elaborate ceremonials with which he was greeted, not knowing that he was being used as a stand-in in a rehearsal for the visit of King George VI later that year. It was after that ego-gratifying reception that Roosevelt, questioned about his cordiality to Somoza, was said to have remarked, "He may be a son of a bitch, but he's *our* son of a bitch." And a loyal one at that.

Nicaragua declared war on the Axis powers two days after

the U.S., which had the fiscal advantage of permitting Somoza to seize ranches owned by German citizens. During World War II, the U.S. established a couple of bases on the territory of its Central American ally and re-armed the National Guard. Somoza's younger son, also named Anastasio, was enrolled in West Point, while his eldest son, Luis, attended university in Lousiana.

Though Somoza was more than willing to extend his tenure to a third consecutive term, pressure from the American embassy in the post war years required the installation of a puppet successor, an elderly uncle. While Costa Rica and Guatemala were transforming themselves into liberal democracies, and even El Salvador was experiencing a moment of possible opening, the Nicaraguan dictator continued to amass his fortune. His financial empire, estimated to be worth more than $100 million by the mid-1950s, ranged from *haciendas* totaling hundreds of thousands of acres to an at-last-successful chain of automobile agencies. Having reoccupied the presidential palace in 1949, Somoza announced in 1956 that he would seek an additional term. In Leon, the traditional center of Liberal party strength, the dictator's two-decade reign came to a violent, sudden end when a young poet and revolutionary, Rigoberto Lopez, pulled out a revolver and emptied it into Anastasio I.

The presidency was inherited by the late dictator's eldest son, Luis Somoza, while command of the National Guard went to his namesake, Anastasio Jr. It was during Luis' term of office that the Cuban Revolution of 1959 occurred, led by Fidel Castro. The reverberations were considerable, inspiring Pedro Joaquin Chamorro, editor and publisher of *La Prensa*, Nicaragua's only independent newspaper, to launch an insurrection from Costa Rica which was quickly put down. When U.S. opposition to Cuba advanced beyond the talking stage, the ever-loyal Somoza dictatorship was only too willing to have Nicaragua used as a major staging area for the CIA-sponsored Bay of Pigs invasion in 1961. Its farcical failure nonetheless had the consequence of bolstering Nicaragua's position in Washington's eyes as a frontline of defense against communism. In accordance with the desire to maintain a semblance of constitutionalism during the period of U.S. President John Kennedy's "Alliance for Progress," Luis Somoza did not seek a second term in office; instead, an old family retainer was elevated to the post in 1963.

At about the same time, three young men announced the formation of the Sandinista National Liberation Front (FSLN). They were Carlos Fonseca, 26, Silvio Mayorga, 25, and 30-year-old Tomas Borge, whose father had fought with Sandino. They met in the late 1950s at the University of Leon law faculty where they began to fashion an ideological synthesis of Sandinism and Marxism. "We identify with socialism, while retaining a critical attitude to the socialist experiences," is the way Fonseca, the prime theorist of the trio, described the heterodox beliefs the fledgling guerrillas thought applicable to the Nicaraguan situation. Strategically, they took their inspiration from the *foco* tactics of small armed bands as practised by Castro in Cuba. In 1963, with no political preparation of the populace, no help from other social institutions (the church was still in its preliberationist phase), and no way to effectively communicate its message to the public, a first, unsuccessful guerrilla operation was started and quickly dispersed in the Coco River region.

In 1967, the year of Luis Somoza's fatal heart attack, his younger brother, Anastasio II, acquired the presidency and undivided power in Nicaragua. He was a popular choice in Washington. His West Point background, his cooperation during the Bay of Pigs venture, his preference for speaking English, and his loud devotion to all things American (a style sardonically characterized by poet Ernesto Cardenal as "Miami kitsch") made him a welcome guest at the Pentagon and at U.S. Southern Command headquarters in Panama. He had several American congressmen at his disposal and was favorably regarded in the White House, having financially contributed to Lyndon Johnson's presidential campaigns, and then further obliged the Texas Democrat by sending a battalion of the National Guard to complement the U.S. Marine invasion of the Dominican Republic in 1965; nor was he any less welcome to Johnson's successor, Richard Nixon, to whose campaign Somoza reportedly contributed a million dollars. Not only did the new dictator display the family trait of insatiable greed (adding to the dynasty's holdings a fishing and seafood processing business, export-import ventures, warehousing establishments, monopolies in cement and structural steel, and a vast expansion of the family cattle ranching business), but he was also able to quickly boast that the last of the Sandinistas had been wiped out near the Indian village of Pancasan, where twenty guerrillas, including FSLN founder Silvio Mayorga, were killed in a three-day battle.

Yet behind the facade of seeming eternality exuded by the Somoza dictatorship, a set of economic-political conditions was developing that would provide the basis for the revolutionary crisis of the 1970s. After World War II, cotton had overtaken coffee as the country's major export, in turn generating spinoffs in light industry such as agricultural chemicals and textiles. Throughout the period 1950-70, Nicaraguan growth rates expanded at an impressive 6 percent clip, stimulated by the post-war capitalist boom, the Central American Common Market and the initial impact of the Alliance for Progress. Nonetheless, as so often occurs in Third World development, the pattern of growth was as uneven as the distribution of its benefits.

The emerging primacy of cotton merely accelerated the concentration of land ownership; by 1975, 1.5 percent of the landowning population owned 40 percent of arable soil, with the Somoza family exercising dominance. Conversely, the peasants experienced increasing proletarianization. Between 1960 and 1977, the agricultural population fell from 60 to 44 percent as huge impoverished barrios rose on the outskirts of the cities. Half the population lived on an annual income of $286 per capita; more than half the people were illiterate; infant mortality rates were among the highest in the hemisphere. Even for the subordinate bourgeoisie, the paternalistic rule of Somoza became increasingly intolerable, especially after a major earthquake destroyed most of Managua and caused some 10,000 fatalities. Millions in reconstruction aid went directly into the pockets of the Somoza clan; the rest provided profits for the dictator's various reconstruction enterprises.

From the top of Tiscapa hill, most of sprawling Managua, with its downtown devastated by earthquake, is visible. This vantage point was the nerve center of the Somoza dictatorship: at its base were the Military Academy, artillery emplacements, the barracks of the dictator's personal armored battalion, the Basic Infantry Training School (commanded by Anastasio III), and the National Guard communications center. Dug into the base was the massively fortified air-conditioned bunker from which the dictator directed military operations against the FSLN. On Tiscapa itself sat the Presidential Palace, surmounted by anti-aircraft batteries. Beneath the palace were the cells housing the regime's political prisoners.

It was to these cells that the captured Tomas Borge was brought near midnight on February 4, 1976. Upon arriving at the Secret Police enclave, they covered the guerrilla leader's head with a hood of coarse linen. Borge was given orders to strip, and then handcuffed. The officer in charge asked the prisoner for his name. "When I told him," Borge later recalled, "his silence was eloquent." A member of the FSLN leadership had fallen into the hands of the regime.

For the FSLN, the years preceeding Borge's capture had been a time of military quiescence, ideological division, and flashes of spectacular resuscitation. With many of its young cadre imprisoned—Daniel Ortega among them—the sorely tried guerrilla group abandoned all military activity for four years, beginning in 1970. When the crisis struck, it was the non-Somozaist middle and upper classes who first responded. After the 1972 earthquake, the multiple contradictions of Nicaraguan economic and political life coalesced. The external market-dependent economy was squeezed by the recession; an inflation rate of under 2 percent before 1970 ballooned to nearly 10 percent; the workers who weren't hit by factory closures and massive layoffs engaged in sharply contested strikes to defend their standard of living; state debt quadrupled; the response of the regime was savage repression. Exasperated by Somoza's grand larceny of earthquake relief funds, the bourgeois opposition sought to unify its efforts, at least to the extent of boycotting the 1974 presidential elections; though Somoza was, of course, re-elected, the rate of abstentions was noteworthy. In mid-December 1974, a first popular front alliance—the Democratic Liberation Union (UDEL)—was formed by the half-dozen parties and trade union confederations that had opposed the electoral farce; it brought together workers and liberal capitalists in support of a moderate democratic program.

Less than two weeks later, the Sandinistas dramatically recommenced military operations with the capture of high-ranking Somoza officials at a Christmas party; these were then exchanged for political prisoners and the publication of lengthy communiques denouncing the regime. When the rescued Daniel Ortega and his fellow former captives were taken to the airport for a flight to Cuba, the crowds that lined the route and cheered them provided an indicator of the depth of popular support to be tapped.

Within the FSLN, once again belying conventional monolithic stereotypes, the Sandinistas were wracked by a debate over political perspectives which was gripping the entire Latin American revolutionary movement after a decade of uninterrupted defeats, the most recent of which had been the CIA-inspired overthrow of Salvador Allende's Popular Front government in Chile in 1973. For the Sandinistas, the result was temporarily fractious, with three organizationally distinct "tendencies" emerging in 1975-76. The active reappearance of the FSLN, however, gave Somoza a pretext for imposing a state of emergency in late 1975, utilizing martial law and press censorship.

The interrogation of Borge began at dawn. Handcuffed to a hoop inlaid into the wall, and kept naked in a room whose intense chill was maintained by a droning air conditioner, the prisoner was ordered to provide details of the network of "safe houses" used by the Sandinistas in Managua. The questions alternated with beatings during the first two-week phase. "There was no place on my body where they did not hit me, including my face and testicles," Borge testified afterward. There was little sleep, no food, and a water ration of one glass every twenty-four hours. The prisoner attempted to hold onto his dissolving sense of time, calculating the hours by the changing shifts of his captors.

As the weeks lengthened into months, the regimen of torture varied. The beatings gave way to long stretches of being kept standing all day in the air-conditioned interrogation room. The phases of brutality were interspersed with brief periods of sleep and food. Even then, every afternoon the official questioner faithfully asked Borge, "Are you prepared to talk?" Each time, he answered, "I have nothing to say." Invariably, the ritual exchange ended with Borge's interrogator warning, "The situation will worsen for you."

The worst of it, strangely enough, was not the physical violence. After a week of not visiting the air-conditioned torture chamber, Borge was taken there again and handcuffed to the hoop in the wall as usual. The prisoner waited. The hours passed. Nothing happened. Then the door opened abruptly and a small bag containing food was thrown in. The pattern was established. Day after day, the naked prisoner remained chained to the wall, listening to the monotonous, penetrating whine of the air conditioner. Three times daily a food bag was flung into the room, and once, in the evening, he was taken to the toilet next door.

It went on for five weeks. "These were the hardest days for me," Borge remembered. "After a week I wished they would come to question me again, even though it meant new beatings. As the days passed by, this longing became more urgent." Borge now faced a more difficult interrogator, the one within his own mind. He answered a mental anguish, more painful than beatings, with dreams. "I imagined a united Central America, crossed by ample highways. College campuses filled with happy people, complete with laboratories and huge libraries. Cooperative cattle farms...Smiling, agile and generous children." He survived. "In my visions I saw Carlos Fonseca, looking at our people with his near-sighted blue eyes, from a wooden platform, raised at one of the extremes of a joyous multitude." One morning his wardens came in, bathed the prisoner with a hose and gave him clothes. The worst was over.

There was one other memorable moment in an imprisonment that would last nearly three years. Toward the end of December 1976, the commander of the prison came to Borge's cell, jubilant, with a copy of the government paper, *Novedades*, in his hands. He gave the prisoners the news. "Carlos Fonseca is dead," he announced. The founder of the FSLN had died in combat. There was a moment of stunned silence.

"You're wrong, colonel," Borge finally replied. "Carlos Fonseca is one of the dead who never dies."

The colonel grudgingly conceded, "You guys are something else."

As novelist Gabriel Garcia Marquez wrote of that day in August 1978, "The plan seemed too simple to be sane: take the National Palace in Managua in broad daylight with a force of only twenty-six, and hold the members of the House of Deputies hostage in exchange for the release of all political prisoners."

Only a year before, Somoza appeared to be in complete

control. Social peace had been imposed, the limited effectiveness of the UDEL coalition was apparent, and the FSLN was fragmented. The dictator felt confident enough to accede to the nagging demands of Jimmy Carter's administration to lift the state of emergency in the name of human rights. A month later, in October 1977, the Sandinistas attacked National Guard barracks throughout the country, from Ocotal in the north to San Carlos near the Costa Rican border, demonstrating that the repression had solved nothing. In November, Pedro Joaquin Chamorro's *La Prensa* published a full-page appeal in which twelve well-known national figures called for a democratic alternative to the regime. Rather than making any concessions to the renewal of oppositional activity, Somoza characteristically opted for catastrophist politics. On January 10, 1978, in Managua, opposition newspaper editor Chamorro was assassinated.

It was the spark that ignited the revolutionary crisis. Some 120,000 demonstrators attended the funeral procession of the slain editor. Henceforth, over the next eighteen months, there would be a continual succession of mass demonstrations, general strikes, and partial insurrection. But it was the crazy masterstroke at the National Palace that signalled the end for a dictator whom the scheme's architect, FSLN commander Eden Pastora, called, perhaps prematurely, "the last Marine."

At about noon on August 22, 1978, two military-green Ford trucks pulled up to the side entrance of the columned facade of the banana parthenon where the Chamber of Deputies was going through the annual ritual of debating the budget. Three squads of soldiers, armed with Uzi sub-machine guns and Garand rifles and garbed in olive green National Guard uniforms sewn by guerrilla tailors, rapidly clambered down from each of the trucks. At the east entrance, Pastora, the leader of the operation, code-named Commander Zero, barked out to the police guards at the entrance, "Out of the way! The boss is coming!" The guards parted. Zero, followed by his men, bolted up the wide staircase to the first floor, continuing to scream in the barbarian fashion of the National Guard when they announced the arrival of Somoza. With the barrel of his G-3 rifle, Zero pushed open the wide glass door of the Blue Room where he found the forty-nine ashen-faced deputies staring at him in absolute bewilderment. Zero sprayed the ceiling with bullets, yelling, "The Guard! Everyone hit the floor." The terrified deputies threw themselves down behind their desks. Meanwhile, in other parts of the palatial administrative center, Commander One, 30-year-old Hugo Torres, and Commander Two, Dora Maria Tellez, 22, quickly rounded up the 2,500 officials and workers on duty. The guards had been disarmed with minimal shooting and the enormous building was locked from the inside with heavy chains. As planned, the whole operations had taken less than five minutes.

As he sat down to lunch in the air-conditioned basement of his private bunker, Anastasio Somoza received the incredible news of the capture of the better part of his government. His immediate reaction was to order an indiscriminate barrage on the National Palace, complete with strafing helicopters. Moments later, the phone rang. One of the captured deputies, a cousin of Somoza's, was on the line to relay the FSLN's message: cease firing or the execution of hostages begins.

The negotiations took two days. All the Sandinista demands but one were met: safe passage to Panama, release of political prisoners (among them, Tomas Borge), broadcast of FSLN communiques and a $500,000 cash indemnity. The Sandinista commandos also demanded that the route to the airport be kept clear. It was one demand that couldn't be met. Although Somoza vainly posted National Guards along the road to prevent any demonstration of popular support, as the school bus carrying the guerrillas and released prisoners traveled toward the airport, thousands of people poured into the streets to cheer the daring victory, an event recorded by international television. Inside the bus, a deputy about to be exchanged at the airport who was sitting beside Commander One, Hugo Torres, was noticeably taken aback by the explosion of popular euphoria. "Look at that," Torres quipped. "It's the only thing money can't buy."

In September 1978, FSLN columns launched the insurrection. The fall of the dictator would not be accomplished until nine months hence. The outcome, though perhaps appearing inevitable from hindsight, was in actuality uncertain, extraordinarily complex at the political level (especially as the Carter regime desperately maneuvered to rescue Somozaism, if not Somoza himself), and most of all bloody, claiming as many as 50,000 victims.

The September insurrection fell short. It had been reluctantly undertaken by the FSLN. "We could not say no to the insurrection," Daniel Ortega explained afterward. The popular opposition had grown to such a size that "we could not oppose this torrent-like movement; all we could do was stand at its head." As columns of guerrillas and civilians retreated under aerial bombings of the towns, Somoza's forces pressed ahead with savage reprisals, taking some 6,000 lives. Once again, the dictator enjoyed the illusion of victory.

Somoza's bourgeois opponents, now expanded into an organization called the Broad Opposition Front (FAO), also thought its hour had come. The show of FSLN strength, though temporarily abated, forced the Carter administration to establish an international mediation commission. The talks dragged on into the beginning of 1979. The American idea was "Somozaism without Somoza"—a democratic capitalist regime excluding the FSLN, maintenance of the National Guard, and guarantees for Somoza property while removing him from office. When Somoza rejected these proposals in January 1979, Carter had little choice but to suspend economic and military aid to the intransigent dictator, in a bid to hasten the collapse of his regime, while maintaining the hope that the pieces would be picked up by a moderate opposition.

In fact, it was a program already bypassed by events. The FAO began to splinter; its political authority gradually eroded; Sandinista slogans calling for dissolution of the National Guard and the expropriation of the Somoza empire were clearly more in tune with public opinion. At the same time, the FSLN succeeded in reunifying its three tendencies into a single force and turning its attention to the development of a new structure, the National Patriotic Front. By spring 1979 the leadership of the mass movement had changed hands. The military offensive was immediately resumed.

On July 19, 1979, the Sandinista columns marched into Managua in triumph. From the declaration of the final offensive in early June to the flight of Somoza two days before the FSLN victory, the National Guard fell back as town after town was taken by its inhabitants, led by the youthful guerrillas garbed in red-and-black neckerchiefs. A U.S. State Department bid to the Organization of American States in late

June to land a hemispheric "peace keeping" force in Nicaragua was soundly rejected, both by Latin American dictators fearful of such a precedent and by more constitutional regimes opposed to another invasion by U.S. Marines. The credibility of this salvage attempt was seriously undercut as American TV viewers watched the public execution of U.S. newsman Bill Stewart that month. By July 16, the major cities of Nicaragua—Leon, Esteli, Matagalpa, Masaya—were in FSLN hands. The next day Anastasio Somoza was on a plane to Miami (a year later he was dead in Paraguay, shot by assassins). In Leon, on the eve of the triumph, Daniel Ortega, about to march into Managua, watched old footage on television of Sandino waving his hat.

For North Americans, post-revolutionary Nicaragua remains as wreathed in mystification as Sandino's mountain fortress of El Chipote was hidden in clouds. Though the story of what happened in Nicaragua after July 19, 1979, is yet to be told, occasionally, as in Carleton Beals' interview with Sandino a half century ago, something equivalent to a shaft of sunlight penetrates the miasma of propaganda.

In mid-1983, shortly after President Reagan's bellicose address to the joint session of Congress, Americans were permitted an unmediated glimpse of the forbidding Sandinistas in, of all places, the pages of *Playboy* magazine. Sandwiched between the magazine's usual glossy fare were the voices of Tomas Borge, Nicaragua's minister of the interior, poet and Minister of Culture Ernesto Cardenal, and novelist and junta member Sergio Ramirez.

"After George Shultz replaced Haig, we had hopes to start afresh," Ramirez told *Playboy* interviewer Claudia Dreifus, in response to her question about the sincerity of the Sandinistas' desire to negotiate with the Americans. "With Haig, there wasn't even a dialogue, because he always barked at us," Ramirez continued. "With Enders, it was more a litany of the things we were supposed to do—and then threats if we didn't obey. We have been spoken to in one of those two ways for more than fifty years."

A couple of months after Shultz' appointment in July 1982, Ramirez related, the new secretary of state was hosting a reception in New York for U.N. delegates. Nicaraguan

Foreign Minister Father Miguel D'Escoto was on the diplomatic list. "At the head of the receiving line, there was Shultz, shaking everybody's hand. Father D'Escoto was announced, he put out his hand—and Shultz refused to shake it. Father D'Escoto plunged on, asking him if the two governments couldn't simply meet to discuss things. Shultz refused to say a single word," Ramirez reported. "That incident shows us the mental and ideological problems the Reagan people have. They despise us. As a people. As a revolution. From their viewpoint, we deserve only annihilation. Why should they waste their time speaking with such a small, weak country?"

"Despite all that, do you still want your position to be better understood by the U.S. public?" asked interviewer Dreifus.

"You know," replied Ramirez, "we have never forbidden any representative from the U.S. to enter the country. I've spoken with at least twenty delegations during the past four years, and we've always given the same explanations, because they have always asked the same things. We've never said, 'What are you people doing here? Why don't you solve *your* problem of racial discrimination. Why don't you solve the problem of chicanos in the U.S.?' That would be stupid on our part." Further, U.S. Ambassador Anthony Quainton was treated with full diplomatic courtesy, Ramirez asserted. "This is one of the few countries in the world where a U.S. ambassador can go to a barbershop to have his hair cut and be completely unconcerned for his safety. He can even act in amateur theatrical productions. I don't know whether Ambassador Quainton is a good or a bad actor but he takes part in community theatre here."

Tomas Borge couldn't resist. "He must be a better actor than Reagan," said the FSLN founder.

Ernesto Cardenal declared, "We would be very happy here to receive Reagan's son, who is a ballet dancer."

"Besides, he's unemployed," Ramirez added.

Borge suggested that it would be interesting to have President Reagan visit. "So that he could see, even with his atrophied vision, the reality we are living."

"No, Tomas, it wouldn't do any good," Ramirez cut in. "It would probably be like the Pope's visit, when he didn't *see* anything. You can attribute that statement to Father

Cardenal,'' Ramirez told *Playboy*. "Only *cardenales* can speak about Popes.''

The interviewer turned from the banter to Reagan's congressional address in April 1983. She quoted the president's discovery of the geographic proximity of Managua to several major American cities. "What was your reaction to that?''

"Those are the same ideas that were behind President Monroe's doctrine,'' Ramirez replied. "That theory of influence due to geographical proximity was what impelled William Walker in 1855 to come to Nicaragua and try to conquer Central America. The important thing about that speech was that Reagan seemed to be personally declaring war on us. I think that Washington and Jefferson would have blushed, because it wasn't for this that the founders of North America fought their revolution.''

"After a speech like Reagan's, do you ever ask yourselves what is going through the mind of the president of the United States?'' Dreifus asked.

"I don't think he thinks,'' said Cardenal. "It all sounds like some wild-West movie he's acting out. He's playing the cowboy who kills all the 'bad guys' in Nicaragua.''

"I think of Reagan as a sort of Frankenstein's monster,'' Ramirez added. "Within Reagan's mind, I don't think there's any one person but, rather, a mixture of any number of extremists who have dwelt in academic and corporate catacombs. Reagan is a character of this period in North America the same way Colonel Sanders was a character representing Kentucky Fried Chicken—just an image with a whole apparatus behind it.''

"What Sergio is saying is absolutely right,'' agreed Borge. "Reagan, or his image, is entirely determined by economic interests. Such is the degree of power of advertising in the U.S. that the people could just as easily elect Coca-Cola as president. And that's what we believe America did—swallowed Reagan as if he were Coke.''

At that point, Ernesto Cardenal had a question of his own for *Playboy*. "By the way, do you know anything about those monkey movies of Reagan's?''

"Monkey movies?'' asked the interviewer. "Do you mean his film *Bedtime for Bonzo*?''

"Yes, I think that's it,'' said Ramirez. "It's an old movie in which Reagan plays a person who controls a monkey. It's very difficult to get hold of prints of that movie."

"Are you saying that the collective leadership of the Sandinista government," asked Dreifus somewhat incredulously, "has been trying to get prints of *Bedtime for Bonzo*?"

"Yes," Borge answered. "But we haven't been able to. The movie deals with a monkey, and the monkey's master is Reagan. So this is a wonderful allegory—almost a premonition."

9 No Safe Harbor

> *I am pissed off... The President has asked us to back his foreign policy. Bill, how can we back his foreign policy when we don't know what the hell he is doing?... Mine the harbors of Nicaragua? This is an act violating international law. It is an act of war. For the life of me, I don't see how we are going to explain it.*
>
> —Senator Barry Goldwater,
> April 1984

From the halls of Montezuma to the shores of Tripoli, as the opening line of the U.S. Marine Corps marching song sweepingly put it: by mid-August 1983, a scant two weeks after the House of Representatives rebuffed the administration's not-so-secret war in Nicaragua, Ronald Reagan had scattered a remarkable portion of his troops, ships and planes around the globe. Contingents from every branch of the service were deployed on three continents, well within shooting range of various world hot spots in Lebanon, Chad, and Central America.

Teddy Roosevelt, the president whose 1904 Corollary to the Monroe Doctrine had inspired a half dozen of his successors, including Reagan, to try their hand at Latin American intervention, also had some terse advice on styles of bellicosity. "Walk softly and carry a big stick," urged the old Roughrider. Certainly, Reagan was busily brandishing the big stick, showing the flag and flexing more military muscle than any Commander-in-Chief since Vietnam.

In the Mediterranean, the carrier *Eisenhower* was steaming up and down the shores of Tripoli, Libya in a bid to persuade Colonel Muhamar Khadaffi to keep his hands off neighboring

Chad. In Beirut, Lebanon some 1,800 Marines were hunkered behind sandbags as part of a four-nation peacekeeping force. Another thousand Americans were keeping the peace in the Sinai Desert. In Egypt, 5,500 U.S. troops were repelling imaginary invaders in Operation Bright Star while a deployment of F-16s whizzed overhead in Operation Prize Falcon; in nearby Sudan, another uneasy Libyan neighbor, a thousand men and two state-of-the-art AWACS radar planes were going through their paces in Operation Natural Bond; in Somalia, 2,800 troops were demonstrating amphibious tactics in Operation Eastern Wind.

But it was in the vicinity of the halls of Montezuma that Reagan's most dramatic and hotly debated military gambit was underway. The advance force of 250 U.S. soldiers had landed in Honduras to begin months of elaborate military exercises that would ultimately involve 5,500 American troops. The U.S. Navy was stationed off both the Pacific and Caribbean coasts of Nicaragua. The Seventh Fleet carrier *Ranger* and its seven escort ships, which had taken up residence off the Nicaraguan coast were about to be relieved by the battleship *New Jersey* while the aircraft carrier *Coral Sea* was chugging across the Atlantic toward the eastern seaboard of Central America. It was that bit of gunboat diplomacy that had riled congressmen sufficiently to turn down Reagan's request for another dollop of arms aid to the Nicaraguan *contras* and their CIA handlers.

While the big stick was much in evidence, it was less clear that the self-appointed policeman of the world was walking or talking softly. As conservative Senator Barry Goldwater would complain six months later, at the moment of maximum confusion, "How can we back his foreign policy when we don't know what the hell he is doing?" The official version of the administration's posture toward Nicaragua's Sandinistas and El Salvador's FMLN guerrillas was called the "two-track approach"—balancing off the display of thunderbolts with moments of diplomatic persuasion. But on given days, puzzled observers didn't know whether to listen to individual freelancers like special envoy Richard Stone who was meandering through Central America talking to rebels and rightists, or to try and reconcile the rhetoric coming out of both sides of the government's mouth while Congress sat in the middle disapprovingly pursing its lips, or to just lean back and be dazzled by a three-ring circus featuring military fireworks, presidential pronouncements, interagency spats, and Henry Kissinger's commission bringing up the rear.

Even at his folksy soft-spoken best, the president managed to sound ominous. Four days after the press reported in late July 1983 that Reagan had approved a National Security Council (NSC) scheme calling for a substantial increase in American military involvement in Central America and preparations for a possible blockade of Nicaragua, the president held a news conference to reassuringly insist that the current spate of wargames was simply aimed at providing "a shield for democracy." However, Reagan couldn't resist adding, "The Soviets and the Cubans are operating from a base called Nicaragua. This is the first real Communist aggression on the American mainland." And when asked whether he could rule out the use of U.S. troops in the region, Reagan merely reiterated his past comment that presidents "never say never."

When it came to speaking softly to Congress, the administration voice ranged from a mumble to a rumble. National Security Adviser William Clark had obviously spoken too softly when he failed to mention that the country was about to send its armada to Nicaragua, thereby incurring sufficient congressional rancor to cause the legislators to slap down the latest request for aid to the *contras*. (By autumn, Clark was on his way out as national security adviser and headed over to the Department of the Interior to plug the hole left by the resignation of the inept James Watt; his successor was Robert "Bud" MacFarlane, much to the chagrin of U.N. Ambassador Jeane Kirkpatrick, who was reported to have coveted the cloak-and-dagger post for herself.)

On the other side of the decibel register, there was no mistaking the tone of Undersecretary of Defense Fred Ikle's speech in mid-September 1983. It came in the temperature-raising wake of the downing of a Korean Air Lines commercial flight by the Soviet Union, a gory incident resulting in 269 deaths. The administration, despite the objections of some State Department officials arguing the "walk softly" position, decided to go on the attack against congressional opposition to its Central American policy. "As long as Congress keeps crippling the president's military assistance program, we will have a policy always shy of success," said the hawkish Ikle, whose script was reportedly approved by Clark, Defense Secretary Weinberger and CIA boss Bill Casey. "We must prevent consolidation of a Sandinista regime in Nicaragua that would become an arsenal for insurgency," he warned. "If we cannot prevent that, we have to anticipate the partition of Central America. Such a development would then force us to man a new military front line of the East-West conflict right here on our continent."

As for the president himself, his main contribution seemed to be the invention of a nagging codex to the Roosevelt Corollary to the Monroe Doctrine, which could be capsulized as: when it comes to asking Congress for funds for Central American intervention, presidents never take no for an answer.

At first, the new hardline pitch appeared to be making progress. Reagan issued a new presidential "finding" authorizing continuing covert action in Nicaragua for the purpose of putting pressure on the Sandinistas to end support for Central American revolutionary movements (a formula designed to calm fears that the U.S. shared the *contras'* intentions of overthrowing the Nicaraguan government); days later the Senate Intelligence Committee voted in favor of $19 million in new covert aid. However, a month later, in mid-October 1983, Speaker of the House "Tip" O'Neill turned thumbs down on the bid for renewed funding. "I believe that the U.S. should not be engaged militarily in trying to overthrow other governments," said the senior legislator.

Despite a last minute letter from Secretary Shultz to the Congress (an aid cutoff, he warned, "would virtually destroy" any chance of getting the Sandinistas to behave) and a presidential defense of the secret war ("I do believe in the right of a country when it believes that its interests are best served to practice covert activity," declared Reagan), the House of Representatives brushed aside the administration's appeals and voted on October 20 to cut off U.S. support for the Nicaraguan *contras*. The vote was 227 to 194, a thirty-three-vote margin identical to the one in July. The administration, said House Intelligence Committee chairman Edward Boland, the chief sponsor of the aid cutoff measure, must stop "waging war in Nicaragua—and make no mistake about it, this is exactly what the United States is doing. Military victory

220

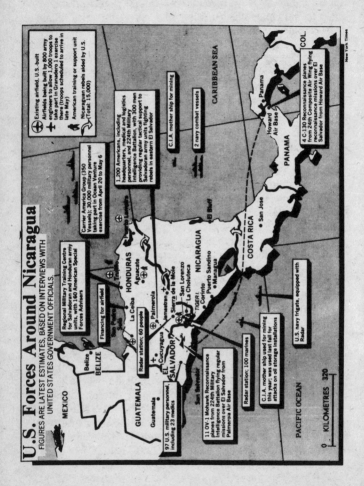

U.S. Forces Around Nicaragua

FIGURES ARE LATEST ESTIMATES, BASED ON INTERVIEWS WITH UNITED STATES GOVERNMENT OFFICIALS.

Existing airfield, U.S.-built

Airfields being built by 800 army engineers to allow 1,000 troops to take part in Granadero I exercise there (troops scheduled to arrive in late May)

American training or support unit

Nicaraguan rebels aided by U.S. (Total: 15,000)

MEXICO

GUATEMALA

BELIZE

Belize

Guatemala

97 U.S. military personnel, including 23 medics

San Salvador

EL SALVADOR

11 OV-1 Mohawk Reconnaissance planes from 224th Military Intelligence Battalion flying regular missions over El Salvador from Palmerola Air Base

Regional Military Training Centre for Salvadoran and Honduran army units, with 160 American Special Forces Advisers

Financing for airfield

Radar station; 60 people

HONDURAS

La Ceiba

Trujillo

Aguacate

Palmerola

Jamastran

Sierra de la Mole

San Lorenzo

La Choluteca

El Cucuyagua

TIGER I.

Corinto

Puerto Sandino

Managua

NICARAGUA

Carrier America Group (350 Vessels); 30,000 military personnel taking part in Ocean Venture exercise from April 20 to May 6

1,200 Americans, including headquarters, medical and logistics personnel, and 224th Military Intelligence Battalion, with 300 men providing radar and tactical support to Salvadoran army units fighting rebels in eastern El Salvador

Radar station; 100 marines

C.I.A. mother ship used for mining this year; was used last fall for attacks on oil storage installations

U.S. navy frigate, equipped with Radar

Bluff

COSTA RICA

San Jose

PACIFIC OCEAN

C.I.A. mother ship for mining

2 navy combat vessels

CARIBBEAN SEA

PANAMA

Panama

Howard Air Base

COL.

4 C-130 Reconnaissance planes from 24th Composite Air Wing flying reconnaissance missions over El Salvador from Howard Air Base

0   KILOMETRES   320

New York Times

is the administration's bottom line.''

Ronald Reagan and George Shultz were engaged in a covert operation. The cover story was that they were weekend golfers, getting in a few rounds of relaxation at the Augusta, Georgia National Golf Club. Though it was the day after the House rebuff on *contra* aid, the president and his secretary of state (with NSC adviser MacFarlane and Treasury Secretary Donald Regan along to round out the foursome) weren't worrying about Nicaragua as they scrambled in and out of sand bunkers and tromped through the rough. In fact, they were plotting the invasion of Grenada.

Reagan had long been obsessed with the tiny Caribbean island and its left-leaning revolution led by Prime Minister Maurice Bishop. Even before becoming president, he had groused about the nutmeg-producing Grenada being a base for communist subversion. And as recently as his April 1983 special address to Congress, Reagan had declared, "It is not nutmeg that is at stake in the Caribbean and Central America. It is U.S. national security." Only days before, an internecine squabble within the island's ruling New Jewel Movement handed Reagan a golden opportunity to roll back the communist tide and to make use of his shiny, expensive arsenal in a more realistic test than that afforded by Honduran wargames. In mid-October a central committee coup led by Bishop deputy Bernard Coard seized power and put the prime minister under house arrest. On October 19, Bishop was freed by a crowd of his supporters and carried to a rally in the center of St. George's, the island's capital. Shortly afterward, troops opened fire on the crowd, killing a score of people, among them the popular Bishop.

Events moved quickly from there. By the next day, while the House was jawing over covert operations aid, Vice President George Bush had convened a Special Situation Group meeting in the White House. The presence of 700 American students at a Grenadan medical school provided the age-old pretext of protecting "American lives and property." A naval task force, headed by the carrier *Independence*, which was on its way to Lebanon with 1,900 Marines, was diverted to Caribbean waters. In Barbados, leaders of the island nations of the Organization of Eastern Caribbean States (OECS) were quickly rounded up in order to pass a resolution asking the

U.S. to do something about Grenada.

Erstwhile golfer Shultz was awakened at 2:45 a.m. on Saturday, October 22, with an urgent cable from Barbados informing him that the OECS resolution had been passed, thus providing legal cover for U.S. military operations. Shultz called Bush in the White House at 3:30. The vice-president rousted other NSC officials and middle-of-the-night invasion planning commenced. As one participant later described it, "Everyone was gung-ho." The president was awakened at 5:15 a.m. to hear Shultz and MacFarlane explain the invasion scheme. That day, the nation's two top secret agents deliberately continued to play golf to avert suspicion that anything was up. At 2:30 a.m. on Sunday, the president, who was known to prefer regular hours, was again awakened. This time there was shocking news from another front line: American and French military quarters in Beirut, Lebanon had been bombed by Shiite Moslem suicide truck drivers. In the carnage, more than 200 Americans lay dead. For some, the Beirut tragedy was cause for considering jettisoning the Grenada mission. For Reagan, who flew back to Washington, the Beirut bombing provided a cover of secrecy for further invasion planning. Said the president: "We cannot let an act of terrorism determine whether we aid or assist our allies in the region. If we do that, who will ever trust us again?"

At 5:30 a.m. on Tuesday, October 25, a group of U.S. Navy Seals, trained in special seaborne operations, slipped silently ashore a Grenadan beach and crept up the hill overlooking the quaint eighteenth-century capital of St. George's as it prepared to seize Government House, the island's formal seat of power. Simultaneously, and more noisily, 400 Marines aboard troop helicopters from the assault ship *Guam* roared into the island's only functioning airstrip. A half hour later hundreds of U.S. Rangers, the Army's elite special forces, parachuted onto the uncompleted airport at Point Salinas where they met surprisingly stiff resistance from Grenadan militia and armed Cuban construction workers. For the first time since the end of the Vietnam War, the U.S. had committed its troops to a combat attack. That morning, President Reagan was in the White House press-briefing room, solemnly asserting that America was not going to be pushed around. Grenada "was a Soviet-Cuban colony being readied as a major military bastion to export terror and undermine democracy,'' explained the president in a nationally televised address two days later. By then U.S. troops had secured the former British colony at the cost of the lives of a dozen American servicemen and several hundred underarmed enemies. ''We got there just in time.''

That's not what most of the rest of the world thought. For the next several days, various world forums reverberated with denunciations of ''bayonet democracy,'' international leaders shrugged in the face of *realpolitik* but nonetheless distanced themselves from the American aggressors, and numerous U.S. politicians and professors uneasily pondered the actions of their trigger-happy president. Even Britain's Margaret Thatcher, notwithstanding her own island war, told her parliament that she had urged Reagan to reconsider his invasion plans the day before the troops hit the beach. France lifted an eyebrow, describing the assault as ''a surprising action in relation to international law.'' At the United Nations, where a midnight Security Council emergency session took place the day after the invasion, Nicaraguan representative Hugo Tinoco wanted to know ''since when is it legal for several states to get together and agree to invade another country with which they are not at war?'' U.S. representative Jeane Kirkpatrick replied with her familiar accusation that Nicaragua's delegate was projecting his own country's wish to interfere in the affairs of neighboring states onto the U.S. (''Nicaragua is trapped in the—Thomas Hobbes said it— restless striving for power that ceases only with death''); but it was hardly an idle question. As New York *Times* columnist Tom Wicker, among many others, pointedly asked, ''Was Ronald Reagan's invasion of Grenada a trial run for an invasion of Nicaragua?''

The president, however, was much less interested in international reviews than in how the Grenada invasion was playing at home. The former movie actor had once portrayed Notre Dame University football coach Knute Rockne whose rallying cry was, ''Win one for the Gipper.'' For Americans, who had been assiduously schooled to admire winning far more than how the game was played, the moral-legal tangle raised by the invasion was far less important than the outcome. As for the impact of the Grenadan adventure on the issues at hand, it didn't take long for congressmen to detect which way the euphoric wind was blowing. On November 3, the Senate, by voice vote, approved continued aid for covert operations in Nicaragua. Two weeks later, the House, after twice voting against further funding for the *contras*, ended up reversing itself and joining the Senate to appropriate $24 million for the not-so-secret war. It was unclear whether the liberals believed they had made some sort of a trade off with the conservatives (Representative Boland apparently thought so, satisfied with a rider prohibiting the CIA from dipping into contingency funds), or whether they had simply been caught up in the flag waving generated by Reagan's Caribbean conquest. The amount allotted was only half of what the CIA wanted, but it was enough to keep the president's "freedom fighters" in the field until June 1984. At which point, the Great Communicator could always come back and not take no for an answer again.

When the twin-engine Cessna swooped in over Sandino Airport in the pre-dawn of September 8, 1983, most residents of Managua were still asleep. A few minutes earlier another Cessna had buzzed the capital and dropped a bomb near the home of Foreign Minister Reverend Miguel D'Escoto. Though the target was apparently a communications center in D'Escoto's neighborhood, the bomb missed, no one was injured, and the plane flew off in the darkness. Meanwhile, at the airport, about ten kilometers outside the city, the second aircraft attacked the main terminal and an adjacent air force base with 200-kilogram bombs. One tore up the hangar of Aeronica, the national airline, and shrapnel and flying debris ripped through the terminal, injuring three people and killing an army reservist. Along the runway, Nicaraguan soldiers opened fire with anti-aircraft guns as the plane made another pass at the main terminal control tower. The propeller-driven plane was hit, twisted crazily, and then crashed at the base of the tower, killing the pilot and copilot, and touching off a fire that engulfed part of the terminal.

The dead fliers were identified later that day as Agustin Roman, a Nicaraguan who had once worked for Aeronica, and Sebastian Muller, an air force deserter. Nicaraguan authorities said that flight plans and other documents found in the wreckage showed that the two planes had taken off from a small airport near San Jose, Costa Rica. Although responsibility for the first air strike in the not-so-secret war was taken by Eden Pastora's Revolutionary Democratic Alliance (ARDE), both the Costa Rican government and Pastora denied that the flights had originated from Costa Rican territory, in a bid to preserve that country's image of neutrality.

Nicaraguan leaders placed the blame not so much on the *contras* as on their U.S. sponsors. Said Father D'Escoto, who was in Panama attending Contadora peace talks, "The only true responsibility is President Reagan's, who has conceived, directed and financed the counter-revolutionary groups he calls freedom fighters." The first international observers to get a first-hand look at what U.S. aid to the *contras* was doing were two American senators; Colorado's Gary Hart and William Cohen of Maine were aboard a U.S. Air Force C-140 transport about to touch down in Managua when the attack began. After their flight was diverted to neighboring Honduras, the senators returned later in the day to inspect the bombed airport. One of the possible culprits was also spotted in the vicinity that day; Defense Secretary Caspar Weinberger was in Honduras, praising regional efforts to fend off communism as he wrapped up a three-day Central American tour. "We must not stop now," said Weinberger. "Just a little bit more in the way of help could make a world of difference."

Though there were many clues strewn about the scene of the crime, it would take a while for anyone other than the Nicaraguans to notice the fingerprints and other telltale signs. In retrospect, it appeared perfectly obvious. Although Reagan had denied it, the report in late July that the U.S. was considering a blockade or "quarantine" of Nicaragua ought to have been a first indicator. However, when the battle groups of the U.S. fleet did nothing more than intimidatingly drop anchor off the coasts of Nicaragua, the quarantine idea was given few second thoughts, nor was there speculation as to the possible indirect forms such a quarantine might take.

A second clue that appeared about the same time as the quarantine notion was the admission that the *contra* operation, after a year of intense activity, was proving ineffective. In fact, the *contra* failure had Nicaraguan officials worried. "We are in more danger now because the *contras* are being repulsed," said one Sandinista leader in late July. "The U.S. will need to choose options that guarantee success."

Though another large-scale *contra* ground offensive was launched in August, and was one of the factors that caused the Sandinistas to impose a controversial military conscription program, the invaders were soon driven back to their Honduran bases. The CIA, in its secret report to congressional intelligence committees in September, admitted that, by themselves, the *contras* stood no chance of inflicting either a military or political defeat on the Nicaraguan government. With Congress growing restive as the October 1983 deadline for Fiscal Year 1984 funding neared, the CIA decided that a highly visible economic sabotage campaign offered the best chance for retaining the *contra* budget and providing, as *Time* magazine put it, "a relatively inexpensive way to attract attention" to the anti-Sandinista cause.

The day after the airport attack, ARDE planes shelled oil and chemical storage facilities at the Nicaraguan Pacific port of Corinto; the same week Nicaraguan Democratic Force (FDN) *contras* from the north hit the oil pipeline terminal at Puerto Sandino, another Pacific harbor. In the first weeks of October, the campaign to decimate Nicaragua's major ports was stepped up. Specially outfitted speedboats known as "piranhas" blew up fuel storage tanks in the Caribbean anchorage of Benjamin Zeledon on October 2. The same tactic, this time backed by air cover, was used ten days later at Corinto, destroying millions of gallons of fuel and forcing the evacuation of the city's 25,000 inhabitants. Within days, Puerto Sandino was hit a second time, as was Puerto Cabezas on the Caribbean.

By then, reporters had spotted CIA footprints. Thumbing through registration papers and other scraps of information, the amateur public detectives who double as journalists had traced the wrecked Cessna 404 that bombed the Managua airport to Investair, a leasing company in Mclean, Virginia, home of the CIA. The manager of the firm, Edgar Mitchell, said his company bought the plane in 1982 and sold it in June 1983 to a Panamanian company, but he declined to answer questions about himself. However, a secretary at the Virginia offices provided scribbling sleuths with a San Francisco phone number which was answered by Mrs. Mitchell who offered the information that her husband had previously worked in Arizona for Intermountain Aviation. Intermountain, as reporters quickly learned from a 1976 declassified Senate

Intelligence Committee report, was one of the CIA's largest proprietaries; it provided "a variety of nonattributable air support activities which were available for quick deployment in support of CIA activities." When the media phoned Mrs. Mitchell's number for more details the next day, the number had been disconnected. The press then tried its luck with Investair's marketing director, Mark Peterson, but he was close-lipped too. However, a background check on Peterson revealed that in the late 1970s he had been an official of Air America, another CIA front operation. The shadowy grade-B movie network of CIA connections was duly reported in early October, though it attracted little attention. In a sense, the 1982 revelations of the CIA-sponsored covert war had "normalized" the intelligence agency's involvement in the *contra* caper. The discovery of further details tended to evoke shrugs that said, So what else is new?

It also became apparent that month that the U.S., as the Nicaraguans had worriedly suggested, was pursuing other "options." The weekend in late October that Reagan and Shultz were brandishing sand wedges and putters on a Georgia golf course while plotting the Grenada invasion, the military chiefs of staff of El Salvador, Guatemala, Panama and Honduras met secretly in Tegucigalpa. The subject of the gathering of the Central American Defense Council (CON-DECA)—an association of regional warlords recently revivified with the help of U.S. General Paul Gorman of the American Southern Command—was to consider whether "legal instruments" may "permit the security and armed forces of Panama and the other Central American countries to participate in the action for the pacification of Nicaragua."

Although Caspar Weinberger, when asked whether the U.S. was urging the revival of CONDECA, offhandedly replied, "Not that I know of," other American sources claimed that the Pentagon had played a key role in the group's resuscitation as part of the administration's long-range plan to deal with Nicaragua through a regional approach. Weinberger now blandly told reporters, "If the countries concerned are in favor of it, it seems to me that's a legitimate thing for them to want to do." Presumably, that's not exactly what he said to defense department counterparts when he toured Central America the month before. The news of the secret meeting, coming in the wake of the Grenada conquest, predictably

U.S.-backed *Contra* Forces

A STUBBORN CONTRA OFFENSIVE

Antileftist rebels recruited, trained and financed by the CIA have fought stubbornly but have attracted little support in Nicaragua. Their current strategy: attacking the country's feeble economy—in part by mining ports.

Ib Ohlsson—NEWSWEEK

aroused only mild interest.

Nor was much notice taken of a *contra* announcement in January 1984 that they had mined the harbors of Nicaragua; it was overshadowed by the concurrent appearance of Henry Kissinger's report on Central America, a document which simply prescribed more of the same for the region. In fact, it was not until the Soviet oil tanker *Lugansk* was blasted by a mine in Puerto Sandino harbor on March 20, injuring five sailors, that the disruption of international shipping attracted any substantial attention. By then, there had been explosions in the Atlantic port of El Bluff in late February, damaging two fishing boats and wounding seven crew members; as well, during the first week of March, a Dutch dredging vessel and a Panamanian freighter carrying baby food had been hit in Corinto harbor.

The Russians delivered a formal protest note to the American charge d'affaires in Moscow, and the Soviet press agency Tass quoted a Nicaraguan security official, Manuel Calderon, as having said that an American naval ship had been sighted cruising near Puerto Sandino ten days before. "It cannot be excluded that the mines were planted by the Americans," said Calderon. The Nicaraguan suggestion of direct U.S. involvement in the mining was promptly dismissed as preposterous.

The official U.S. reply to the Soviets expressed regrets for the damaged tanker, but disclaimed any responsibility; after all, said the administration, the danger "was well known from previous incidents." Further disassociating themselves from any hint of a hands-on relationship to the harbor incidents, the State Department pointed out that the mines were "relatively unsophisticated" and obviously "handmade" by anti-Sandinista insurgents.

A New York *Times* editorial replied, "Imagine the roles reversed: an American ship in the Arabian Gulf strikes a mine planted by a Soviet-led operation. Is it any answer to be told the Gulf was knowably dangerous and that, in any case, American arms sales to the region were the real source of the trouble?" Columnist Tom Wicker was even harsher: "The mines were sown at Puerto Sandino by *contras* who are funded, armed, supported, partly trained and largely organized by the CIA for the express purpose of overthrowing the Nicaraguan government. The Reagan administration piously denied any responsibility for the mines, but that's like saying Mr. Reagan is not responsible for the CIA... It's sheer hypocrisy, too," Wicker continued, "for Mr. Reagan to push a guerrilla insurgency against Nicaragua while denouncing such tactics in El Salvador and condemning 'state terrorism' directed against U.S. forces in Lebanon." Asked the angry columnist, "What does he imagine the efforts of the CIA-directed *contras* amount to, if not state terrorism?" Reagan's critics were close, but they were still missing a crucial piece to this particular whodunit puzzle.

Interest in the mining controversy temporarily waned as attention in late-March 1984 turned to a more overt U.S. operation in Central America, the Salvadoran presidential election. In any case, days before the Soviet ship was hit, the Senate Intelligence Committee had approved an administration request for another $21 million to tide the *contras* over until Fiscal Year 1985 proposals were considered. Dastardly deeds notwithstanding, it appeared there was a good chance the president would not have to take no for an answer on behalf of his *contra* proteges.

In between the chaotic first round of the Salvadoran presidential race in March and the run-off in May 1984, and while the media was hot on the trail of the No Safe Harbors case in Nicaraguan waters, the Honduran military took the opportunity to stage a mini-coup. Now that Honduras had been coated with a patina of democracy that included a figurehead civilian president, shakeups in the ranks replaced official, full-scale coup d'etats.

The abrupt ouster of General Gustavo Alvarez on March 30 was unlikely to result in any drastic alteration in the course of Honduran affairs. Nonetheless, even minor seismic rearrangements of personnel in volcanic Central America created a situation that Washington could hardly afford to ignore. In the last three years, the Reagan administration had pumped more than $300 million into the region's poorest country in order to transform it into the newest outpost of Fortress America. The decision to turn Honduras into what at times resembled a single, gigantic, border-to-border military base went back to the Carter regime and the political problems created by the concurrent successful Sandinista triumph in Nicaragua and the rise of the FMLN in El Salvador in 1979-80.

But it was during Ronald Reagan's tenure that the Pentagon radically changed its relationship with the Honduran military.

The chief U.S. operative in the country was the ambitious proconsul John Negroponte, whose burgeoning embassy staff of 150 occupied two spacious and well-fortified buildings which faced each other across one of Tegucigalpa's main thoroughfares. Consistent with the high priority chores of assuring collaboration between the Honduran and the Salvadoran armed forces, with providing a sanctuary for 10,000 Nicaraguan *contras*, and preparing for such dire scenarios as the partition of Central America as suggested by Fred Ikle, Negroponte's domicile was upgraded from a sleepy backwater Class 4 mission to a bustling Class 2 embassy, outranked in Latin America only by the American outposts in Mexico and Brazil.

Negroponte's first act, apart from handing newly elected President Suazo Cordova a shopping list of American demands, was to pick a military chieftain in January 1982. The promotion of Colonel Alvarez to head the armed forces so drastically violated Honduran military protocol—which stipulates that to occupy the nation's highest military post, the candidate already had to be a general—that it was evident to the disgruntled top echelon of the Honduran officer corps that Washington was the decisive factor in the choice. Alvarez' lowly ranking was soon remedied as he was vaulted to five-star general, and in November 1982 the country's legislative body meekly elevated the head of the Honduran armed forces to the position of commander-in-chief, an authority which, until then, had always rested with the president. Alvarez was nothing if not enthusiastic in his dramatic recitation of the domino theory liturgy. "Only when El Salvador has fallen, and Honduras and Guatemala follow, only when all of Central America is communist, when it is already too late, we will realize how important this war to the death is," he intoned. Of course, when he became too zealous—as on one occasion when he decided to invade Nicaragua—Negroponte could always jerk his leash, leaving the general to briefly sulk, "The U.S. wants vassals, not allies."

Although the Reagan administration would doggedly insist that U.S.-Honduran military maneuvers were strictly "routine," in fact, the Reagan administration had hit upon a deviously clever means of stationing several thousand U.S.

troops in Central America while preserving the "deniability" factor. Given the need to be attentive to the post-Vietnam sensibilities of an already wary American public, policy packaging became as important as the product. Hence: the U.S. was not backing a rightwing military regime in El Salvador, rather it was shoring up a frail political "center" against extremists of the left and right; in Nicaragua, the U.S. was not engaged in an illegal naval blockade, it was merely the sponsor of a group of "freedom fighters" littering the country's harbors with floating boobytraps.

Similarly, in Honduras, the U.S. wasn't stationing troops, it was conducting "extended" wargames that had no fixed termination date. The program was slated to begin with Operation Big Pine in December 1982, but the exposure of the CIA's not-so-secret war and Reagan's inclusion of Honduras on the itinerary of his Latin American trip forced a brief postponement. The one-week Big Pine maneuvers got underway on February 1, 1983 and, dwarfing all previous "routine" joint exercises, involved 4,000 Honduran troops, 1,600 U.S. soldiers, a fleet of ships complete with landing craft, and squadrons of air cover.

It was the announcement of Big Pine II in July 1983, however, that marked a qualitative change in U.S. troop involvement in Central America. The duration and magnitude of U.S. sea, air and land force commitment to Big Pine II made its namesake look like an overnight camping trip. Two full naval battle groups, 5,600 U.S. soldiers and a scheduled run of six months (eventually extended through March 1984, and then continued under a new name, Grenadero I) were only part of the scheme. It also featured a vast multi-million dollar building program which included the extension of three airfields, a military hospital, a radar base in the Gulf of Fonseca, roads, port facilities and communications centers.

Added to Honduras' own rapidly expanding army, 10,000 or more resident *contras*, several thousand visiting Salvadoran soldiers, and uncounted numbers of covert agents, military advisers, and footloose multinational mercenaries, had transformed Central America's most impoverished country into the world's largest military base. Although there were a few muted congressional protests about improper spending and evasion of legislative control over foreign military assistance (the Honduran construction blitz was financed by

Defense Department funds designated for military maneuvers, on the grounds that the installations were temporary), the Reagan team had pulled off an unprecedented military deployment at minimal political cost.

Despite President Reagan's Vulcan-like assurances that he was but hammering out a "shield of democracy," the Sandinista government was thoroughly alarmed at the armoring of Central America. In contrast to periodic announcements by the U.S. of communism's aggressive intentions (thus supplying a pretext for arming Nicaragua's neighbors to the teeth), the revolutionaries in Managua stubbornly refused to conform to Washington's relentlessly hyped image of incipient totalitarians. From July 19, 1983, when Daniel Ortega marked the fourth anniversary of the revolution with a comprehensive peace proposal, to February 21, 1984, the half-century commemoration of the assassination of Sandino when the Nicaraguan junta announced that its slated 1985 elections would be moved up to November 4, 1984 (two days before the American presidential contest), the Sandinistas presented a portrait of a government attempting to maintain a precarious pluralism under wartime conditions. Although Managua's concessionary gestures were frequently dismissed as merely a tactical response to a developing domestic crisis, and were greeted in Washington with barely disguised cynicism ("The Sandinistas are on the ropes—keep the pressure on," was the way one Reagan official described the prevailing mood of the administration), a comparison of U.S. and Nicaragua policy initiatives during 1983-84 left little doubt as to whether it was the revolutionaries or the American empire who were the instigators of Central American turmoil.

Meanwhile, in Tegucigalpa the weekend before the commencement of the Grenadero exercises at the end of March 1984, a disgruntled Honduran military made its decision. General Alvarez was in San Pedro Sula, the country's industrial center, meeting with his rightwing business backers. After a party that lasted until 2 a.m., the groggy and unshaven Honduran strongman arrived at the local airport for his return to Tegucigalpa. His comrades in arms had other travel plans for him. Alvarez was arrested, handcuffed and hustled aboard an airplane for the ninety-minute flight to Costa Rica. By Saturday morning, March 31, the former unofficial dictator was nursing more than a mild hangover.

The middle of the following week, as planes buzzed overhead, the Honduran Congress voted unanimously to elect 43-year-old air force head General Walter Lopez as commander of the country's armed forces. Although Washington's initial reaction to the purge was an expectation of business as usual in the garrison state, some Hondurans appeared to feel differently. As the Grenadero exercises noisily rumbled ahead, 4,000 demonstrators marched through the streets of Tegucigalpa, denouncing government oppression and demanding an end to the U.S. military presence; it was the first significant public protest in the country in more than two years. General Lopez took the hint. By July 1984, the Hondurans were asking for a revision of the 1954 bilateral military agreement with the U.S., as well as a bigger economic payoff for turning their country into a shooting range, and they were wondering if their heavy-footed American patrons could make an effort to tiptoe more discreetly across the bullet-pocked landscape.

From the sound of the explosion, the innocent observer might have assumed that the CIA had laid the mines in Washington's Potomac River rather than in the waters of Nicaragua's harbors. The latest secret in the not-at-all-secret war blew up in the faces of its perpetrators on April 8, 1984 on the front page of the New York *Times*.

"Americans working for the CIA on a ship off Nicaragua's Pacific coast," said the bulky Sunday *Times*, "have been supervising the mining of Nicaraguan waters in recent months." The intelligence ship carrying the American bombers bobbed on the horizon outside the fifteen-kilometer territorial waters limit recognized by the U.S. It launched small, high-powered speedboats manned by an elite group of Latin American commandos who careened to within two or three kilometers of the Nicaraguan shoreline and placed the sophisticated mines (assembled in El Salvador and Honduras with the help of American technicians) in the shipping lanes of Nicaragua's ports. It was an overt act of war. The key word in the account of this terrorist modus operandi was "Americans." As the *Times* pointed out, "the planting of the mines directly involves Americans and is under their immediate control," thus marking the "first time since the U.S. began supporting

Nicaraguan rebels that Americans have become directly involved in military operations against Nicaragua.''

Although to the uninitiated there seemed to be little difference between hiring Nicaraguan *contras* to do the dirty work and doing it yourself, in the delicate protocols of international law, a thin but crucial line had been irrevocably crossed. As one exasperated Republican member of the Senate Intelligence Committee explained, ''We have carefully monitored these activities to insure that, whatever else happened, Americans didn't get into combat-type operations against Nicaragua. That distinction has now been lost.'' To make matters worse, it appeared that the nasty new secret had also been kept secret from the Senate and House oversight committees. Despite federal law requiring the CIA to keep Congress informed about covert operations, neither the Senate nor the House committee had been informed about the mining operation until recent weeks, and no one could recall CIA director William Casey mentioning anything about American participation. Added the baffled Republican senator, ''When an American is on the mother ship in a mining operation, he's involved directly in military activities. It's irrelevant whether the ship is in international waters.''

Almost predictably, the bombshell revelation came in the midst of the Reagan administration's annual spring offensive against Central America. The 1984 version of the exercise had eschewed the usual rhetorical display of sudden perceptions of a ''crisis'' and the inevitable ''White Paper.'' In Nicaragua, the *contras* were making their way through the mountains while the mines went off; in El Salvador, the Americans were boosting the presidential candidacy of their favorite; and in Honduras, the Grenadero exercises, despite the minor disruption of an unofficial coup, were using up surplus U.S. ammunition at an unprecedented pace.

Nonetheless, just days before the exposure of the mining crime, President Reagan had gone on the offensive against his congressional opponents. ''Unfortunately, many in the Congress seem to believe they are still in the troubled Vietnam era, with their only task to be vocal critics, not responsible partners in developing positive, practical programs to solve real problems,'' said the president as he blamed the legislators for lousing up his foreign policy. ''We must restore bipartisan consensus in support of U.S. foreign policy,'' Reagan urged.

"We must restore America's honorable tradition of partisan politics stopping at the water's edge." The president would soon get more bipartisan consensus from the water's edge than he had bargained for, especially once Congress discovered what the waters actually contained.

By mid-day Sunday, April 8, the U.S. ship of state had taken a direct hit, and was listing badly, even as various officers on the bridge ordered a full steam reverse. Some of the crew were busy sealing off other rapidly flooding compartments. The same day the mining story appeared, the *Times* ran another front-page article claiming that the Reagan administration was drawing up "contingency plans... for the possible use of U.S. combat troops in Central America if the current strategy for defeating leftist forces in the region fails." Defense Secretary Caspar Weinberger, who was appearing on ABC's "This Week" that morning, vigorously denied that plans to use the combat troops had been developed or were being drawn up. "No, they are not," said Weinberger. The next day the *Times* confirmed its story. Senior administration officials, said the paper, "affirmed that the Defense Department, in a significant shift in thinking, had accepted a political policy of being prepared to use American combat troops in Central America."

Over at the State Department administration lawyers were up to their ankles. Having broken the law, the U.S. government now decided to flout it. The Reagan administration announced that it would not accept World Court jurisdiction in disputes involving Central America for the next two years. While the orchestra of the *Titanic* could be faintly heard playing on the deck, a State Department official down in the bilge said the move had been made because of information that Nicaragua was about to drag the U.S. to the International Court of Justice in The Hague. Under World Court rules, a nation can refuse to be judged by the court, but only before a case is brought before it. "We had to do it very rapidly,"' said the official. "If they filed before we moved, we'd be stuck." The wily Nicaraguans had a habit of embarrassing the U.S. before international bodies. Just the previous week, the U.N. Security Council had voted thirteen to one in favor of a resolution condemning outside military intervention in Nicaragua, including the mining of harbors, forcing the U.S. to exercise its veto power to quash the measure. "We did not want to turn the World Court into a big propaganda forum," said the State Department official in charge of the bilge pumping operation.

Replied Princeton University professor of international affairs Richard Ullman, in one of a wave of articles flooding the opinion pages of U.S. newspapers that week, "Like the American officer who ordered a Vietnam village destroyed in order to 'save' it, the Reagan administration is boycotting the World Court to prevent it from being 'misused' by Nicaragua." Referring to the author of *1984*—the dystopian novel receiving considerable attention in the year for which it was named—Ullman added, "George Orwell would not have been surprised at such language." The professor also noted that the bill currently before the Congress to provide another $21 million for the *contras* "bears a doublespeak label that would have choked even Orwell's dictators—the Central America Democracy, Peace and Development Initiative."

On Monday, House Speaker Tip O'Neill said that the Democracy, Peace and Development Initiative was doomed. "I can't conceive of it passing the House," O'Neill asserted. "Up to this point, I have contended that the Reagan administration's secret war against Nicaragua was morally indefensible. Today it is clear that it is legally indefensible as well," he added. At least that's the decision Nicaragua would be seeking, said Sandinista Foreign Minister Reverend Miguel D'Escoto that day as he announced that he had filed suit against the U.S. The complaint, which charged the U.S. with "training, supplying and directing military and paramilitary actions against the people and government of Nicaragua" in an effort "to overthrow or destabilize the government of Nicaragua," asked the World Court to order the U.S. to stop supporting operations against Nicaragua immediately and to pay reparations for the loss of lives and property. Even though the court had no power to enforce its decisions other than moral suasion, the State Department admitted that the move to evade jurisdiction—the first time since the U.S. joined the court in 1946 that it had taken such an action—"will be regarded as a concession that the U.S. is currently violating international law in its mining of the harbors."

In Tuesday morning's mail, CIA director Casey received a letter from Senate Intelligence Committee chairman Barry Goldwater. The elderly conservative, who had run for the presidency in 1964 on the chilling slogan that extremism in the defense of liberty was no vice, was in a state of apoplectic rage. "All this past weekend," he told Bill Casey, "I've been trying to figure out how I can most easily tell you my feelings about the discovery of the president having approved mining some of the harbors of Central America. It gets down to one, little, simple phrase: I am pissed off.

"Bill, this is no way to run a railroad and I find myself in a hell of a quandry," Goldwater continued. "The president has asked us to back his foreign policy. Bill, how can we back his foreign policy when we don't know what the hell he is doing? Lebanon, yes, we all knew that he sent troops over there. But mine the harbors in Nicaragua? This is an act violating international law. It is an act of war. For the life of me, I don't see how we are going to explain it."

As the ship continued to take on water, Casey was called up from the covert depths of the hold. In the rooms of the Senate Intelligence Committee, electronically swept for bugging devices, old men, full of self-righteous sound and patriotic fury, argued the significance of the secret war. The press had long since ceased making fun of the geriatric Russians (their interim leader, Yuri Andropov, had died in February, and was replaced by an equally aged apparatchik, Konstantin Chernenko). Just as the House resistance to *contra* aid was led by two sprightly congressmen in their seventies (Clarence Long and Edward Boland), that morning the elderly and sometimes forgetful Goldwater faced off with the rumpled Casey, speaking on behalf of his septuagenarian president. In two bitter confrontations with groups of senators who were indignant over both the agency's policy and its failure to adequately inform the oversight committees, Casey continued to be less than forthcoming. As one Republican legislator said, "Casey wouldn't tell you if your coat was on fire—unless you asked him." Even under attack, Casey insisted, "I do not volunteer information. If you ask me the right questions, I will respond." "It was disastrous," reported Tennessee Democrat Jim Sasser from the closed door sessions. Said a Republican senator, "He was arrogant, confused, unknowing and did a miserable job of explaining this problem."

That night Ronald Reagan got some bipartisan consensus. In an overwhelming vote, the Senate approved a resolution introduced by Senator Ted Kennedy that said: "It is the sense of Congress that no funds heretofore or hereafter appropriated in any act of Congress shall be obligated or expended for the purpose of planning, executing or supporting the mining of the ports or territorial waters of Nicaragua." Although the "sense of the Senate" measure was nonbinding, the support of Senate Republican leader Howard Baker and forty-one other members of the president's party allowed Kennedy to justifiably claim, "The Senate took a first step to halt President Reagan's secret war in Nicaragua." The next day the House of Representatives passed a similar resolution.

Reagan feigned indifference. "If it is not binding, I can live with it," the president said. "I think there is a great hysteria about this whole thing. We are not going to war." Deputy Secretary of State Kenneth Dam, hauled up before the House Foreign Relations Committee, offered a novel defense of the mining. Though he repeatedly refused to acknowledge that the U.S. was directly involved, he said that if it were the case, it could be justified under the collective self-defense clause of the U.N. Charter. "Collective self-defense is a ground for use of force," said Dam. U.N. Ambassador Jeane Kirkpatrick, speaking to the American Society for International Law that week, made a similar claim and said that "to portray Nicaragua as a victim in the current situation is a complete, Orwellian inversion of what is actually happening in Central America." The international lawyers were unpersuaded by her closing argument. For the first time in the seventy-eight-year history of the society, it voted overwhelmingly to condemn an action of the U.S. government, and urged Reagan to reconsider his decision to turn aside the World Court. The most that White House loyalists could hope for was that the ten-day Easter recess that began at the end of the week would mitigate congressional rage, and that something might yet be salvaged of the Salvadoran and *contra* aid bills still pending. "We have got to get the members out of town for ten days and let them cool off," said House Republican leader Robert Michel.

During the recess, there was little inducement to cool off. While a debate raged over what CIA director Casey had or hadn't told the Senate (it came down to a couple of muffled references to the mining about a month before the furor), Senate Intelligence Committee co-chairman Daniel Moynihan announced he would resign in protest, but later agreed to stay on after an apology from Casey. In Nicaragua, the war briefly heated up when the *contras* seized the isolated southern town of San Juan del Norte, and grandiosely announced plans to form a provisional government, only to find themselves retreating into the Costa Rican jungle when the Sandinistas quickly retook the outpost. President Reagan did his bit to cool things off by escalating the rhetoric. "If Central America is lost, then our own borders will be threatened," said Reagan in a speech on April 17. "Today, a faraway totalitarian power is committing enormous resources to change the strategic balance of the world by turning Central America into a string of anti-American, Soviet-styled dictatorships." With that calming gesture, the president departed the overheated galley before the stewing congressmen returned, and took a slow boat to China where, despite being hosted by the dreaded communists, there was a respite from questions about Nicaragua.

Back from the hustings in late April 1984, the day that the World Court sat to hear the Nicaragua case, members of Congress reported that the folks back home were confused and concerned. "Support for the covert war against Nicaragua has diminished," said Texas Democrat Jim Wright. New Mexico Representative Bill Richardson had been asked by his constituents, "Don't you have any guts? How can you permit the president to disregard international law?" According to Louisiana Democrat Buddy Roemer, "There's a lot of confusion: who are the good guys, who are the bad guys, and what is America's legitimate role?" A CBS/New York *Times* opinion poll at the end of the month confirmed the congressmen's impressions. Only one American in three supported President Reagan's policies in Central America, while nearly half the respondents said they were afraid those policies might drag the U.S. into a war. Response to the mining of Nicaraguan harbors was even more negative. By a margin of 67 percent to 13 percent, those questioned disapproved of the covert action. At the same time, however, Americans continued to show little knowledge of the situation—only 19 percent of those surveyed could identify which side the U.S. was supporting in Nicaragua.

In early May, after the Salvadoran presidential run-off at last produced a victory for the candidate identified as the good guy by the Reagan administration, the president again took to national television to sell his Central American policy to the public over the heads of his stubborn legislators. Evoking a "Communist reign of terror" in Nicaragua, the word "communist" was uttered incessantly. "If we do nothing, or if we continue to provide too little help," said Reagan in a key passage of his pitch, "our choice will be a Communist Central America with additional Communist military bases on the mainland of this hemisphere, and Communist subversion spreading southward and northward. This Communist subversion poses the threat that 100 million people from Panama to the open border on our south could come under the control of pro-Soviet regimes." Reagan's vision of a Red tide left Representative Clarence Long unmoved. "The president makes a speech every other month that Central America is going to go Communist, but that doesn't ring a bell with the people," said the controller of the House purse strings.

The next day, May 10, the World Court, in a unanimous decision, ruled that the U.S. should immediately halt any attempts to blockade or mine Nicaraguan ports and that the country's political independence "should be fully respected and should not be jeopardized by any military or paramilitary activities." Despite a State department avowal that the U.S. "respects the Court and the rule of law and intends to act accordingly," the CIA had no intention of obeying the injunction; its problem was to end the squabbling among those seeking to jeopardize Nicaragua's political independence.

For months, *contra* leader Eden Pastora had complained about CIA threats to cut off aid to his ARDE group unless he agreed "to align with the genocidal Somocista guard that is on the northern border, supported by the CIA and the darker forces of the U.S." Other ARDE members were less queasy about the "darker forces." At the end of May 1984, they voted to join the Honduran-based *contras*. Pastora, however, dissented. The next day he called a news conference at his jungle headquarters to denounce the deal. Someone decided to shut up the maverick *contra*. Just as the conference got underway, a bomb went off killing five journalists, but only slightly wounding its intended target, Pastora.

Nicaragua wasn't the only country worried about its political independence. That same month, the Washington *Post* disclosed a State Department document advocating that the administration move swiftly to fill a small military aid request from Costa Rica with the argument that it could lead to a significant shift from Costa Rica's "neutralist tightrope act and push it more explicitly and publicly into the anti-Sandinista camp." Officials from the economically strapped Central American democracy (it had received $211 million in U.S. economic aid in 1983) reported that U.S. embassy pressure on President Luis Monge had "been increased ten-fold over the last two months." Although an embassy official issued a pro forma denial that "any pressure had been exerted in any way to obtain a change in Costa Rican policies," Costa Rican officials said they had been told privately by Ambassador Curtin Winsor that the U.S. would be reluctant to give new economic aid until the "Nicaraguan cancer" was eliminated from the area.

Meanwhile, in the House of Representatives, the legislators were still trying to convince Reagan that "no" meant no. On May 24, the congressmen approved an emergency military aid package for El Salvador, but a similar request for more money for the *contras* was voted down 241 to 177, a margin nearly twice as large as previous rejections. "We'll continue to work for full funding," said a never-take-no-for-an-answer White House aide.

Although it had long since been forgotten, the original rationale for launching the undeclared war against Nicaragua was to "interdict" the alleged flow of arms to Salvadoran guerrillas. On June 10, 1984, a spy came in from the cold to say that it was all a lie. David MacMichael, a 56-year-old former CIA employee whose job was to assess intelligence reports about the alleged Nicaraguan arms flow to Salvadoran rebels, now challenged the very foundation of the Reagan administration's policy. "The whole picture that the administration has presented of Salvadoran insurgent operations being planned, directed and supplied from Nicaragua is simply not true," declared the ex-CIA man. "There has not been a successful interdiction, or a verified report of arms moving from Nicaragua to El Salvador since April 1981." MacMichael, the only CIA analyst in recent years to make a public break with the agency, said he decided to speak out when he concluded that "the administration and the CIA have systematically misrepresented Nicaraguan involvement in the supply of arms to Salvadoran guerrillas to justify its efforts to overthrow the Nicaraguan government.''

The White House decided to try again. In late June, the bid for *contra* aid was sneakily included in an omnibus supplemental spending bill that featured $100 million for a domestic summer jobs program, a measure the administration was certain the Congress wouldn't dare turn down in a re-election year. They were wrong. On June 25, the Senate voted eighty-eight to one to delete *contra* aid from the summer jobs bill. Republican Senate leader Howard Baker attempted to keep up the morale of his troops. ''Keep your powder dry, fight this fight where you have got a chance to win,'' said Baker with an eye to future requests. However, *contra* aid program supporter Senator John East replied, ''I have been here long enough to know what all these code words mean. It is over. It means there will be no more aid.''

That's not what Reagan thought. In mid-July, the president called Nicaragua a ''totalitarian dungeon'' as the administration opened a last ditch offensive against the Sandinistas. It included everything from speeches at the Organization of American States to a new White Paper to accusations that Sandinista leaders were involved in cocaine smuggling into the U.S. A week later, the White House threw in the towel and announced it was abandoning its attempts to get additional money for the *contras* in 1984. The House of Representatives made it official on August 2, 1984, voting 294 to 118 against supporting the *contras*.

Of course, there was still Fiscal Year 1985. If the president could get himself re-elected in the November 1984 race, he would be back.

10 Our Man in San Salvador

President Duarte is our kind of man.
— Representative Clarence Long,
May 1984

If, as U.N. Ambassador Jeane Kirkpatrick liked to complain, America's enemies were paranoid, then it equally might be argued that the mental illness afflicting the Reagan administration was manic depression. Indeed, it had been the symptoms of a severe depression, manifested by Kirkpatrick after her visit to El Salvador in February 1983, that launched a hectic perception of renewed crisis in Central America. By mid-August 1983, however, U.S. military advisers in El Salvador were once again riding up the emotional rollercoaster in the three-year-old civil war. Although advisers disliked using the word "optimism," said one battlefield report, nonetheless "a mood of optimism has replaced an equally palpable mood of pessimism that prevailed earlier in the year."

Only a couple of weeks before, in late July, the Defense Department urged President Reagan to more than double the number of military advisers in El Salvador from fifty-five to 125, and to permit them to accompany Salvadoran troops in the field, hardly a sign of confidence about progress in the war. While the president mulled it over, he sent Congress the fourth in a series of semi-annual certifications of human rights progress in the country ruled by the military and Roberto D'Aubuisson's National Assembly. Despite the official seal of approval, the U.S. embassy "grim-gram," as diplomatic staffers called it, reported from San Salvador that political deaths in the past six months had risen 12 percent to 1,054 (two other human rights organizations in the country put the toll at closer to 3,000). "Everyone is going to give us holy hell for the increase," admitted outgoing Ambassador Deane Hinton (confirmation of his replacement, Thomas Pickering, was temporarily held up by Senator Jesse Helms, who apparently doubted if the former Nigerian ambassador was hardline enough for the Salvador posting). As well as the discouraging body count, a report on the land reform program said that one out of every eight farmers had been evicted from land they were in the process of purchasing under the redistribution scheme. On top of that, casualty figures indicated the army was getting mauled, with 2,300 deaths in the past year (more than double the number reported for the year before that). Questioned about the grounds for certification, administration members became testy. Snapped one senior State Department official, "This law was written about El Salvador and not Utopia."

What cheered up the American counterinsurgency advisers in late summer was the acceptance of a "National Campaign Plan" by General Vides Casanova, the defense minister who had replaced General Garcia. Formulated by U.S. Special Forces experts in Panama, it was a classic counterinsurgency program, complete with an aggressive military thrust coupled to a plan to win the hearts and minds of the peasantry, and virtually indistinguishable from its Vietnamese and Guatemalan predecessors. At last, the Salvadoran military had agreed to the sure-fire solution that the Americans had been pressing upon them for two years.

Operation Well-Being began in June when 5,000 government troops swept into San Vincente province. A few days later and amid great publicity, Vides Casanova arrived on the scene to kick off a civic action program that in no time flat had established medical clinics, opened schools, and roused public support. A month after it began, the zone was officially declared cleansed of rebels. Said departing Ambassador Hinton, a booster to the end, "Right now the army has it all its way and it's damned good."

By August, the upbeat advisers found cause for satisfaction in the fact that "70 percent of the army has been in the field almost continuously since the National Campaign began." There were other heartening omens. "To a civilian it may sound strange, but one encouraging sign is that second lieutenants are starting to die out there. That means they are making mistakes and their own mistakes are killing them, but they are leading the men and being aggressive." Presumably, the FMLN guerrillas were also encouraged by such signs. Nonetheless, "it is going well, better than hoped for," declared the American helpers. Apparently, it was going well enough that President Reagan, in the midst of his annual August vacation at his California ranch, decided not to provoke Congress by asking to send more advisers into the fray.

The euphoria was short-lived. By the end of the month there was new fighting in San Vincente. The rebels had occupied five nearby towns and, on September 3, two battalions of the FMLN Arce Brigade launched a spectacular attack on the eastern provincial capital of San Miguel, the nation's third largest city. They shelled army, police and National Guard barracks, occupied the city for twelve hours, and destroyed bridges, warehouses, and gasoline depots, as well as inflicting heavy casualties. Although newly arrived Ambassador Pickering, echoing the official optimistic mood, said, "San Miguels are bound to happen," other American officials admitted that the assault dealt the army a psychological "bloody nose," and demonstrated the guerrillas' superior tactical and intelligence capabilities ("Boy, have they got an intelligence system," marvelled one American adviser). Defense Secretary Caspar Weinberger, visiting the region that week, also accentuated the positive. "The government troops have had increasing success and are returning increasing amounts of the country to civilian control and that is a very good tendency."

However, wishing couldn't make it so. The main thrust of the FMLN's fall offensive focused on overrunning villages and hamlets guarded by the Civil Defense squads (a key part of the National Campaign plan). By the end of September, seven of the country's most strategic provinces were engulfed in the offensive. Although *contra* raids against Nicaraguan ports and the administration's high-profile adventures in

Lebanon and Grenada were grabbing the headlines in autumn 1983, by the end of October, *Newsweek* reported that "El Salvador's FMLN have coordinated more than sixty attacks in recent weeks. The FMLN campaign undermined the Salvadoran government's plan to extend pacification by securing an area militarily, then sending in teams to provide essential services and encourage local people to rebuild the economy." Rather than pacification, it was the guerrillas who were scoring "impressive victories," said the magazine.

The depression set in the following month. "U.S. advisers are glum," said the dispatches reporting a new string of rebel attacks. "The guerrillas have the initiative now, no one can question that," said one adviser. Another just gloomily nodded his head when asked if he thought the U.S. should pursue a political solution rather than a military one. Two recent battles illustrated why the military advisers were reaching for the Valium. One town of 8,000 about fifty kilometers from the capital was being defended by 180 government soldiers when the FMLN attacked. Instead of staying to fight, the soldiers fled to a nearby town and changed into civilian clothes. "A 180-man unit in a defense position should be able to hold out and stay and fight," muttered the American overseer. A similar situation occurred in Ciudad Barrios, a town of 20,000 in the eastern province of San Miguel. Six hours after the guerrilla assault commenced, the eighty National Guard defenders fled the scene. By mid-November, the frustrated Salvadoran army had reverted to what it did best—mounting "search-and-massacre" missions.

An equally frustrated Reagan decided he was tired of making pseudo-certifications. On November 30, he quashed a bill from Congress to extend the semi-annual verifications of progress. "In the present circumstances," Secretary of State George Shultz told reporters after Reagan's veto, "unless there were a change between now and the middle of January, I think it would be very difficult to sign a certification." As if to underscore the point, in mid-December D'Aubuisson's National Assembly pushed through a constitutional measure that cut by about half the amount of land available for future redistribution. Said a bitter Christian Democrat critic, "I congratulate the National Assembly for succeeding in definitely ending agrarian reform."

There was worse to come. December 1983 was marked by a series of FMLN successes, from the occupation of major coffee plantations to the destruction of a strategic military communications center in Morazan province. During the last week of the year, 20,000 Salvadoran soldiers were marched into the field in the government's largest offensive of the war. While the army was busily beating the bush, the insurgents did it again: on December 30, the FMLN captured the U.S.-designed El Paraiso military base in Chalatenango, the first time in the war that the rebels had overrun a major military installation. Two days later on the Pan American Highway, the guerrillas hit the Cuscatlan suspension bridge that spanned the Lempa River, severing the last major link to the eastern third of the country. The battle was over in two hours. Although the guardsmen suffered only a few casualties, they panicked and fled after their lieutenant fell dead. The guerrillas jeered at the departing soldiers through bullhorns: "*Feliz ano*"—Happy New Year.

Upon the appointment of Henry Kissinger, "an unemployed secretary of state" as one of his less kindly critics called him, to head the president's Bipartisan Commission on Central America, even gung-ho *Time* magazine admitted that while the commission's job was "ostensibly, to give advice on long-term American policy in Central America," in fact, it had "a clear-cut political purpose: justifying the deeper extended commitment in Central America, both military and economic" that the Reagan administration had already decided to undertake. In short, the fix was in. As Representative Norman Mineta complained, "People are already relating Nicaragua to Vietnam. Now comes the man who gave us the bombing of Cambodia to deal with Central American problems. It doesn't make any sense."

The undaunted and energetic commissioner promptly settled into his first floor suite at Foggy Bottom and set a whirlwind pace. Within weeks he had conferred with congressional leaders, top-ranking Latin diplomats, the Contadora group, and envoys from all the Central American countries. Amid all the activity, Kissinger still found time to settle the critical issue of where his car would be parked in the State Department garage: right next to George Shultz's. Before the six-month consensus-making exercise ended, the twelve-man group of mostly conservative Republicans and Democrats heard hundreds of witnesses and managed to squeeze in a week-long tour of the object of their deliberations where they chafed under a history lecture from the Sandinistas and were shocked by the bloodthirsty D'Aubuisson in El Salvador.

On January 10, 1984, Kissinger dropped a 132-page report on the president's desk that was, as one State Department official described it, "by and large, an endorsement of what administration policy is." The report called for more of everything, amounting to a proposal to pour an additional $8 billion in aid into Central America over the next five years. While the report, as expected, endorsed the "mini-Marshall plan" favored by commission instigator Kirkpatrick, and urged an end to death squad killings in El Salvador, at its core was acceptance of the position that "the U.S. has a vital interest in combatting Marxist revolution." Thus, it contained a demand for more guns, ammunition and helicopters for friendly governments, especially El Salvador, where the commission recommended spending some $400 million in military aid in 1984-85. It was a message that Reagan welcomed. "I'm impressed with the depth of the analysis and the creativity of the recommendations," said the president.

Not everyone was similarly impressed. As one typical foreign newspaper editorial put it, Reagan "has just been urged to pour a little oil on burning waters. That's the gist of Henry Kissinger's advice on how to deal with the conflagration in Central America. Basically, it's the same kind of advice that got the U.S. mired in Vietnam two decades ago. The Kissinger commission's recommendations seem to have emerged from a time warp. Sadly, it's what Reagan wanted to hear." In Managua, Daniel Ortega noted, "Every time an American president wants to justify an aggression, he resorts to a commission." Similar commissions, remembered Ortega, were formed after the Cuban revolution in 1959 and the invasion of the Dominican Republic by U.S. Marines in 1965. "They are not commissions to resolve problems, but to justify aggressive policies," said the Sandinista leader.

Although the report had a fairly narrow readership of government officials and interested academics, given that it provided the first full-scale rationale for U.S. intervention since Jeane Kirkpatrick's "Dictatorships and Double Standards'' in 1979 it deserves at least a moment's reflection.

At its intellectual heart was an examination of the "considerable controversy as to whether the basic causes of the crisis are indigenous or foreign.'' Having observed the failure of Reagan's efforts to explain the "trouble in our backyard'' as solely due to the machinations of the "evil empire'' across the sea, Kissinger produced a more subtle answer: "The crisis is the product of both indigenous and foreign factors. It has sources deep in the tortured history and life of the region, but it has also been powerfully shaped by external forces.'' The problem for the commission was to sort out the diverse causes, remedying the legitimate "indigenous factors'' with generous dollops of economic aid and democracy, while extirpating the illegitimate "foreign'' sources by means of military might.

Although the foundation of Kissinger's argument was a historical overview that recounted the region's colonial legacy of poverty and inequality, the rise of oligarchic rule in the late nineteenth century, and the unsuccessful post-Depression reformist challenge to the old order, this "scandalous rewriting'' of the past, as critic William LeoGrande called it, required a glaring omission. Having delineated a set of conditions that would give rise to revolutionary aspirations, wrote LeoGrande, "one would expect this historical overview to trace the evolution of these revolutionary movements—the defection of the youth from the decimated reformist parties to the guerrillas, the growth of militant urban mass organizations, the role of the church in organizing rural Christian Base Communities...But that is not how the report's history proceeds. It does discuss the growth of insurgency—'communist insurgency'—but not the development of Central America's revolutionary movements. Instead, the focus shifts suddenly to Cuba and its 'effort to export revolution to Central America.'''

The intent, argued LeoGrande, was obvious: to blame Cuba for the growth of insurgency, while at the same time delegitimizing the region's indigenous revolutionary movements. Of course, for Kissinger to make that case, many inconvenient facts had to be buried. For example, critic LeoGrande pointed out, "when guerrillas in Nicaragua, El Salvador and Guatemala were developing into serious contenders for power during the mid-1970s, the Cubans were not engaged in Central America. The hiatus in Cuban involvement in Latin America between 1968 and 1978 is too well established to deny, so the report simply states that Castro once again became active in the 'export of revolution' in 1978 because he saw 'new opportunities' in Central America.'' With that sleight of hand, Kissinger erased ten years of history, precisely those years in which the Central American movements grew indigenously without Cuban aid.

Beyond blaming Cuba, the main issue was "indigenous" versus "foreign" factors. In Kissinger's view, not only were legitimate grievances against the oligarchic order to be acknowledged, but the U.S. should be identified with the need for change. "The U.S. is not threatened by indigenous change, even revolutionary change in Central America," wrote Kissinger. "All that remains," added LeoGrande, "is to define this distinction in a way that will allow the commission to brand the revolutionary movements as 'foreign'... If the report granted that these movements are indigenous, it would be much more difficult to make recommendations to defeat them and still contend that the U.S. is not the guardian of an antiquated and unjust status quo." That, by the way, was one of the reasons why revolutionary history had to be excluded, because it tended to show that the Central American movements indeed grew out of the brutal and horrendous conditions that the report readily acknowledged.

The report offered four reasons why the revolutionary movements had to be treated as foreign rather than homegrown. First, they had a "foreign ideology," Marxism; second, they had received aid from Cuba and the Soviet Union; third, wretched conditions, by themselves, do not produce revolution; and finally, the movements have been able to survive for a protracted period. Despite Kissinger's reputation as a dazzling intellect, the argument was both weak and specious.

Report critic LeoGrande took the elements of the case one by one. Not only was it absurd to think that any late twentieth-century revolution (apart from such theological upheavals as those in Iran) could be entirely removed from Marxism (even the report admitted, somewhat contradictorily, that Marxism was one of the intellectual traditions that had emerged in the region), but the commissioners ignored the amalgam of Marxism, radical Christianity and anti-imperialism that was specific to Latin American thought, i.e., the very thing that made it an indigenous ideology; moreover, "the very assertion that ideas—whether those of Marxism or of democratic liberalism—can ever be 'foreign' is an affront to the concept of freedom of thought." Similarly, it made equally little sense to define a revolution as foreign simply because the revolutionaries received help from abroad; certainly, the commission made no claim that substantial assistance from France during the American revolution had undercut its indigenous character.

Reasons three and four were interlinked. "Whatever the social and economic conditions that invited insurgency in the region," said Kissinger's report, "outside intervention is what gives the conflict its present character. Of course, uprisings occur without outside support, but protracted guerrilla insurgencies require external assistance. Indeed, if wretched conditions were themselves enough to create such insurgencies, we would see them in many more countries of the world." Although nodding in the direction of easily crushed local uprisings, the report came dangerously close to saying that successful resistance must be externally generated; carried to its illogical extreme, the report was arguing there could be no such thing as an indigenous guerrilla war. The ability of a revolutionary movement to survive, said the report, was itself proof of its foreignness. "The elegance of these arguments has to be envied," LeoGrande sardonically noted. "If one takes them seriously, 'indigenous revolutionary movements' becomes a null set."

LeoGrande was quite willing to concede that it is "possible to distinguish between authentic revolutionary movements and those that are the artificial creation of external powers engaged in subversion." To do so, however, one had to examine the history of the movement. LeoGrande offered a set of criteria by which such a judgment might be made. "Did the movement emerge and develop primarily out of the socio-political milieu of the nation? Does it have a significant degree of popular support? Does it have autonomy from any external power in making decisions about its politics and strategy?" In sum, was external aid an adjunct that strengthened a pre-existing movement or was it a primary motivating force without which no such movement would exist?

"The history of Central America leaves little doubt,"

observed LeoGrande, "that the revolutionary movements of the region were well advanced before they received any significant outside aid from Cuba or anywhere else." In short, they were indigenous. If one wanted to find a genuine example of a "foreign" movement, LeoGrande pointed out that "the counter-revolutionary forces fighting against Nicaragua did not exist before 1982, when the CIA assembled and armed them." The *contras* did not have popular support; their strategy was designed by a foreign power; if Congress made its cutoff of *contra* aid stick, the movement would collapse. "Thus if any insurgency in Central America is a product of external intervention, it is this one."

Neither the ironies nor the deconstruction of Kissinger's shoddy reasoning ever reached the American public. Before the report faded from view, about the only aspect of it that received public attention, apart from Reagan's formal request in February 1984 for $8 billion to pay for the proposals, was a squabble over whether or not the additional $300 million in military aid to El Salvador should be "conditional" upon political and human rights progress (the liberals favored "conditionality," Kissinger opposed it). Given that only a month earlier Reagan had vetoed a continuation of the fraudulent certification process, it seemed a moot question.

The situation in El Salvador was, admittedly, a mess. The patented American solution to such problems was money. But to pry the money out of a reluctant Congress, there had to be "progress." And the all-American symbol of progress was the demonstration of democracy at the ballot box. Of course, the "good guy" had to win the election, but presumably, that could be managed.

First, however, the Reagan administration discovered death squads. Of course, it had stumbled upon death squads before; in fact, it was thought that one of the factors leading to the dismissal of former Ambassador Deane Hinton was his too-vigorous denunciation of them in autumn 1982. Now, a year later, with the felicity of one entering a second childhood, the administration discovered them again as though they had never been noticed before.

In mid-November 1983, Under Secretary of Defense Fred Ikle, in one of those speeches billed as a "major policy statement," charged that "the death squads of the violent right'' were benefiting the leftist guerrillas and ''more must be done'' to restrain them. A week later, Ambassador Thomas Pickering was saying the same thing to Salvadorans. The unwillingness of the Salvadoran government to take action against the death squads, said Pickering, ''runs an extremely serious risk'' of provoking a cutoff of aid. The State Department even had a list of twenty-eight Salvadorans suspected of running the operation. ''None of us can afford to continue in the self-deluding belief that nothing is really known about the shadowy world of these individuals,'' the ambassador said. Finally, on December 11, Vice-President George Bush was dispatched to El Salvador where he told provisional President Magana, ''I ask you as a friend not to make the mistake of thinking there's any division in my country on this question.'' He added, ''It is not just the president, it is not just me or the Congress. If these death-squad murders continue, you will lose the support of the American people and that would indeed be a tragedy.'' If there wasn't any noticeable progress on death squads in El Salvador, perhaps the Congress would be satisfied with progress on the subject in the White House.

It was almost spring in Washington, and in almost-spring an old administration's fancy turns to crisis. President Reagan had announced a few weeks earlier that he would run for re-election in November to ''finish the job.'' In mid-February, there was another personality squabble among the Central American team. Special envoy Richard Stone had apparently incurred the wrath of Assistant Secretary of State Langhorne Motley, and after only eight months on the job—mostly devoted to ineffectual efforts to promote talks between the Salvadoran government and the rebels—he was replaced by Harry Shlaudeman, a diplomat who had been second in command at the U.S. embassy in Chile in 1973 while the CIA was helping to overthrow the Allende government. For the most part, the 1984 version of the annual pre-spring offensive was the real thing: the CIA was blowing up ships in Nicaraguan harbors, thousands of U.S. troops were practicing in Honduras, and the American flotilla was sailing in menacing circles off the Central American coast.

While all this was real enough, in El Salvador a presidential election was in the offing which was clearly not the real thing, notwithstanding the energetic tours of the hustings by frontrunners Jose Napoleon Duarte and Roberto D'Aubuisson. On February 21, 1984, the day the Nicaraguans announced they would hold presidential elections at the same time as the Americans, Secretary of State George Shultz was getting hot under the collar in a Senate committee room as he attempted to explain why the Reagan administration was considering providing El Salvador with emergency military aid without waiting for Congress. "We're concerned that the Salvadoran armed services will run out of key materiel in the next few months during which they are likely to face increased guerrilla efforts to disrupt the March 25 presidential elections," said the secretary in a tone that hinted at crisis.

By mid-March, President Reagan was injecting a note of urgency into a request for $93 million worth of emergency military aid for El Salvador, without which, he implied, it would be impossible to hold secure elections. "We can't afford to let political partisanship jeopardize our security interests or undercut the opportunity for El Salvador to build its democracy," said the president. As invariably happened when such claims were sounded, the Salvadoran chief of staff, Colonel Adolfo Blandon, assured everyone the next day that the elections would "take place no matter what. Even if the U.S. doesn't send more ammunition, there will be elections." In the end, the Senate chopped the aid request by a third and decided not to vote on it until after the Salvadoran contest, apparently wanting to know who the winner would be before spending the taxpayers' money.

Meanwhile, on the campaign trail, the contenders were hurling insults among the ruins. "Christian democrats and the guerrillas represent two different tactics of communism," said ARENA standard-bearer D'Aubuisson. "The first one to get into power will call the other, and together they will give the country to the USSR." Replied Duarte, "D'Aubuisson sees communists under the bed, on the table, when he's awake and in his dreams. His theory that the tragedy of El Salvador will be resolved by total war is pure demagoguery." The third man in the race, National Reconciliation party candidate Francisco "Chachi" Guerrero, a 58-year-old lawyer, described himself as "an ordinary man caught between two messiahs."

Given that its U.S. mentors were trying to instill a tradition of old-fashioned electioneering into Salvadoran politics, it was only par for the course when the campaign even produced a hint of scandal. A former Salvadoran military official turned up in the U.S. in the midst of the speechmaking to implicate D'Aubuisson and a clutch of high-ranking Salvadorans in acts of murder and terrorism. Among the charges: the organizer and director of the death squads was none other than D'Aubuisson himself; the death-squad network had been shaped by leading security force officials, including D'Aubuisson patron Colonel Nicolas Carranza, currently chief of the Treasury Police; former Nicaraguan National Guardsmen had been used by D'Aubuisson to carry out some of the killings; and Defense Minister Eugenio Vides Casanova was directing a cover-up in the 1980 slayings of the four American churchwomen which had been ordered by his cousin, Colonel Oscar Casanova. The degree of detail provided by the informant made the bloodchilling charges more than merely plausible. Unsurprisingly, the revelations had no effect on the election. If American politicians could run for office under clouds of tax evasion, drug use and sexual misdemeanors, why shouldn't Major Bob, accusations of mass murder aside, also get his chance? In any case, as Jeane Kirkpatrick told a Senate committee the day after the accusations were made, the evidence was inconclusive. "I think it is nondefinitive and it involves anonymous informers and that sort of thing," said the brains of the Reagan administration.

Election day, despite a U.S. expenditure of $8 million to ensure fair elections (not counting $2 million spent by the CIA to ensure a Duarte victory), was a disaster. "Everything is in complete disorder," moaned a voting official. Said a foreign observer, explaining the muddle and chaos, "To avoid fraud and collusion, the system was made so complicated that many ordinary people couldn't find their way through it." By Monday night, March 26, twenty-four hours after the polls had closed, the $3.4 million Wang computer system had yet to count a single vote. Despite the disarray, there was always one official election observer to be found attempting to put the best possible face on the farce. "To us it is not a question of whether the Wang computer can wang in with the figures," mused Gordon Fairweather, the aptly named head of the three-member Canadian observer team. "Whatever the motivation for voting, it must have been meaningful to the more than one million who voted."

It took the better part of a week to discover that nobody had won. That is, no candidate managed to garner more than 50 percent of the vote needed for victory. While Duarte was the clear leader with about 45 percent of the ballots, Major Bob had secured a solid 30 percent of the tally, and PCN candidate Chachi Guerrero brought up the rear with a pivotal 20 percent of the vote, meaning that a runoff election between Duarte and D'Aubuisson would be required in early May to determine a winner.

Although the electoral demonstration didn't produce a victor, as many observers noted, the temporary loser was clearly the Reagan administration. Whereas the 1982 legislative election in El Salvador handed the U.S. a considerable propaganda victory, the turmoil and inconclusive results of the 1984 contest dealt its sponsors a setback. As one characteristic middle-of-the-road editorialist noted, "Whoever is finally elected will find it difficult to clothe himself in a mantle of popular legitimacy." The main problem was Washington's man in San Salvador, Napoleon Duarte. As the same editorial observed, Duarte "failed during his 1980-82 stint as president either to curb the rightwing death squads or to negotiate with the guerrillas. Mr. Duarte's years in office showed just how subordinate, even helpless, the president is in relation to El Salvador's true power centers within the military." How, asked the pundits, could victory in a disputed election invest Duarte with more authority than he had last time? "There is therefore no reason to expect a better performance by him in his second term," concluded the dismal forecast.

In the interim between electoral rounds, while American public attention was absorbed by the discovery of direct U.S. involvement in mining Nicaragua harbors, the mechanics moved in and untangled the computer circuitry. President Reagan became slightly more hysterical about the need for immediate Salvadoran military aid; at one point he told Congressmen, "Some members of the El Salvador Army may have to go on missions with only one clip of ammunition." The House of Representatives refused to budge, voting to delay action on Salvadoran aid until after the May runoff. In the end, Reagan invoked his emergency powers to send $32 million to the "good guys."

On May 6, 1984, the technicians at the computer terminals finally got it right. America's man in San Salvador, Napoleon

Duarte, at last won one for the Gipper. Although his 54 to 46 percent victory over Major Bob was hardly a landslide, especially given the forces represented by D'Aubuisson, nonetheless the hallucinatory triumph had exactly the effect on Congress desired by the White House. Just to hammer home the point, Reagan took to national television three days after the Duarte win to chastise Congress for not doing enough. "Helping means doing enough," said the president in his best bedtime-story voice. "So far, we have provided just enough aid to avoid outright disaster, but not enough to resolve the crisis, so El Salvador is being left to slowly bleed to death." Despite the guilt-inducing image of negligence, the preliminary House vote the next day was a squeaker. "We are facing a communist revolution in our own backyard," said Representative William Broomfield, voicing the cliches of the conservative position. Representative Stephen Solarz replied, for the confused liberals, "The American people don't want any more Cubas in Central America, but neither do they want any more Vietnams." The tally was 212 to 208 to do more or less what Reagan wanted.

The following week Duarte was brought to Washington to make a personal pitch before the definitive House vote on aid. The Congressmen found the ebullient Salvadoran president-elect charming, sincere and persuasive. "I'm putting my life on the line," Duarte told the legislators. "Do not leave me standing alone." On May 24, while turning down additional emergency funds for the Nicaraguan *contras*, the House, by a vote of 267 to 154, agreed to provide $61 million in instant military aid for the Duarte regime. Said Representative Clarence Long, formerly a stubborn opponent of more money down the drain, "President Duarte is our kind of man."

As rain pounded down on the roof of the courtroom in Zacatecoluca, El Salvador at the unearthly hour of 4 a.m. on May 24, 1984, the jury of three men and two women stood in front of the bench and prepared to deliver their verdict.

Three and a half years after Ita Ford, Maura Clarke, Dorothy Kazel and Jean Donovan had been dragged from a lonely airport road, sexually assaulted, and then murdered, five former National Guardsmen were on trial for the crime. Seldom had the wheels of justice ground more slowly. Although the Salvadoran military had surrendered the accused to a civilian court in February 1982, more than a year after the slayings, it was not until nine months later, in November, that Judge Bernardo Rauda decided there was sufficient evidence to try the Guardsmen. A trial was expected in January 1983, but once again the case was entangled in judicial red tape. In March 1983, an appellate court judge ruled that the trial could not proceed until a lower court provided additional evidence concerning the subsidiary charges of assault.

The Reagan administration decided in June 1983 to send retired U.S. Judge Harold Tyler to conduct an on-the-scene inquiry into the interminable delay. The move was clearly intended to placate congressmen on the eve of the president's semi-annual certification of progress. Nonetheless, in October, Congress turned the screws a little tighter by voting to block a portion of Salvadoran aid pending a decision in the case. Three weeks later Judge Rauda, for the second time, ordered a trial.

On December 3, 1983, the third anniversary of the killings, Judge Tyler filed his report. Although Tyler told many people that he had deliberately kept out of his files anything that could be considered secret, the State Department immediately classified the report as secret, specifically refusing to give it to the anguished families of the victims on the grounds that leaks might jeopardize the trial proceedings. Not until mid-February 1984 were the report's contents filtered to the media. The main thing Tyler found was a cover-up. "The first reaction of the Salvadoran authorities to the murder," the judge wrote, "was, tragically, to conceal the perpetrators from justice." Tyler suggested that Salvadoran Minister of Defense General Eugenio Vides Casanova, commander of the National Guard at the time of the murders, may have been aware of the cover-up which began, apparently, within a day or two of the crime.

The families of the murdered women renewed their request for copies of Tyler's report. The State Department replied with a modest proposal to add insult to injury: the families could ask for security clearances; if they passed the test, they would have to sign a nondisclosure agreement promising never to divulge what they read; then they could come to Washington and read the report. The families declined to jump through the hoops.

In the rainy pre-dawn in the Zacatecoluca courtroom, the

jurors were asked of each charge, "Do you have the clear conviction" that each guardsman is guilty? "Yes," the jury spokeswoman replied on all charges. "We are in unanimity. They are all guilty." A month later, in June, Judge Rauda sentenced former sergeant Luis Colindres and the four other men to the maximum thirty years in prison for killing the churchwomen.

The verdict and sentence, coming in the wake of President Duarte's election, was quickly taken by the Reagan administration as another sign of democratic progress in its client state. However, as William Ford, a brother of one of the victims, noted, "The families and the American people now have to deal with the question of who ordered, who directed, who covered up, who paid for these crimes." There seemed little likelihood those questions would be answered, just as there was even less possibility that the families of the 40,000 people who had been killed in El Salvador in recent years would get the answers to their questions.

Despite the pro-Duarte sentiment in Congress that would ensure additional military aid for Fiscal Year 1985, it was clear little had changed. In late June 1984 it was revealed that the month before a plot had been afoot to assassinate Ambassador Thomas Pickering, who had been named by Senator Jesse Helms as having interfered in the Salvadoran election on behalf of Duarte. General Vernon Walters, the Reagan regime's Mr. Fixit, was immediately dispatched to San Salvador to "read the riot act" to the case's prime suspect, Roberto D'Aubuisson. Days later, the sore-headed presidential runner-up was touring Washington and being feted by his American patron, Senator Helms.

Elections notwithstanding, the FMLN guerrillas had not faded away, except to turn up again at unexpected moments. On June 28, in a pre-dawn assault, the rebels briefly captured the nation's most important power dam, Cerron Grande on the Lempa River, in an impressive display of their undiminished capabilities. The rightwing National Assembly hadn't disappeared either. The day after the battle at the dam, the ultra-conservative legislative majority voted to halt the remaining part of the land reform program. Nor had the killings ceased. Although the State Department reported to Congress on July 13, 1984 that Salvadoran extra-judicial executions had occurred at a reduced rate of ninety-three per month for the first five months of 1984, compared to an average of 140 per month in 1983, that same day Salvadoran Roman Catholic officials said that 134 people were killed by government death squads in the first month of President Duarte's administration.

In reflecting on U.S. foreign policy in Central America from 1980 to 1984, one of its most striking characteristics is the limited political range of the debate in which it was and continues to be fashioned. That is, the language of American liberalism and conservatism, with its "bipartisan" acceptance of the fundamental values of capitalism and with the exaltation of particular political forms (especially elections) over substance, marks the boundaries of acceptable discussion. Intellectual traditions available in Europe and even in other parts of North America are absent from the U.S. forum. In Canada, for example, one finds at the formal level of politics the embodiment of a social democratic ideology that at least ensures, however inadequately, a hearing for the Nicaraguan revolution or for the cause of the Farabundo Marti National Liberation Front in El Salvador. In the U.S., expressions of even moderate non-capitalist views are relegated to the non-governmental sidelines of Central American solidarity committees and small circulation specialized publications. Insofar as the American public professes views on Central American questions (a Harris poll published in *Business Week* on August 6, 1984 found that, by a margin of 65 percent to 33 percent, Americans felt Reagan was "risking another Vietnam by interventionist policies in Central America"), they tend to be couched in terms of self-interest rather than having a basis in principles or values.

To make matters worse, the limitations of the debate are exacerbated by the discussion taking place in a context of ahistorical consciousness; America's lengthy and dubious record of intervention is conveniently lost in a pervasive and collective amnesia. Repeatedly, the primary finding of American public opinion polls about Central America is popular ignorance. Despite the most sophisticated apparatus in the world for the dissemination of information, Americans simply don't know which side the U.S. is on in El Salvador or Nicaragua. Unsurprisingly, American deliberations on Central American policy, whether dominated by liberals or conservatives, tend to be contradictory, inconsistent and subject to momentary enthusiasms for short-lived trends or charismatic political figures. For example, as late in the debate as July 30, 1984, Representative Clarence Long, a key legislative opponent of additional aid to the Salvadoran regime, announced, in what was described as a significant shift of opinion, after meeting President Duarte in Washington that he now supported $300 million in military and economic aid for El Salvador in Fiscal Year 1985. Duarte, declared Long, "persuaded me he's caught between the radical left and the radical right and he needs some support. I want to give him a chance."

The characterization of Salvadoran political forces, especially in the period 1979-82, provides a concrete example of the framework of liberal/conservative perspectives. Only at Foggy Bottom could a regime consisting of the right-of-center Christian Democratic remnant led by Duarte, and the vast apparatus of the military, headed at the time by Colonel Garcia, be regarded as the center; only there could the forces of the FDR/FMLN be consigned to the role of an insignificant left extremism ("without popular support," as the 1981 State Department White Paper insisted), and those of the death squads be treated as an independent extremist right.

For outside observers, the alignment appeared somewhat different. In this version, the right is comprised of an array of sectors extending beyond formal state institutions. At its liberal margin are the Duarte-led Christian Democrats. At its heart is the military apparatus. As well, it counts the oligarchy, though there are political differentiations within this ruling class. At its extreme right are elements of the military, particular oligarchs, and such figures as Roberto D'Aubuisson, who finance and direct the operations of state terrorism. What this force lacks in numbers, it makes up in fiscal and institutional power, particularly its control of the economy and the state. The key point, however, is that this complex of state-military-private sector-terrorist apparatus, irrespective of its occasional internal policy differences, is a coordinated social force. The same can be said of the leftist ensemble of "social" Christians, organized peasants and workers, social democratic and Marxist political formations, and guerrilla armies.

Such a bifurcated characterization is unacceptable to the

Americans (especially the Reagan administration), since it accords these forces the status of "sides" in a civil war (as they are seen by Mexico, for example). But civil war is precisely what the Reagan regime must refuse to recognize, for then its efforts to secure legitimacy for the government would be seen, not as support for the "center," but as an attempt to impose victory for one side in the conflict. Hence, the ready willingness to accept a cosmetic explanation of the death squads as an independent rightwing force, and the corresponding effort to minimize the left as "terrorists," or to split it by claiming that its political forces are "dupes" of international communism. Such a view, as became evident, forecloses on the one option for a solution short of military victory—political negotiations. Since such negotiations imply an actual sharing of power, the long-term outcome of such a solution would likely be some form of socialism, a result unacceptable to the Americans, who equate all such forms with Soviet communism.

Nor was it merely the Reagan administration and its conservative supporters who held such views; the fundamentally similar perspective of American liberals illustrates the tendency toward convergence in the liberal/conservative debate, a "bipartisanship" which is more deeply rooted in American political thought than the "consensus" President Reagan sought to manipulate into existence. This is not to say that liberals and conservatives are one and the same, as some leftist analysts tend to argue. In fact, the urge to conflate these views, rather than seeing them as a differentiable but limited range of thought, can be fatal to those most directly affected by the policies that emerge from the liberal/conservative debate. There is no doubt that an alternative to the "hardline" policies of the Reagan administration, even the alternative available within the constricted range of choices presented to American voters, would be of significant importance to the lives of Central Americans.

Nonetheless, it is this convergence of basic views that goes some way toward explaining the erratic performance of liberals in the U.S. Congress during the period under review. Sometimes, they were adamantly opposed to further commitments of American resources in El Salvador, at other times they were easily cajoled into cooperation with the Reagan administration's schemes. For the most part, they contented themselves with patently ineffective "conditioning" of such aid, as in the acceptance of the farcical certification procedure. Invariably, they prefaced their admonitions against "another Vietnam" with the patriotic assurance that they too sought to prevent "another Cuba." At no time did American liberals propose a significantly different policy than the one imposed by Reagan, notwithstanding their more sincere disposition toward negotiations than the charade-like gestures of the administration. Similarly, regarding Nicaragua, liberals could applaud the romantic aspects of the overthrow of tyranny, and oppose such violations of the rule of law as the mining of Nicaragua's harbors, but once the Sandinista revolution failed to behave in ways recognizable in the U.S. context, wariness and disenchantment set in. Again, there was no liberal policy proposal toward Nicaragua beyond a laissez-faire grudging tolerance of its existence. In the end, then, liberal acceptance of a Duarte-type solution begs the question. For, even if Duarte, after much coaxing and coaching, turns out to be a moderate democrat, and even if the army can be toilet-trained to regard democracy with benign neutrality, what will be the benefits for the people of El Salvador? Will a relatively authoritarian democratization in the mode envisaged by Jeane Kirkpatrick, which leaves in place the structures of capitalism and the oligarchy, significantly improve the lot of Salvadorans, the mass of whom will remain landless peasants or proletarianized dwellers in urban shantytowns? Hardly. Despite the Kissinger Commission's claim that "the U.S. is not threatened by indigenous change, even revolutionary change in Central America," the liberal inability to countenance the possibility of justified revolution remains a fundamental constraint on the prospects of American foreign policy in Central America.

While perspectival complexities are a key to the American policy impasse necessitating extended analysis (far more so than the brief schemata offered here), other judgments on the outcome and the prospects of Reagan administration policy initiatives can be made succinctly.

The Nicaraguan case, above all, is relatively clearcut. Not only did the Reagan administration impose upon the Nicaraguans the same economic quarantine American governments have maintained against Cuba for more than two decades (in the process, significantly contributing to a self-fulfilling prophecy of emerging authoritarian tendencies in the ostracized regimes), it also launched an undeclared, and by almost all standards, immoral, war against a legitimate government with which it had no justifiable dispute. Jeane Kirkpatrick's protestations of "projection" aside, the not-so-secret war was the sole demonstrable example of "foreign intervention" in the region during this period. In mining Nicaraguan harbors, the U.S. crossed the line between immoral "sponsorship" of war and direct involvement in it, thereby almost certainly breaking international law. Compounding the crime, the U.S. openly contradicted its devotion to the "rule of law" by refusing to recognize the jurisdiction of international legal bodies.

The insincerity of the Reagan administration's pursuit of other policy options, particularly economic aid and support for political negotiations, leaves one with little choice but to conclude that the American government's intention of seeking a military solution to Central American conflicts remains dominant. Neither the Caribbean Basin scheme, nor the "mini-Marshall Plan" contained in the Kissinger Commission report, offer more than a cover for the continuing provision of military hardware to favored regimes in the region. In any case, not even at a theoretical level do these proposals offer any prospect of freeing the region from the grip of impoverished capitalist dependency. The occasional nods toward the negotiating efforts of the Contadora group, as well as the Reagan administration's own forays into mediation, if not demonstrably hollow, at best produced no reduction of tensions.

The rationale for U.S. intervention—that conditions in Central America pose a threat to the "vital national security interests" of the U.S.—remains a rhetorical contention rather than a proven thesis. The quarter-century existence of communist Cuba a few kilometers off the American mainland has not noticeably endangered the U.S. However, in terms of prospects, American intervention has indeed increased the danger of wider war. Not only has the U.S. sponsored and directly participated in a war against Nicaragua, it has also thoroughly militarized Honduras, revived the specter of CONDECA as an amalgamated Central American army to be launched against America's ideological opponents, and churned out a variety of plans—the partial revelations of which are sufficient to make observers shudder—that could ultimately lead to direct U.S. troop involvement in a Central American war if all else fails. The prospect of the re-election of Ronald Reagan in autumn 1984 increases the danger exponentially.

In contemplating the record, one is left with the question: Why is the U.S. in Central America? The answer to that query, ultimately, must be cast in moral syntax: It shouldn't be. In another sense, the answer is provided by the Reagan administration itself. In one of those rare instances of taking a government at its rhetoric, the answer is, as Reagan and his advisers proclaim, to prevent a socialist transformation in Latin America. In accepting this face-value explanation, it is necessary, of course, to strip away a good deal of verbiage about Soviet "subversion," international communist conspiracies, dark Cuban intentions, and the like. It's also important to recognize that other factors, such as the export of capital, deserve as much consideration as allegations concerning the "export" of revolution.

Left to their own devices, the military and pseudo-democratic dictatorships of Central America would in due course fall before the revolutionary movements in El Salvador, Guatemala, and eventually Honduras. Inevitably, that would bring into being various, as yet undetermined, forms of socialism. Some of those might turn out to be as totalitarian as Jeane Kirkpatrick imagines all socialism to be; on the other hand, some of those socialisms (in the plural) might emerge as relatively recognizable in relation to the rhetoric of its proponents, and more importantly, might significantly improve the lives of Central Americans.

It is more difficult to answer the further question, What rights does the U.S. have to intervene in Central America in order to prevent socialism? Leaving aside specious concerns about national security, we are quickly brought to a realm of political metaphysics. It's perhaps best to content ourselves with the simpler answer that, in terms of what the U.S. professes its principles to be, it has no right to violate anyone's national sovereignty.

Finally, there is the now-familiar image of falling dominoes, conjured up by Cold War American politicians since the 1950s. Insofar as the invocation of a domino theory suggests forces independent of the will of actual groups of Central

Americans, it's of a patronizing piece with much of the rest of the vocabulary used by U.S. officialdom to describe life in the hemispheric isthmus. The concept condescendingly suggests the political incapacity of the region's inhabitants to determine their own fate. In that sense, it's no different than the possessive depiction of Central America as "our backyard," or the repeated allusions to the "Soviet-Cuban threat" as a means of ignoring the indigenous forces for revolution. However, insofar as the domino theory is an authentic foresight of things to come, then one's only objection is its authors' complacent exclusion of the last domino that must fall, America itself.

Notes

My primary sources for the record of daily events are the New York *Times*, the Washington *Post*, the Toronto *Globe and Mail*, *Time*, *Newsweek*, *Maclean's*, the *Guardian* (New York) and *Barricada Internacional*. Unless otherwise cited, all quotes in the text are taken from the foregoing.

Chapter One

The account of the deaths of the four American churchwomen is taken from daily press dispatches, the newsweeklies, and versions in Arnson, Bonner, and Armstrong and Shenk (see bibliography for references). The brief discussion of Jimmy Carter's Latin American policy makes use of the former president's memoirs. Jeane Kirkpatrick's essay, "Dictatorships and Double Standards" is available in the volume with that title and, more readily, in Gettleman *et al*, which also contains Tom Farer's rebuttal. Luis Maira's reply to Kirkpatrick is found in Diskin.

Chapter Two

The biographical materials on Alexander Haig are primarily from *Time* and *Newsweek*; the description of the period as Kissinger's aide is taken from Hersh. The 1981 State Department White Paper is reprinted in Gettleman *et al*, as are the James Petras and Washington *Post* critiques of that document.

Chapter Three
The account of the FMLN "final offensive" and the subsequent narrative is based on the analysis in Armstrong and Shenk, Bonner, Arnson and Buckley.

Chapter Four
The review of El Salvadoran political history primarily depends on the interpretation of Armstrong and Shenk, but also makes use of materials in LaFeber, Bonner, and Buckley.

Chapter Five
The account of Haig's resignation makes use of the former secretary of state's memoirs. Descriptions of FMLN operations come from Bonner's series of dispatches in the New York *Times* as well as his subsequent book, Clements, and White.

Chapter Six
Guatemalan historical materials are based on the NACLA volume, LaFeber, and Kinzer and Schlesinger. The account of the counter-insurgency campaign during the Rios Montt dictatorship borrows heavily from White.

Chapter Seven
Ortega's and Kirkpatrick's speeches at the U.N. are found in Rosset and Vandermeer. The biographical material on Daniel Ortega is based on an interview in *Playboy*. The account of *contra* operations relies on White.

Chapter Eight
The account of Beals' meeting with Sandino is based on Beals' dispatches published in *The Nation* in 1928. The review of Nicaraguan political history primarily relies on the interpretations of Black, Weber, and LaFeber.

Chapter Nine
The revelation of CIA involvement in the mining of Nicaraguan harbors first appeared in the New York *Times*.

Chapter Ten
The account of the National Campaign relies on White. The critique of the Kissinger Commission report follows the analysis in LeoGrande.

Bibliography

Allman, T.D., "Rising to Rebellion," *Harper's*, March 1981. One of the first and most widely-read accounts of the Salvadoran civil war.

Americas Watch Committee and the American Civil Liberties Union, *Report on Human Rights in El Salvador* (Vintage, New York, 1982). One in a series of thoughtful reports on human rights violations in Central America.

Amnesty International, *Amnesty International Report 1983* (Amnesty International, London, 1983). One in a series of annual surveys of human rights conditions throughout the world.

Anderson, Thomas, *Matanza: El Salvador's Communist Revolt of 1932* (University of Nebraska, Lincoln, Nebraska, 1971). A history of the traumatic, formative event in Salvadoran politics.

Armstrong, Robert, and Janet Shenk, *El Salvador: The Face of Revolution* (South End, Boston, 1982). A popularly written, readable and astute interpretation of Salvadoran political history; recommended.

Arnson, Cynthia, *El Salvador: A Revolution Confronts the U.S.* (Institute for Policy Studies, Washington, 1982). A useful account of the Salvadoran revolution, critical of U.S. intervention.

Baloyra, Enrique, *El Salvador in Transition* (University of North Carolina, Chapel Hill, North Carolina, 1982). Scholarly account of Salvadoran politics from a liberal perspective.

Beals, Carleton, "With Sandino in Nicaragua," *The Nation*, March 28, 1928 (and subsequent issues). A classic series of journalistic dispatches containing interviews with Sandino and providing a unique flavor of Sandino's guerrilla war against the U.S. Marines.

Black, George, *Triumph of the People* (Zed, London, 1981). An excellent account of the Nicaraguan revolution from a materialist perspective; recommended.

——"Central America: Crisis in the Backyard," *New Left Review* 135, September 1982. An enlightening analysis of the current situation from a Marxist perspective.

Bonner, Raymond, *Weakness and Deceit: U.S. Policy and El Salvador* (Times Books, New York, 1984). A critical account of U.S. foreign policy in El Salvador by a New York *Times* reporter, based on extensive first-hand information and containing considerable declassified U.S. government documentation; recommended.

Boron, Atilio, "Latin America: Between Hobbes and Friedman," *New Left Review* 130, November 1981. An intelligent analysis of the current situation, featuring a particularly useful discussion of the relationship between capitalism and democracy.

Brecher, John, John Walcott, David Martin and Beth Nissen, "A Secret War for Nicaragua," *Newsweek*, November 8, 1982 (reprinted in Rosset and Vandermeer). The journalistic scoop that blew the cover on the CIA's covert war against Nicaragua.

Buckley, Tom, *Violent Neighbors: El Salvador, Central America and the U.S.* (Times Books, New York, 1984). An impressionistic account of Central American current affairs and history by a *New Yorker* journalist; makes the mistake of identifying Central America rather than the U.S. as the "violent neighbor."

Carter, Jimmy, *Keeping Faith* (Bantam, New York, 1982). A memoir by the underrated former U.S. president.

Chomsky, Noam, *Towards A New Cold War* (Pantheon, New York, 1982). The title essay, "Resurgent America," and a lengthy "Introduction" all contain a carefully reasoned, densely documented polemic interpretation of Reagan foreign policy.

——and Edward Herman, *The Washington Connection and Third World Fascism* (South End, Boston, 1979).

Clements, Charles, *Witness to War: An American Doctor in El Salvador* (Bantam, New York, 1984). A beautifully written account of a year's experience working as a physician in the Guazapa region of El Salvador that provides the best account of the FMLN available in English; recommended.

Didion, Joan, *Salvador* (Simon and Schuster, New York, 1983). An impressionistic account of a visit to El Salvador in mid-1982 that successfully conveys the atmosphere of terror and which, because of Didion's reputation, was politically important in bringing the issues to the attention of a broader audience.

Diskin, Martin (ed.), *Trouble in our Backyard* (Pantheon, New York, 1983). A useful collection of writings about Central America, including Luis Maira's "Reagan and Central America," and essays by Tommie Sue Montgomery, Richard Fagen and Steven Volk, among others.

Elman, Richard, *Cocktails at Somoza's* (Applewood, Cambridge, Massachusetts, 1981). A reporter's journal of experiences in Nicaragua.

Evans, Rowland and Robert Novak, *The Reagan Revolution* (E.P. Dutton, New York, 1981). A panegyric hailing the arrival of the Reagan administration by two conservative columnists.

Fried, Jonathan, Marvin Gettleman, Deborah Levenson and Nancy Peckenham (eds.), *Guatemala in Rebellion* (Grove, New York, 1983). One of a series of useful volumes containing historical material, analytic essays, documents and newspaper accounts about Guatemala.

Galeano, Eduardo, *Guatemala: Occupied Country* (Monthly Review, New York, 1969).

——*Days and Nights of Love and War* (Monthly Review, New York, 1983). A literary work, part-journal, part-journalism, by the Uruguayan writer and political activist; recommended.

Gerassi, John, *The Great Fear in Latin America* (Macmillan, New York, 1965). One of the first works in the present period to offer a thorough critique of U.S. domination of Latin America.

Gettleman, Marvin, Patrick Lacefield, Louis Menashe, David Mermelstein and Ronald Radosh (eds.), *El Salvador: Central America in the New Cold War* (Grove, New York, 1981). An excellent anthology of Salvadoran materials, including Jeane Kirkpatrick's essay, "Dictatorships and Double Standards"; recommended.

Gilmour, David, *Lebanon: The Fractured Country* (Sphere, London, 1984).

Grossman, Karl, *Nicaragua: America's New Vietnam?* (Permanent Press, Sag Harbor, New York, 1984). A journalistic account of a visit to Nicaragua featuring extended interviews with various people representing a broad spectrum of Nicaraguan political opinion.

Haig, Alexander, *Caveat: Realism, Reagan, and Foreign Policy* (Macmillan, New York, 1984). A loyalist memoir by the former secretary of state.

Herman, Edward, *The Real Terror Network* (South End, Boston, 1982). An analysis of contemporary terrorism that argues, contrary to U.S. propaganda, that the system of terror operates at peak efficiency in U.S.-sponsored "authoritarian" states.

Hersh, Seymour, *The Price of Power: Kissinger in the Nixon White House* (Summit, New York, 1983). A definitive account of the former secretary of state and national security adviser's tenure, richly detailed, and illuminating with respect to the process of U.S. policymaking; recommended.

Immerman, Richard, *The CIA in Guatemala: The Foreign Policy of Intervention* (University of Texas, Austin, Texas, 1982).

Jonas, Susanne and David Tobis (eds.), *Guatemala* (North American Congress on Latin America, New York, 1974).

Kinzer, Stephen and Stephen Schlesinger, *Bitter Fruit* (Doubleday, Garden City, New York, 1981). An excellent account of the overthrow of the Arbenz regime in Guatemala; supplants earlier accounts to stand as the current definitive work on the subject; recommended.

Kirkpatrick, Jeane, *Dictatorships and Double Standards* (American Enterprise Institute/Simon and Schuster, New York, 1982). Contains the celebrated essay by the Reagan administration's guru on Latin American policy as well as other pieces in a similar neo-conservative vein.

——*The Reagan Phenomenon* (American Enterprise Institute, Washington, 1983). Speeches and papers by the Reagan administration's ambassador to the U.N.

Kissinger, Henry *et al.*, *Report of the National Bipartisan Commission on Central America* (Washington, January 1984). A generally conservative justification of the Reagan administration's policies in Latin America; should be read in conjunction with LeoGrande's critique.

Kwitny, Jonathan, *Endless Enemies: The Making of an Unfriendly World* (Congdon and Weed, New York, 1984). A readable account from a liberal perspective by a *Wall Street Journal* writer about America's self-destructive foreign policy; marred by the author's quirky defense of capitalism.

LaFeber, Walter, *Inevitable Revolutions: The U.S. in Central America* (Norton, New York, 1983). A useful survey history of Central America and U.S. foreign policy there; the best historical overview currently available; recommended.

LeoGrande, William, "Through the Looking Glass: The Report of the National Bipartisan Commission on Central America," *World Policy Journal*, Winter 1984. A devastating critique of the Kissinger Report; recommended.

Lernoux, Penny, *Cry of the People* (Penguin, New York, 1982). An account of the changing role of the Catholic Church in Central America in the struggle for human rights.

Millett, Richard, *Guardians of the Dynasty* (Orbis, Maryknoll, New York, 1977). An account of the Nicaraguan National Guard under Somoza.

Montgomery, Tommie Sue, *Revolution in El Salvador* (Westview, Boulder, Colorado, 1982).

North American Congress on Latin America, *NACLA Report on the Americas* (bi-monthly; NACLA, 151 West 19th Street, 9th Floor, New York, New York, 10011).

O'Shaughnessy, Hugh, *Grenada: Revolution, Invasion, and Aftermath* (Sphere, London, 1984). An account of recent events in Grenada by a correspondent from the London *Observer*.

Oye, Kenneth, Robert Lieber and Donald Rothchild (eds.), *Eagle Defiant: U.S. Foreign Policy in the 1980s* (Little, Brown, Boston, 1983). A collection of papers, including Abraham Lowenthal's "Ronald Reagan and Latin America," which argues that Reagan's Latin American policy is not strikingly different from his predecessor's and is relatively moderate compared to its initial zealous rhetoric; written before the invasion of Grenada and the revelation of CIA involvement in blowing up Nicaraguan harbors, it stands as a caution to authors of instant history.

Poulantzas, Nicos, *Fascism and Dictatorship* (New Left Books, London, 1974). Marxist theoretical discussion of capitalist state forms under exceptional circumstances.

Randall, Margaret, *Doris Tijerino: Inside the Nicaraguan Revolution* (New Star, Vancouver, 1978). An account of the development of the Sandinista movement by a prominent activist.

——*Sandino's Daughters* (New Star, Vancouver, 1981). A particularly useful volume of oral histories and interviews with Nicaraguan women that provides one of the few "unmediated" accounts of events there; recommended.

——(ed. and trans.), *Breaking the Silences* (Pulp, Vancouver, 1982). An anthology of twentieth century poetry by Cuban women.

——*Christians in the Nicaraguan Revolution* (New Star, Vancouver, 1983). Dialogues among Christian activists in Nicaragua; contains an informative introduction and a valuable discussion of Ernesto Cardenal's religious activities.

Rosset, Peter and John Vandermeer (eds.), *The Nicaraguan Reader* (Grove, New York, 1983). A useful anthology of historical materials, essays, and reportage about Nicaragua.

Schmidt, Steffen, *El Salvador: America's Next Vietnam?* (Documentary, Salisbury, North Carolina, 1983). A journalistic interpretation of current Salvadoran events from a Christian Democratic perspective.

Selser, Gregoria, *Sandino* (Monthly Review, New York, 1981). A biography of the Nicaraguan nationalist leader.

Stein, Herbert, "The Reagan Revolt That Wasn't," *Harper's*, February 1984. One of several current critiques by economists of Reagan's economic policies.

Walker, Thomas (ed.), *Nicaragua in Revolt* (Praeger, New York,

1982). A useful collection of scholarly papers assessing the first eighteen months of the Nicaraguan revolution.

Wiarda, Howard, *The Continuing Struggle for Democracy in Latin America* (Westview, Boulder, Colorado, 1980). An analysis of the region by an influential neo-conservative scholar.

Weber, Henri, *Nicaragua: The Sandinist Revolution* (Verso, London, 1981). A brief account of the Nicaraguan revolution from a Marxist perspective; recommended.

White, Richard Alan, *The Morass: U.S. Intervention in Central America* (Harper and Row, New York, 1984). An excellent account of U.S. involvement in Central America emphasizing the use of counterinsurgency strategies; recommended.

Index